Energy and Environment:
The Four Energy Crises

G. Tyler Miller, Jr.

*Professor of Human Ecology and Coordinator
of Environmental Studies*

St. Andrews Presbyterian College

Wadsworth Publishing Company, Inc.
Belmont, California

© 1975 by Wadsworth Publishing Company, Inc., Belmont, California 94002. All rights reserved. No part of this book may be reproduced, stored in a retrieval system or transcribed, in any form or by any means, electronic, mechanical, photocopying, recording or otherwise, without the prior written permission of the publisher.

ISBN 0-534-00407-5

L. C. Cat. Card No. 74-31817

Printed in the United States of America

1 2 3 4 5 6 7 8 9 10 – 79 78 77 76 75

Designer: Gary A. Head

Production Editor: Mary Arbogast

Science Editor: Jack C. Carey

Technical Illustrators: Darwen Hennings, Vally Hennings, John Waller

Preface

Ecologist Garrett Hardin has stated that the basic principle of ecology is: everything is connected to everything. We are slowly beginning to realize that energy and its flow through all living things is the primary common denominator that connects everything to everything. Thus, understanding some of the basic principles of energy and the consequences of its use and misuse must be a prime requisite for understanding what we can and cannot do on this planet.

This book is a nontechnical introduction to energy and environment—it can be used as a supplement for introductory courses in biology, geography, chemistry, and man and environment or as a basic text for short courses on energy and environment.

The purpose of this book is to look at the two basic energy laws—you can't get something for nothing, and you can't even break even—and use them to evaluate our energy options. Reams of words have been written about the energy crisis of 1973. I shall not dwell on the details of this crisis nor engage in the "find the villain" game that is our first response to most crises. Instead this book is designed to evaluate our future options for the energy crises coming during the next few decades.

The book's tone is neither gloom-and-doom pessimism nor technological optimism, both of which encourage or allow inaction or withdrawal. We live on an exciting "hinge of history" with many alternatives and hopeful choices still available. Indeed, I believe that during the next fifty years we must and can make the transition to an earthmanship society, one that recognizes (in the words of Rolf Edberg) that "the earth does not belong to us, but we to the earth." Such a transition can happen only if we accept and act according to the realities of energy and ecology.

Major Features

Concepts used throughout   Basic energy principles are developed in a nontechnical manner early in the text and then used to connect many of the complex and seemingly unrelated energy facts, problems, and possible options.

Guest editorials   Five prominent scientists have written short original editorials for this book. These normally focus on specific issues to provoke discussion.

Documentation and manuscript review   Key points are documented throughout the book and listed in an extensive bibliography of over 500 references. In addition, an annotated list of further readings is suggested for each chapter. These references allow you to check the reasoning behind environmental statements. They provide you with starter references for term papers, reports, or further study of topics that may interest you.

Because of the complexity of energy issues, no author or small group of authors can provide the necessary expertise in all areas. To compensate for this problem, some 13 reviewers have helped to improve the quality of this book and insure that it is accurate and up-to-date. Each chapter has been reviewed in detail by at least one recognized expert in that area. In addition, the entire manuscript has been carefully analyzed by seven reviewers who teach environment related courses in colleges and universities.

Analysis of solutions and future orientation   The arguments on both sides of major environmental issues are discussed. Then the merits, demerits, and "tradeoffs" of alternative solutions are examined. Discussion questions further emphasize the pros and cons of important issues and help us to understand the impact of personal life styles on the environment. To stimulate critical thinking and action, I have outlined plans for dealing with aspects of the present and future energy crises. This plan is divided into short range (present to 1985), intermediate (1985 to 2000), and long range (2000 to 2020) proposals. It is not presented as "the" answer to our complex energy problems. Instead it is my response to the responsibility of putting forth concrete proposals so they can be analyzed, debated, accepted or rejected and, most importantly, improved.

Illustrations   Special emphasis has been placed on creating illustrations that: (1) simplify complex interrelationships, (2) relate important ideas such as matter cycling and energy flow to living organisms and human concerns, and (3) demonstrate with maps and other devices our use of resources and the resulting impact on air, water, and land.

As you struggle with the crucial and exciting issues discussed in this book, I hope you will take the time to correct errors and suggest ways of improving the quality of the text. Information feedback and open discussion of issues between readers and an author are vital elements in an earthmanship society.

Acknowledgments

I wish to thank all of those who took the time to point out errors and to suggest many improvements. The deficiencies remaining are mine, not theirs.

I have tried to give credit for the ideas of others but, like any writer, I have absorbed information from others without recognizing or remembering the source. I would be most appreciative if any who feel they have not been recognized for their contributions would notify me so that I might acknowledge them in any future editions of this book.

It is with great pleasure that I extend special thanks to the prominent scholars who took time out of their busy schedules to write guest editorials for this book or to provide very helpful reviews (see the lists later in this section).

My sincere thanks also go to Mrs. Ruth Y. Wetmore for her skill and patience in typing and for improving the text when it didn't make much sense. It is a rare author who has the services of an expert typist who is also an editor and author. Finally, I wish to thank my sons Greg and David Miller for serving as my assistants in assembling the manuscript and to my wife Marlene for her encouragement, support, and help in those crucial times any author experiences.

One of the pleasures of writing this book has been the opportunity to work with members of Wadsworth Publishing Company. I am particularly indebted to Ms. Mary Arbogast for her careful editing and numerous improvements in the manuscript, to Darwen Hennings, Vally Hennings, and John Waller for their exciting and innovative art work, and to Gary Head who acted as designer for the book. But above all I wish to thank Jack Carey, science editor at Wadsworth. In addition to producing numerous helpful ideas in brainstorming sessions lasting into the wee hours of the morning, he is one of those rare and creative editors who knows how and when to use positive reinforcement to help an author struggling to give birth to a manuscript.

G. Tyler Miller, Jr.
Laurinburg, N.C. 28352

Reviewers

Guest Editorialists

Reviewers of the Entire Manuscript

Virgil R. Baker, Professor of Geography, Arizona State University

Arthur C. Borror, Professor of Zoology, University of New Hampshire

Ted L. Hanes, Associate Professor of Botany, California State University, Fullerton

William W. Murdoch, Associate Professor of Biology, University of California, Santa Barbara

John E. Oliver, Professor of Geography, Indiana State University

Grace L. Powell, Associate Professor of Geography, University of Akron

Donald E. Van Meter, Associate Professor of Natural Resources, Ball State University

Chapter Reviewers

Ian G. Barbour, Professor of Religion and Physics, Carleton College

David R. Inglis, Professor of Physics, University of Massachusetts

Harry Perry, Consultant and Senior Specialist in Environmental Policy, Legislative Reference Service, Library of Congress

John E. Stanley, Department of Environmental Sciences, University of Virginia

Kenneth E. F. Watt, Professor of Zoology and Senior Investigator, Institute of Ecology, University of California, Davis

George M. Woodwell, Senior Ecologist, Brookhaven National Laboratory

John P. Holdren, Assistant Professor, Energy Resources Program, University of California, Berkeley

David R. Inglis, Professor of Physics, University of Massachusetts

Glen T. Seaborg, University Professor of Chemistry and Associate Director of the Lawrence Berkeley Laboratory, University of California, Berkeley

Kenneth E. F. Watt, Professor of Zoology and Senior Investigator, Institute of Ecology, University of California, Davis

Alvin M. Weinberg, Director of Energy Research and Development, Federal Energy Administration

Contents

Prologue

Passengers on Terra I, the only true spacecraft, it is time for you to hear the annual State of the Spaceship report. As you know, we are hurtling through space at about 66,600 miles per hour on a fixed course. Although we can never return to home base to take on new supplies, our ship has a marvelous and complex life-support system that uses solar energy to recycle the chemicals needed to provide a reasonable number of us with adequate water, air, and food.

There are about 4 billion passengers on board, with more than 151 nations occupying various sections of the ship. This cultural diversity, along with the diversity of animal and plant life on board, is essential for the long-term ecological stability of our life-support system. Paradoxically, this diversity of human cultures also threatens us. The present lack of trust and cooperation and the continued fighting among some groups can destroy many, if not all, of us. Only about 12 percent of you are American and Russian, but your powerful array of weapons and your unceasing efforts to build even more destructive weapons must concern each of us. You have argued that the arms buildup will help us all by insuring peace through mutual deterrence. Some have wondered whether your real purpose is to protect your luxury cabins and services.

Let me briefly summarize the state of our passengers and of our life-support system. One-quarter of you have occupied the good to luxurious quarters in the tourist and first-class sections. You have used about 70 to 80 percent (some say 90 percent) of all supplies available this past year. Most of the Americans have the more lavish quarters. Even though they represent only about 5.5 percent of our total population, they used about 35 percent of this year's supplies. They have even returned a small fraction of the ship's resources to some of the 3 billion of you traveling in the hold of the ship to help you increase your standard of living. However, the supplies and matter recycling capacity of our craft are limited, and energy resources cannot be recycled. Now, many of you are questioning whether or not there are enough resources for a significant number ever to move from the hold to the tourist and first-class sections, in spite of glowing technological assurances from the Americans. And even more important, many of you are asking why you have to travel in the hold of the ship.

I am saddened to say that things have not really improved this year for the 75 percent of our passengers traveling in the hold. Over one-third of you are suffering from hunger, malnutrition, or both, and three-fourths of you do not have adequate water or shelter. More people died from starvation and malnutrition this year than at any time in the history of our voyage. This number will certainly rise as long as your soaring population growth wipes out any small gains in food supply and economic development.

Although the records are not clear, some believe that our voyage began long ago with only two passengers. A plot of the length in time of our voyage versus the increase in passengers from the original two passengers to the 4 billion now on board yields a curve in the shape of the letter J. The most important fact molding our lives today is that we have gone around the bend on the J curves of increasing population, resource use, and pollution. At the present rate, our population will double to over 8 billion passengers in the next 36 years.

No one knows the maximum number of persons our ship's supplies and recycling systems can support. Some of our engineers say the upper limit is 10 to 15 billion passengers—a number we could reach in only 40 to 50 years. One highly optimistic engineer believes we could support 45 billion passengers. Unfortunately, these estimates are for maximum levels, with almost everyone living in misery just barely above starvation. So we must consider a more important question: What is the optimum population and consumption level that will allow all passengers to have life with freedom, dignity, and a fair share of our finite resources? Some experts estimate this figure to be about 1 to 2 billion passengers, a figure we surpassed long ago.

But the overpopulation of the hold in relation to available food is only part of the problem. In the past few years, we have recognized a second type of overpopulation that is even more serious because it threatens our entire life-support system. This type of overpopulation is occurring in the tourist and first-class sections. These sections are overpopulated relative to the level of consumption and the resulting pollution of our environment. Two J curves of increasing consumption and pollution rise sharply with even a slight growth in population in the tourist and first-class cabins. The 214 million Americans used 35 percent of all of our supplies and produced about 50 percent of our man-made pollution during the past year. Each American tourist and first-class passenger has about 25 to 50 times as much impact on the life-support system as each passenger traveling in the hold. In this sense, the American section is the most overpopulated one on the ship. The Americans and other passengers traveling tourist or first class must reduce their population and simultaneously reduce and redirect their wasteful patterns of consumption, which squander much of our limited supplies. Failure to do this may disrupt, or impair, our life-support system beginning in the first-class cabins.

We are now entering the early stages of our first major spaceship crisis, an interlocking crisis of overpopulation, pollution, resource depletion, and the danger of mass destruction by intergroup warfare. Some have expressed fear that the ship is already doomed, while other technological optimists project a glorious future for everyone. Our most thoughtful experts agree that the situation on this ship is most serious, but certainly not hopeless. They feel that if we begin now, we have about 30 to 50 years to learn how to control our population and consumption and to learn how to live together in cooperation and peace on this beautiful and fragile lifecraft that is our home. Obviously a far greater number of us must begin to act like crewmen rather than passengers, particularly those of you traveling tourist or first class, who have the greatest negative impact on our environment and who have the greatest resources to correct the situation.

1.   John and Susan, two college students, were spending the weekend at a ski resort in Colorado. They had caught the last part of the State of the Spaceship report on the color TV in the ski lodge. "To hell with the ecological crisis," said John as he ripped the tab from his third aluminum beer can. "I'm sick of hearing about it. I've read Ehrlich, Commoner, and a lot of other eco-freaks and it's already too late. My motto is eat, drink, and swing while you can. What's the world done for me?"

"I don't think it's too late at all," observed Susan. "If we can put men on the moon, we can certainly solve our pollution problems. Sure it's going to cost some money, but I'm willing to pay my share. The whole thing is merely a matter of money and technology. John, during Christmas break let's fly to Switzerland to ski. There are too many people here, we always have to wait in line, and all these hideous new ski lodges here have spoiled the view. Besides I want to try out my new skis and shop for a new ski outfit."

2.   In a rotting tenement room in Harlem, Larry angrily switched off the TV, even though he usually kept it on to drown out the noises around him—particularly the scratching sounds of the rats. He dropped out of high school five years ago. For two years he looked for work and then he gave up. "What a lot of crap. This is just another whitey trick to keep us from getting a piece of the action. This ecology thing is just a new form of black genocide. Every summer some liberal college kids come down to help the social workers show us blacks how to use IUDs. What the hell do I care about pollution when my little sister was bitten by a rat last night, my mother has some new disease called emphysema, and we ain't had no heat in this firetrap for months. Tell it to my uncle in Florida who's paralyzed from the waist down from some chemical they used on the fruit trees he was picking. Give me a chance to pollute and then I might worry about it."

3.   In Calcutta, Mukh Das, his wife, and their seven children did not hear the broadcast in the streets where they lived. As Mukh, who is 36, watched his 34-year-old wife patting dung into cakes to be dried and used for fuel, he was glad that seven of his ten children were still alive to help now that he and his wife were in their old age. He felt a chill, and he hoped his children would soon be returning from begging and gathering dung and scraps of food. Perhaps they had been lucky enough to meet another rich American tourist today.

4.   In a Connecticut suburb Bill and Kathy Farmington and their three children, David, Karen, and Linda, were discussing the broadcast. David, a college senior, turned away from the TV in disgust. "This ecology thing is just a big cop-out by people who don't really know what it's all about. In the commune I'm moving into we're going to get back to nature and away from this plastic, racist society of people who don't care."

"That's the biggest cop-out of all," said Karen, a college sophomore. "The only reason you have the freedom to drop out is because you live in an affluent country. Why don't you help rather than trying to escape? The real problem is with the poor Americans in the ghetto who keep having all those children. Why don't you work on family planning in the slums this summer like I'm going to do? I'm even going to get college credit for it."

Bill Farmington, chief engineer for Monarch Power Company, looked sharply at his children. "The problem with all you back-to-the-woods dropouts and misguided liberals is that you don't understand what hard work it takes to keep the world going. If you're so fired up about pollution, David, why don't you walk to your commune rather than driving the car I gave you? Karen, you might consider turning in that snow-

3

mobile you use to recuperate from your hot summer in the ghetto. How do you think I paid for all those things you want? I'm all for clean air and water, but we can't stop economic progress upon which our American way of life is built. Remember last year when we had a lot of eco-freaks and liberal professors trying to stop us from building the new nuclear power plant? Americans are doubling their energy needs every ten years, and we have to provide our customers with the power they want. You're both as bad as those college professors who go around making speeches and writing books on ecology who don't change their own life styles and who don't know what hard physical work is all about. David, cut off that TV, and the one in the kitchen, too. I'm sick of hearing about war casualties, corruption in government, and rioting in India. Linda, it's getting hot in here. Would you please turn up the air conditioning?"

Kathy, his wife, was slowly shaking her head. "I just don't know. This ecological crisis is bad and we all have to pitch in and do something. The problem is I don't know what to do. One scientist says we shouldn't build nuclear power plants, another says we should. One says ban DDT and another says if we do many will die from malaria and starvation. How can we know what to do when experts disagree? I recognize that the population problem is bad in India, Africa, and South America. Remember how horrid it was in Calcutta on our trip last summer? I just couldn't wait to leave. I'm glad we don't have an overpopulation problem in the United States. At least we can afford to have children."

As Linda, a college freshman, got up she was thinking that no one really listened to the speech. "Don't they realize that we are all interconnected with one another and with our spaceship? Can't they see that everyone on Terra I is a unique human being entitled to a fundamental share of the ship's basic resources? To say that environmental reform diverts efforts to provide food, shelter, a meaningful occupation, peace, freedom, and dignity for people is to deny the essential meaning of environment. Like many I'm fearful for mankind, but I really don't think it's too late. When I become a public service lawyer, I plan to devote my life to environmental reform."

This book is dedicated to the growing number of Lindas on Terra I and to Larry, the Das family, and others whose right to human dignity, freedom, and a fair share of the world's resources must be respected.

*Turn off the lights; in the silence of your
darkened home you can hear a thousand
rivers whispering their thanks.*

Clear Creek

1

The Four Energy Crises

1-1 Some Urgent Questions

Suddenly Americans have awakened to find themselves in the midst of an "energy crisis"—a cliche term that greatly oversimplifies the most important, hopeful, complex, and controversial environmental problem we face. As we move from the "find the villain" to the "find a solution" phase we are beginning to see that our dependence on a high rate of energy flow and of wasted energy raises urgent ecological, economic, political, and moral questions.

1. What supplies of fossil fuels do we have remaining in the world and in the United States? If supplies are limited, should we deplete them or save some for future generations?
2. Should we shift from fossil fuels to nuclear power over the next 30 to 50 years? Should we shift from conventional nuclear reactors to breeder nuclear reactors? Can nuclear power plants, nuclear fuels, and radioactive wastes be safeguarded against such possibilities as runaway reactions, highjacking, and inadequate storage?
3. If nuclear power is too dangerous, should we shift back to coal, the only fossil fuel still abundant in the United States? Should we relax air pollution and strip mining regulations to allow increased use of coal?
4. Are there cleaner ways than coal to produce energy at a reasonable cost? Are we devoting sufficient funds and efforts to develop solar, geothermal, wind, or tidal power as viable options before committing ourselves to nuclear and fossil fuel power?
5. Do we really need all of the energy we use? How could energy demand and waste be reduced? Is it right for some individuals, companies, and countries to consume more than their share of the world's nonrenewable energy resources?
6. Since a high flow rate of energy is the single most important characteristic of any industrialized society, why don't we have a national energy policy? How can we develop one for the short, intermediate, and long term?

There is little doubt that these and related questions will dominate much of our lives over the coming decades.[1]

1-2 How Did We Get into This Mess?

Although the problem is enormously complex, five major factors seem to have led to our present situation: (1) our total and our per capita energy consumption have been rising rapidly; (2) the demand for oil and natural gas has outstripped the domestic supply and refinery capacity, producing an increased dependence on imports; (3) because all energy use pollutes to some degree, the increased use of energy has come into direct conflict with our need to preserve the air, water, and land; (4) the lack of a coordinated national energy policy has led to poor long range planning and to conflicting policies on the part of the government and the energy industries (Sporn 1974); and (5) potentially useful energy options such as solar, geothermal, nuclear fusion, wind power, and energy conservation have not been developed (Sporn 1974, Landsberg 1974, Starr 1973).

A human living at survival level needs about 2,000 kilocalories of energy per day (Figure 1-1). But today the average American consumes or, more accurately, degrades

---

[1] For overviews of the energy crisis, resources, and options see Cook 1972, Darmstadter 1971, Faltermayer 1972, Holdren & Herrera 1971, Hottel & Howard 1972, Hubbert 1962, 1969, 1971, Luten 1971, Garvey 1972, National Petroleum Council 1971, Office of Scientific Technology 1972, Rocks & Runyon 1972, Saltonstall & Page 1972, Schurr 1971, 1972, Starr 1971, 1973, Weaver 1972, Wilson 1972, 1972a, Hammond et al. 1973, McLean 1972, Healy 1974, Surrey & Bromley 1973, Shell Oil Co. 1973, U.S. Atomic Energy Commission 1973a, Office of Emergency Preparedness 1972, Large 1973, Joint Committee on Atomic Energy 1973, Bengelsdorf 1971, Theobald et al. 1972, Council on Environmental Quality 1973a, Odum 1971, 1973, Brown 1971, Inglis 1973, Landsberg 1974, Woodwell 1974, Wilson & Jones 1974, Cheney 1974, Hammond 1973a, Udall 1973, Anthrop 1974, Rose 1974, Alfven 1972, *Scientific American* 1971, *Bulletin of the Atomic Scientists* Sept. & Oct. 1971 issues, *Technology Review* 1972, Conservation Foundation 1972a, Lovins 1974, Committee on Interior and Insular Affairs 1971, 1971a, 1972a, Weinberg 1972, Fisher 1974, World Environment Newsletter 1974, 1974a, Steinhart & Steinhart 1974, 1974a, Peach 1973, Environment Information Center 1973, Energy Policy Project 1974, Commoner et al. 1974, Marion 1974, Seager et al. 1975, Clark 1974.

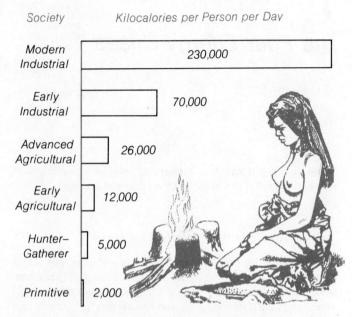

Society   Kilocalories per Person per Day

Modern Industrial   230,000

Early Industrial   70,000

Advanced Agricultural   26,000

Early Agricultural   12,000

Hunter–Gatherer   5,000

Primitive   2,000

1–1   The daily per capita energy consumption at various stages of cultural evolution. (Modified after Cook 1971)

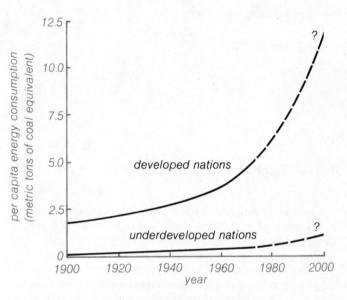

1–2   The gap in per capita energy consumption between the developed nations and the underdeveloped nations is widening. (Source: United Nations)

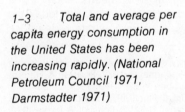

1–3   Total and average per capita energy consumption in the United States has been increasing rapidly. (National Petroleum Council 1971, Darmstadter 1971)

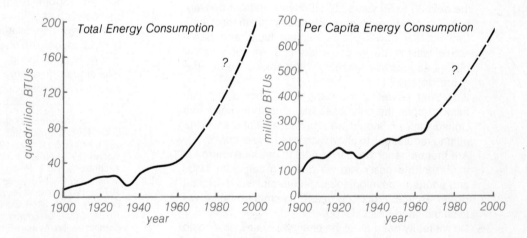

230,000 kilocalories of energy a day—a 115-fold increase over the survival level (Cook 1971).

It is not surprising that one of the most steeply rising J curves in the world and in the United States is energy consumption. World energy consumption increased almost 600 percent between 1900 and 1965 and is projected to increase another 450 percent between 1965 and the year 2000. World oil consumption is now so enormous that during the decade between 1970 and 1980 the nations of the world are projected to consume as much oil as was used in the hundred years between 1870 and 1970 (Udall 1973). Coal has been mined for 800 years, but over one-half of it has been extracted in the past 37 years. Petroleum has been pumped out of the ground for about 100 years, but over one-half of it has been consumed

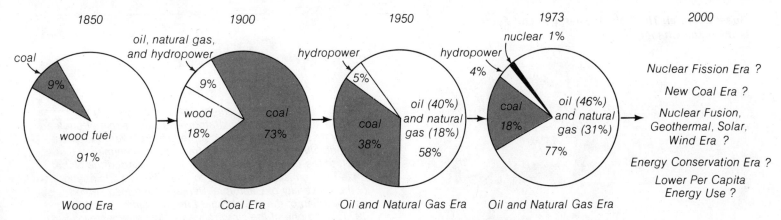

1–4   *Changing patterns in the use of energy resources in the United States. (Data from U.S. Bureau of Census and Resources for the Future)*

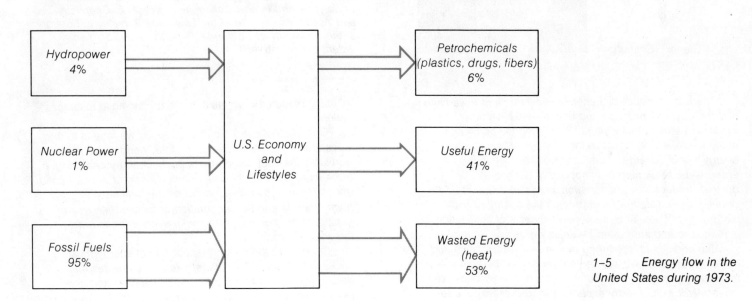

1–5   *Energy flow in the United States during 1973.*

during the past 18 years. In sum, most of the world's consumption of energy from fossil fuels throughout all history has taken place during the past 30 years.

Most of this energy is consumed by the industrial nations. With only 30 percent of the world's people, they use 80 percent of the world's energy and this gap is expected to widen (Figure 1–2). The United States with less than one-sixteenth of the world's population accounts for over one-third of the world's annual consumption of energy (Figure 1–3). In contrast, India with about 15 percent of the world's population consumes only about 1.5 percent of the world's energy. Each year 214 million Americans use as much energy for air conditioning alone as 800 million Chinese use for all purposes,

and we *waste* almost as much energy as 105 million Japanese consume for all purposes (Udall 1973).

Today about 95 percent of all energy used in the United States is based on the fossil fuels coal, oil, and natural gas. Between 1850 and the present we shifted our energy use pattern first from wood to coal and then from coal to oil and natural gas, which now supply some 77 percent of our energy (Figure 1–4). The joyride of cheap fossil fuel energy in the United States seems to be over (Freeman 1971), and we must now adopt a new energy use pattern. We are not running out of energy, but we are running out of cheap oil and natural gas.

In spite of this, over 50 percent of the energy used in this country is wasted (Figure 1–5). Experts (Office of Emer-

*Guest Editorial: The Role of Energy in Our Future
Growth and Change*

Glenn T. Seaborg

*Glenn T. Seaborg is one of America's most distin-
guished scientists, administrators, and proponents of nuclear
energy as our major energy source. He discovered element
94 (plutonium) and eight other transuranium elements. In
1951, at the age of 39, Dr. Seaborg was awarded the Nobel
Prize in Chemistry. From 1958 to 1961, he was Chancellor
of the University of California, Berkeley, and then served
as Chairman of the U.S. Atomic Energy Commission until
1971. He is one of the strongest and most eloquent sup-
porters of nuclear energy as evidenced in his book with
W. R. Corliss, Man and Atom (1971). In 1972 he served as
President of the American Association for the Advancement
of Science and is now University Professor of Chemistry
and Associate Director of the Lawrence Berkeley Laboratory
at the University of California, Berkeley. He is also an
ardent conservationist.*

There is no doubt that energy—how much of it we have
and the ways we produce and use it—will have a
significant effect on our future. In meeting the challenge
of the future, we do not have the choices of "energy or no
energy," or of "energy or environment." Energy is the
essential underpinning of almost all of our society. Industrial production, transportation, communication,
population, knowledge for improving the quality of life—
the growth of these and many other aspects of civilization
is related to and supported by energy growth.

Our choices for the future rest in how we perceive and
use our resources. We are seeing—or should be seeing—our
total energy reserves as a huge, versatile energy pool. We
must treat it with a vastly expanded rationale—expanded
beyond the needs of this spot, these short-term economics,
this point of time, to total global reserves on a very long-
term scale. We must determine which resources could serve
us best for what purposes and the effects of their various
uses on both our natural and man-made environment. In
short, we must begin to think, plan, and act as we have
never done before in making energy work for us without its
inadvertently working against us.

This will require some enormous changes in our
society, nationally and internationally. The longer term
energy resource problem and the shorter term environmental
crises due to the misuse of such resources now challenge
individuals, nations, and the entire international community
to undertake serious energy policy planning. If we are not
thoroughly to deplete many of our irreplaceable natural
resources in a few generations, and at the same time put
those generations in environmental jeopardy by the misuse

of those resources, we must begin to use those resources
rationally.

One of the most difficult challenges we face is to find
ways to ensure that all peoples of the world share more
equitably the vast human benefits that energy can bring. If
we want to see our children live in a world of peace based
not on terror or suppression but on the fulfillment of
human needs and the recognition of human dignity, we
must over the coming years make every effort to narrow
the energy gap.

Contrary to the notion that our use of energy must
necessarily deplete our planet's resources or despoil
nature, I believe that our wise use of energy—and considerably more than we are using now—can restore nature
and rejuvenate man.

Discussion

1. What "enormous changes in our society" do you believe
must be made to deal with the energy problem? How will
these affect you personally?

2. What constitutes rational use of our energy resources?

3. Debate the proposition that the United States should reduce
its consumption of energy by one-third.

4. How would you implement Dr. Seaborg's suggestion that
all peoples in the world share more equitably the world's
energy resources and the benefits energy can bring?

gency Preparedness 1972, Makhigani & Lichtenberg 1972, Hirst & Moyers 1973) estimate that our energy waste could be cut by one-third to one-half (without a loss in life quality) through a mandatory national energy conservation program based on existing technology.

1–3   The Four Energy Crises

Based on the time perspectives of the short term (present to 1985), intermediate term (1985 to 2000), and long term (2000 to 2020), there appear to be four distinct energy crises. Two of these are *real energy crises* based on a true shortage of needed energy resources, while the remaining two are more accurately described as *energy policy crises*. They do not result from an actual global shortage of energy resources but from a fragmented, unwise, or nonexistent energy policy that affects world-wide exploration, distribution, and processing of existing energy sources.

The complex dimensions of the world food energy crisis have been treated by this author (Miller 1972, 1975) and by others (Allaby 1972, Borgstrom 1973, 1973a, 1973b, Brown & Finsterbusch 1972, Wade 1973). The remainder of this book will be devoted to a discussion of the second, third, and fourth energy crises.

The Four Energy Crises

1. Today's Real Energy Crisis—Food: *One-third to one-half of the world's population does not get the basic minimum quantity and quality of 2,000 kilocalories of energy per day needed for good health.*

2. Today's Energy Policy Crisis: *Cheap fossil fuel energy is maldistributed or unavailable because of poor planning and unwise policies of the government and energy industries and because of increased per capita energy use and waste.*

3. The Energy Policy Crisis of 1985: *Failure to develop and coordinate a national energy policy could make the country dependent on outside sources for much of its oil and natural gas (National Petroleum Council 1971) or could force the nation to switch to nuclear fission energy or return to coal before evaluating the potential of solar, geothermal, wind, coal gasification, and energy conservation alternatives.*

4. The Real Energy Crisis of 2000 to 2020: *As economically acceptable supplies of natural gas, petroleum, and uranium begin to dwindle, we will have to shift to essentially infinite and safe energy resources or suffer a sharp drop in per capita energy use. (The policies we are making now will determine how prepared we are for this crisis.)*

*We have for a long time been breaking the
little laws, and the big laws are beginning to
catch up with us.*

A. F. Coventry

2

Some Energy Concepts: Two Spaceship Laws We Can't Repeal

Let us begin by examining some of the fundamental scientific laws of energy, which determine what we humans can and cannot do. If you pick up an apple and then let it go, you automatically expect it to drop to the floor or other surface below it. Why? Because during your lifetime and apparently during the lifetime of all others on this spaceship, unsupported objects have always been observed to fall downward. This description of what we have always observed has been codified in what we call the "law of gravity." This and other scientific laws are descriptions of the orderly behavior of nature based solely on observation of what always happens on our spaceship. (In space or on another planet a different set of laws may, of course, apply.) Unlike legal laws passed by man, we can't repeal these natural limitations on what we can or cannot do. A scientific theory, on the other hand, may be altered or even overthrown. It is an attempt to explain the law. You may doubt Einstein's theory explaining gravitation, but I am confident you would not jump from a ten-story building with the idea that you would not fall or that you would slowly float to the ground.

Yet in a way this is precisely what we have unwittingly been trying to do. We are not trying to ignore the law of gravity, but we have been acting as if we could ignore or repeal two equally fundamental and inviolable energy laws on our spaceship.

2–1 *You Can't Get Something for Nothing: The First Law of Energy*

What energy changes occur when an apple drops to the floor? *Potential energy* is the energy associated with the position of an object relative to some force that can act on it. When the apple is dropped we say that there is a loss of potential energy from a high value (hand) to a low value (floor). The apple has dropped to a state of minimum potential energy relative to its surroundings. (Under other circumstances, it may drop to a lower potential energy — if the floor were on the fifth story of a building, for example.)

Has energy been lost or consumed in this process? It is important to distinguish between the *system* (that is, the collection of matter under study) and its *environment*, or *surroundings* (the rest of the universe). During any process energy may pass from the system to the surroundings or from the surroundings to the system.

According to the *first law of thermodynamics*, also known as the *law of conservation of energy*,

Energy is neither created nor destroyed by any physical or chemical process; it is merely transformed from one of its forms such as heat, light, mechanical, electrical, or chemical energy to another.[1]

If the system loses or gains energy, then an equal amount of energy must be transferred in some form to or from the surroundings. In any process, the total energy of the system plus its surroundings remains constant. In other words, we can't get something for nothing.

In the case of the falling apple, potential energy is transformed primarily into the *kinetic energy* (average energy of motion) of the apple and into the kinetic energy of the air molecules in the surroundings. Temperature is a measure of the average kinetic energy of a collection of molecules.[2] The net effect of the falling apple is to raise the temperature of the air molecules in the immediate surroundings, and we say that some of the energy has been transferred as heat from the system (apple) to the surroundings (air). No energy is created or destroyed; it is merely transformed from one form to another.

Although most of us are familiar with this first law of energy we occasionally forget that we can't get something for nothing. For example, many talk of synthetic foods as a solution to the problem of feeding our growing list of passengers. To make synthetic foods we must use an energy source, normally fossil fuels or perhaps nuclear energy, to force small molecules together to form the large organic molecules that comprise food. The first law requires that we put in at least as much energy as we will eventually get out of the molecules as food energy. And since even our most sophisticated processes approach only 60 percent efficiency, making synthetic foods on a large scale will require more energy than we can get out of it. We will be depleting even more rapidly our dwindling supply of high-energy resources in the form of fossil fuels and uranium and adding enormous amounts of

---

[1] Matter can be converted into energy (witness nuclear power) but this becomes measurable only in nuclear reactions, not ordinary chemical reactions. A more accurate and comprehensive statement would be "Matter–energy can be neither created nor destroyed."

[2] Actually only the absolute, or Kelvin, temperature is a measure of the average kinetic energy of a collection of molecules. The Kelvin temperature is obtained by adding 273 to the temperature in degrees Celsius (°C).

heat and other pollutants to our environment. Additional heat and chemical pollution will be added by building the food plants, extracting and transporting raw materials to the plants, and transporting and distributing the synthetic food to users. There is no such thing as a free lunch on our spaceship.

3-2   If You Think Things Are Mixed Up Now, Just Wait: The Second Law of Energy

Spontaneous processes and increasing disorder   In nature we distinguish two types of processes: *spontaneous processes,* which can occur naturally without an outside input of energy, and *nonspontaneous processes,* which require an energy input from the surroundings. The second energy law summarizes our observations about the direction of energy flow in spontaneous processes.

What are some spontaneous processes? We observe that objects fall to the ground, water flows spontaneously downhill, and heat flows spontaneously from a hot body to a cold body. If you drop a vase to the floor and it shatters, under no circumstances would you expect the random array of fragments to spontaneously re-form the vase. We cannot put Humpty Dumpty together again, at least not spontaneously.

Closer observation reveals that all spontaneous processes have one common element, based on the phenomena of order and disorder. In general, do you observe that things and events tend spontaneously to become more orderly or more disorderly? What is the most probable state of your room—naturally increasing order or naturally increasing chaos? Doesn't keeping your room neat and orderly require continuous effort (energy) on your part?

Vegetation in a natural state such as a jungle appears disorderly, at least as viewed from above in an airplane.[3] Lawns must be cut to keep them orderly. A garden or field, consisting of neat and orderly rows of plants, does not form on its own. Fly over the land and you can immediately see where man has been by the presence of straight lines in fields, roads, and cities. These straight lines represent an ordering process against the apparently natural tendency for more random, or disorderly, growth of vegetation. These ordering activities of man are nonspontaneous processes requiring enormous and continuous inputs of energy to be maintained.

Smoke from a smokestack and exhaust from an automobile spread out spontaneously to become more randomly dispersed in the atmosphere. Chemical wastes are dumped into a river on the assumption that they will be spontaneously dispersed into a more disordered and less harmful state.

Indeed our primary approach to pollution control so far has been that dilution is the best solution to pollution. We dump our wastes into the air, water, or soil and assume that they will spontaneously be diluted to harmless amounts or at

---

[3] The relative degree of order or disorder depends on the level of observation. For example, at the molecular level vegetation is a highly ordered array of molecules.

The spontaneous tendency toward disorder.......

least dispersed far away from us. We are now beginning to realize that *dilution is not always the solution to pollution.* It is a useful application of the idea that disorder tends naturally to increase. However, it contains some fatal flaws.

We have apparently uncovered a driving force in nature for spontaneity, so let us propose a tentative hypothesis:

A system tends spontaneously toward increasing disorder, or randomness.

Now, does this hypothesis always hold true in nature? Can we find any spontaneous process that does not increase the disorder in the system? Isn't a living organism, such as a man, an example of increasing order rather than disorder? A living organism is a highly ordered collection of atoms and cells. So life appears to contradict the tendency toward disorder. But maintaining life is not a spontaneous process. To form and preserve the highly ordered arrangement of molecules and the organized network of chemical reactions in any plant or animal it must be supplied with energy and raw materials from its environment. In other words, order in your body system (or in that of any living organism) is maintained at the expense of a greater increase in disorder in the environment. Man's ability to create disorder in the environment while trying to order part of the world is greater than that of any other organism. The production of food, the manufacturing of various chemicals, clothes, shelter, and other supplies, the burning of fossil fuels to provide heat and to cook foods all greatly increase the disorder of the environment. This disorder most often takes the form of heat (the disorderly, chaotic motion of molecules) and the conversion of relatively large fossil fuel molecules into smaller, air pollutant, molecules such as carbon monoxide.

The second energy law   Thus, when we consider the change in disorder in *both system and surroundings* we find a net increase in disorder even for living organisms. Experimental measurements again and again have revealed that for any spontaneous process, when both the system and its surroundings are considered, there is always a net increase in disorder. With these facts we revise our original hypothesis to include both the system and its environment, or surroundings:

Any system plus its surroundings tends spontaneously toward increasing disorder, or randomness.

This is a statement of the *second law of energy or thermodynamics.*

Scientists frequently use *entropy* as a measure of relative disorder. A disorderly system has high entropy and an orderly system has low entropy. Now, using the term entropy, we restate the second law as

Any system plus its surroundings tends spontaneously toward increasing entropy, *or*

If you think things are mixed up now, just wait.

Notice that the second law makes no predictions about the system alone. It analyzes the entropy, or disorder, changes in both the system and its surroundings. In most "apparent" violations of the second law, the observer has failed to include the greater disorder (entropy) increase in the surroundings when there is an increase in order in the system.

In a system such as our spaceship, the second law determines the ultimate limit of what we can and cannot do. It tells us that maintaining order in the form of life always increases disorder in the surroundings. It also tells us that as we try to support more and more humans at higher and higher levels of energy and resource consumption, the amount of disorder in our life-support system will automatically increase. This is the *entropy trap* (Boulding 1965) that inevitably limits the use of energy on earth.

The second law and useful energy   Another statement of the second law is that *no conversion of energy from one form to another is 100 percent efficient.*[4] In other words, in any energy conversion, some energy is always wasted. Not only can we not get something for nothing but we can't even break even. As energy is transformed from one form to another it is degraded into less and less useful forms until it becomes heat energy, which is the random motion of molecules. This chaotic, disorganized motion of molecules cannot be har-

---

[4] Percent efficiency = $\dfrac{\text{useful energy output}}{\text{total energy input}} \times 100$. If you eat 100 units of energy and you obtain 10 units of useful work, then your percent efficiency is $\dfrac{10}{100} \times 100 = 10\%$. Ninety percent of the input of food or chemical energy ends up as wasted heat energy in the environment.

nessed readily to perform useful work. A useful form of energy is one that has a high capacity for doing work.

For example, photosynthesis in plants converts solar energy to chemical energy, which is stored in the chemicals produced. If you eat plants such as lettuce, this chemical energy is transformed within your body to the energy of motion in muscles and other life processes, and heat energy is given off to the environment. Each energy step is inefficient and adds nonreusable waste heat to the environment. The end result is that all of the ordering processes necessary for life on our spaceship increase disorder, primarily as heat, in our life-support system. The ultimate pollutant in any spaceship is heat, as is discussed in greater detail in Chapter 8.

The ways in which man converts energy are particularly inefficient. For example, the efficiency of the internal combustion engine is about 22 percent. When we deduct friction losses the automobile is only about 10 to 12 percent efficient; 88 to 90 percent of the gasoline or chemical energy used to drive the car is wasted and lost as heat to the environment. If we tried to design the most inefficient engine possible, we would be hard pressed to come up with a poorer one than the internal combustion engine. Converting to steam engines could increase overall automobile efficiency to 30 or 40 percent and could decrease most of the harmful chemical pollutants spewing out of the exhausts of our automobiles. Improving efficiency would then be a major aid, but the second law says we can never reach 100 percent efficiency. As Robert Morse put it, "The second law means that it is easier to get into trouble than to get out of it."

2–3   Life as a Dynamic Steady State

Open and closed systems   In real life there are two major types of systems, open and closed. In an *open system,* both matter and energy are exchanged between the system and its surroundings. Life is maintained by a balanced steady state exchange of matter and energy between the organism and its environment. In a *closed system* energy but not matter is exchanged between the system and its surroundings. Life is possible only with an outside energy input and an internal system for recycling vital chemicals.

An open container of boiling water is an open system. Both energy and matter are being exchanged between the container of water and the surrounding atmosphere. All living organisms are also open systems. We take energy and matter into our bodies, transform them to maintain life, and put heat and waste materials back into our surroundings. Thus, life is an open, or flowing, system, maintained through a balanced exchange of matter and energy with the environment. This balanced input and output maintains the steady state needed for survival. We can therefore describe life in an individual organism as an *open system maintained in a dynamic steady state.*

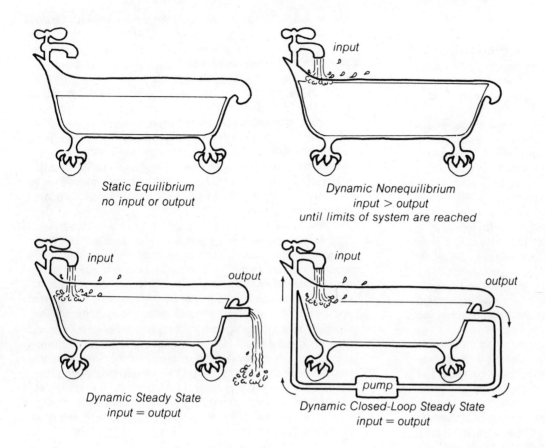

Static Equilibrium
no input or output

Dynamic Nonequilibrium
input > output
until limits of system are reached

Dynamic Steady State
input = output

Dynamic Closed-Loop Steady State
input = output

2–1   Four states of a bathtub—or any system—static
equilibrium, dynamic non-
equilibrium, dynamic steady
state, and dynamic closed-
loop steady state.

The dynamic, exciting steady state   The phrase "steady state" may sound dull and static, but nothing could be further from the truth. When anyone mistakenly equates a steady state society with a static or no-growth society, remind them that every living organism, including human beings, is in a dynamic steady state. What could be more interesting?

A bathtub filled with water or a car tire filled with air is a static state of equilibrium. Suppose you hook up a compressor to the tire or turn on the water to the tub and go off to lunch. You have then created a system like the world today. It is a non-equilibrium system growing and growing and growing. Sometime during your lunch there will be an explosion or a wet floor as the tire or the tub reaches the limits of its finite growth potential. You won't be able to predict when the pop or over-flow will occur but you know it will happen unless you are an awfully fast eater.

A steady state, however, is a dynamic not a static state, in which input and output are balanced. There is continuous motion, or flowthrough, within the limits of the system. For ex-ample, suppose the bathtub has an overflow pipe. By running water in at the same rate as it flows out we maintain the water level in a dynamic steady state somewhere below the top of the tub (Figure 2–1). There is a whole series of different steady states—different possible water levels—as long as we don't exceed the limits of the tub. There is also a series of possible flowthrough rates depending on the sizes of input and output pipes, the supply of water, the capacity of the pump, and the supply of energy to run the input pump. The steady state is a dynamic balance of these variables.

But this system is still linear; water is flowing through the system and presumably being wasted. If water is a scarce item we can close the loop and recycle it to yield a dynamic, closed-loop steady state. In this case we have made an im-portant advance. We no longer need to worry about running out of water. Our major problem now is having enough energy to keep the recycling pump running. We have also decreased pressure on our energy resource supply, because it will take much less energy to pump the water the length of the bathtub than to pump it for miles from a nearby river, reservoir, or ocean. The key words describing a steady state then are *dynamic* and *balanced* not static and unbalanced. The basic problem of society today is making the transition from our present linear or dynamic nonequilibrium state to a dynamic closed-loop steady state, or earthmanship, society.

2–4   Our Misuse of the Term "Spaceship Earth"

Let us examine some closed systems. Consider a closed test tube containing chemicals. It can be heated or cooled and thus gain or lose energy, but the amount of matter in the system remains the same even though the chemicals can react to form different substances.

A person living in a space capsule is another example of a closed system. Once inside the capsule, he can stay alive only as long as there is an energy input from outside (solar energy to recharge the batteries for his power system) and a system capable of recycling the chemicals needed to maintain life. But our man-made space capsules cannot sustain life very long; they must be brought back to earth periodically, converted to an open system, and refilled with supplies. In this sense a space capsule is not a truly self-sustaining closed system, or spaceship. The only real spaceship is the earth. We can never return or go anywhere to take on new supplies. Life on this closed system depends on a delicate and intricate array of chemical recycling systems developed through millions of years of evolution and driven and sustained by energy from the sun.

Unfortunately, the term *spaceship earth* has meaning to most of us because we liken the earth to our man-made spacecrafts. But this is an upside-down view of reality. We should be considering not how the earth is like a spaceship but how a spaceship is like the earth. On our man-made spaceships every natural function can be performed only with the utmost deliberation and rigid control. There is little room for novelty, spontaneity, freedom, or most of the things that make life rich, vivid, or poignant. To survive on a man-made spaceship, everything must be programmed. Our lives would be managed and manipulated by experts, swathed in artificiality, and surrounded by gadgetry. How would you like to spend your entire lifetime on such a voyage?

The term *earthmanship* as used in this book implies a world view and life style that goes beyond the useful but too restrictive spaceship view. Because we have had the spaceship image upside down, we have not cared about the real ship. Our task is not to pilot spaceship earth, not—as Teilhard de Chardin would have it—"to seize the tiller of the world." Instead we must stop trying to steer completely. Somehow we must tune our senses again to the beat of existence, sensing in nature fundamental rhythms we can trust even though we may never fully understand them. We must learn anew that we belong to the earth and not the earth to us. We must control nature to some extent, but we must do so with wisdom, care, and restraint.

2–5   The Second Energy Law and the Environmental Crises

As we shall see throughout this book, the second energy law provides a key both for understanding the energy crises and for understanding how we must deal with them. From a physical standpoint, *the energy crises are entropy, or disorder, crises,* and the second law explains why. It says that any increase in order in a closed system such as the earth will automatically and irrevocably increase the entropy, or disorder, in the environment. We can dig a hole in the ground but the dirt and heat energy produced must go somewhere.

Thus, paradoxically, the more we attempt to order, or "conquer," the earth the greater the stress we inevitably put on the environment. Failure to accept the fact that we can't repeal the first and second laws of thermodynamics and that we must learn to live with the restrictions they impose on us can only lead to a steady and further degradation of the quality of life on this planet.

Why do we think we can ignore or repeal these laws? Part of our problem is ignorance. Most people have never heard of these laws let alone understand their implications. A more important factor is that these laws are statistical or cumulative rather than individual. Everyone accepts the fact that he cannot violate the law of gravity because it limits him and everyone else on a personal level. We have the illusion, however, that we can ignore the consequences of the second law. Each individual's activities increase the disorder in the environment, but individual impact has no major consequence. However, the cumulative impact of all the disorder-producing activities of a large number of individuals can affect the overall life-support system. The limitation and the challenge of the second law of thermodynamics means that we are all interconnected whether we like it or not.

The energy crises are

1. Crises in human values—our attempts to order nature.

2. Entropy crises—our attempts to ignore the consequences of the first and second laws of thermodynamics.

The ecological and human imperative that we must learn from the energy laws is simple and profound: *whenever you do anything be sure to consider its present and possible future impact on your fellow passengers and on your environment.* We must apply this imperative now if we are to prevent a drastic degradation of our lives.

The law that entropy increases—the second law of thermodynamics—holds, I think, the supreme position among laws of nature. . . . If your theory is found to be against the second law of thermodynamics, I can give you no hope; there is nothing to do but collapse in deepest humiliation.

Arthur S. Eddington

Discussion Topics

1. List occurrences in everyday life that illustrate the tendency toward increasing disorder. List any processes that you feel violate this tendency.

2. Criticize the statement: "Any spontaneous process results in an increase in the entropy or disorder of the system."

3. Criticize the statement: "Life is an ordering process and, since it goes against the natural tendency for increasing disorder, it violates the second law of thermodynamics."

4. Which of the following systems has the higher entropy: (a) a deck of cards arranged according to suit and number or the same deck after shuffling, (b) a solid sugar cube or the sugar cube dissolved in hot coffee, (c) a gas or a liquid at the same temperature, (d) students sitting in a classroom listening to a lecture or the same students 30 seconds after the end of the period?

5. Explain how the following nursery rhyme is a statement of the second energy law:

> *Humpty Dumpty sat on a wall*
> *Humpty Dumpty had a great fall!*
> *All the King's horses*
> *And all the King's men*
> *Couldn't put Humpty Dumpty together again.*

6. Discuss the line in Genesis 3:19, "You are dust and to dust you shall return," in relation to the second law of thermodynamics.

7. Explain why the ultimate pollutant on earth is heat.

8. Explain how the energy and environmental crises can be considered (a) crises in human values and (b) entropy crises.

9. Using the first and second laws explain the idea "To exist is to pollute." Does this mean that increasing pollution is inevitable? Why or why not? Does it apply to all types of pollution or only to some?

Further Reading

Angrist, S. W., and L. G. Hepler. 1967. *Order and Chaos*. New York: Basic Books. Excellent nontechnical introduction to thermodynamics emphasizing its fascinating historical development.

Blum, H. F. 1968. *Time's Arrow and Evolution*, 3rd Ed. Princeton, N.J.: Princeton University Press. Discussion of the second law and the evolution of life.

Boulding, Kenneth E. 1964. *The Meaning of the 20th Century*. New York: Harper & Row. Penetrating discussion of our planetary situation by one of our foremost thinkers. See especially Chapters 4, 6, and 7 on the war trap, the population trap, and the entropy trap.

Cook, Earl. 1971. "The Flow of Energy in an Industrial Society," *Scientific American*, September, pp. 83–91. Readable discussion of degradation of energy and energy use.

Lindsay, R. B. 1963. *The Role of Science in Civilization*. New York: Harper & Row. A nontechnical and very readable discussion of the relationships between science and the humanities, philosophy, history, technology, government, and human behavior. See pp. 290–298 for a discussion of entropy and ethics.

Miller, G. Tyler, Jr. 1971. *Energetics, Kinetics and Life— An Ecological Approach*. Belmont, Calif.: Wadsworth. My own attempt to show the beauty and wide application of thermodynamics to life. Amplifies and expands the material in this chapter at a slightly higher level.

Odum, Howard T. 1971. *Environment, Power and Society*. New York: Wiley-Interscience. Important and fascinating discussion of energy use and man.

Thirring, Hans. 1958. *Energy for Man*. New York: Harper & Row. Informative overview of man's use of energy. Read in conjunction with the later work by Odum.

Earth and water, if not too blatantly abused, can be made to produce again and again for the benefit of all mankind. The key is wise stewardship.

Stewart L. Udall

3

Some Ecological Concepts: Energy Flow and Matter Cycling

3-1 The Ecosphere: Our Life-Support System

What keeps all species alive on this tiny planet hurtling through space at 66,000 miles per hour? All life exists only in a thin film of air, water, and soil having an approximate thickness of only nine miles. This spherical shell of life is known as the *ecosphere,* or *biosphere* (Cole 1958, Hutchinson 1970). The ecosphere concept includes every relationship that binds together all living things.

The earth can be divided into three major spherical layers —the *atmosphere* (air), the *hydrosphere* (water), and the *lithosphere* (soil). Our life-support system, the ecosphere, is a thin spherical shell within this system. It consists of three major layers: (1) above us a thin layer of usable atmosphere no more than seven miles (about 12 kilometers) high;[1] (2) around us a limited supply of water in rivers, glaciers, lakes, oceans, and underground deposits; and (3) below us a thin crust of soil, minerals, and rocks extending only a few thousand feet into the earth's interior. This incredibly intricate film of life contains all of the water, minerals, oxygen, nitrogen, carbon, phosphorus, and other chemical building blocks. Because we live in a closed system these vital chemicals must be recycled again and again for life to continue. If we liken the earth to an apple, then all life and all of the supplies necessary for maintaining life are found within the skin of the apple. Everything in this skin is interconnected and interdependent; the air helps purify the water, the water keeps plants and animals alive, and the plants keep animals alive and help renew the air. It is a remarkably effective and enduring system—and endure it must.

3-2 Solar Energy: The Source for All Life

A nuclear fusion reactor The source of the radiant energy that sustains all life on earth is the sun. The sun warms the earth and provides energy for photosynthesis in plants, which in turn provides the food or carbon compounds that sustain all life.

The sun is a medium-sized star composed mostly of hydrogen. At its center, the sun is so hot that a pinhead of heat at this temperature could kill a man 100 miles (166 kilometers) away. Under such temperatures (and pressures) light hydrogen nuclei can be "fused" together to form heavier helium nuclei. In this process, called *nuclear fusion,* some of the mass of the nuclei is converted to energy. The amount of energy released is enormous (see Section 7–1).

The sun is really a gigantic thermonuclear reactor some 93,000,000 miles (155,000,000 kilometers) away that liberates about 100,000,000,000,000,000,000,000,000 (or 10^{26}) calories[2] of energy per second. If we could completely harness this energy, each person on earth each second would have for his own personal use over 70,000 times the annual power consumption of the United States. The sun uses up about 4.2 million tons (4.1 billion kilograms) of its mass every second in producing this enormous amount of energy. We need not worry about the sun running out of fuel, however. In the normal life cycle of stars, the sun is entering middle-age. It has probably been in existence for at least 6 billion years, and there is enough hydrogen left to keep it going for at least another 8 billion years.

The solar electromagnetic spectrum This radiant energy from the sun is traveling at a speed of 300,000 kilometers per second (186,000 miles per second) in the form of *electromagnetic waves* with a whole range of energies (Brown 1971). At this speed the light striking your eyes made the 93 million mile (155 million kilometer) trip from sun to earth in about 8 minutes. What we observe as sunlight and refer to as visible light is only a tiny portion of the continuous spectrum

---

[1] The atmosphere extends much further but life is found only in this thin layer near the earth's surface.

[2] The calorie is a standard unit for heat. It is equivalent to the amount of heat needed to raise the temperature of 1 gram of water from 14.5° to 15.5°C. The calories stated for food values are actually kilocalories, often represented by using a capital C:

1 kilocalorie (kcal) = 1 Calorie = 1,000 calories

A piece of pie listed as 2,000 Calories is actually 2,000 kcal or 200,000 calories. The internationally approved unit for energy is the joule (pronounced *jool*). Calories can be easily converted to joules and vice versa:

1 joule = 4.184 calories
1 kilojoule = 1,000 joules = 4,184 calories

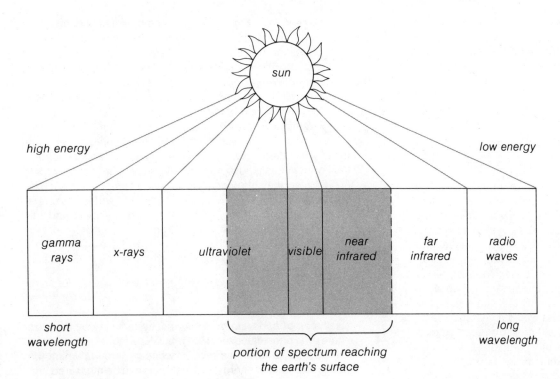

3–1   The electromagnetic spectrum. The sun radiates a spectrum of electromagnetic waves over a wide range of wavelengths and energies, but because of the earth's atmosphere only a small fraction of these actually reaches the earth's surface. (A minor amount of high energy waves also penetrates the atmosphere.)

of energies given off by the sun and known as the *electromagnetic spectrum* (Figure 3–1). These various forms of electromagnetic radiation differ from one another in energy and in *wavelength,* the distance between the crest of one wave and the next. The higher energy, shorter wavelength rays—gamma rays, x-rays, and most ultraviolet rays—are harmful to life. Fortunately, various chemical molecules in our present atmosphere absorb these rays and thus prevent them from reaching the surface of the earth. Without this atmospheric screening process, essentially all present forms of plant and animal life on this planet would be destroyed.

The only portion of the solar energy spectrum used to support life is a narrow band in the visible spectrum. And this energy can be captured and used only by plants containing chlorophyll or chlorophyll-like substances. Even so, plants use 100 times more energy than that used by all man-made machines and make more efficient use of their share of the energy than any man-made machine does.

Global energy flow   The first law of thermodynamics (the law of conservation of energy) requires that eventually the earth must lose energy to space at the same rate that it receives radiant energy from the sun (Miller 1966, Oort 1970, Gates 1971). But although energy in must equal energy out, the useful short wavelength incoming solar energy is degraded to almost useless heat energy with a longer wavelength in accordance with the second law. The earth and its

atmosphere can then be viewed as a giant thermodynamic engine driven by sunlight (Figure 3–2).

The reflectivity and chemical composition of the atmosphere determine which wavelengths of energy will be absorbed and emitted. This in turn determines the average global temperature.[3] Thus, changes in either the chemical composition or the reflectivity of the atmosphere can raise or lower the earth's average temperature. As a result, global climate patterns could be altered with serious consequences for man.

Natural processes such as volcanic eruptions and dust storms can alter the composition and properties of the atmosphere. The question of whether man's activities can alter global climate is receiving increasing attention. Man has been adding massive amounts of carbon dioxide and heat to the atmosphere by burning fossil fuels (gas, oil, coal). Can this lead to a gradual warming of the earth's atmosphere (sometimes called the *greenhouse effect*)? A rise of 2 centigrade degrees (°C) in *average* atmospheric temperature might cause major changes in global weather patterns and a 3° to 6°C rise could eventually melt the polar ice caps, thus flooding a large portion of the world (SCEP 1970, SMIC 1971). Man's activities might also cause a cooling of the earth's atmosphere

---

[3] Obviously temperature varies considerably at different locations and times of the day and year, but the average temperature of the entire earth is maintained by a balanced energy input and output.

through massive additions of soot, dust, and other particulate matter. Such cooling could even trigger a new ice age. The degree to which man may inadvertently be altering the global climate is a current subject of scholarly debate (see Chapter 8). Now let us look at how solar energy is used by living organisms after it enters the ecosphere.

3–3   Ecosystem Structure: What is an Ecosystem?

Levels of organization   Looking at earth from space we see a predominately blue sphere with an irregular pattern of green, red, and white patches on its surface. As we zoom closer these colorful patches are resolved into deserts, forests, grasslands, mountains, seas, lakes, oceans, farmlands, and cities. Each subsection is different, having its own characteristic set of organisms and climatic conditions. Yet, as we shall see, all of these subsystems are interrelated. As we move in closer, we can pick out a wide variety of living organisms. Continuing the magnification process would reveal that plants and animals are made up of cells, which in turn are made up of molecules, atoms, and subatomic particles. One theme running through the universe is that matter is organized in identifiable patterns that vary in complexity from subatomic particles to galaxies. The idea that matter can be classified according to various *levels of organization* is especially useful in helping us identify and understand the function of various components of the ecosphere (Figure 3–3) .

Ecology and ecosystems   *Ecology,* a term coined by Ernest Haeckel in 1869, is derived from two Greek words, *oikos* meaning house or place to live and *logos* meaning study of. Literally then, ecology is a study of organisms in their homes. It is usually defined as the scientific study of the relationships of living organisms with each other and with their environment. One of our most prominent ecologists, Eugene P. Odum (1962, 1971a, 1972), defines it as a study of the structure and function of nature. It considers how organisms and groups of organisms are structured and how they interact with one another and with their environment.

Ecology, unlike other scientific disciplines, takes a broad view. Its message is that of synthesis. *Human ecology* emphasizes the relationships among man and other species and their environment. Because man is also a social and cultural animal, it violates traditional academic and scientific boundaries and seeks to integrate scientific, behavioral, sociological, political, economic, and ethical factors as they relate to man and the environment.[4]

---

[4] This definition is not shared by some who would prefer to restrict the term *ecology* to the strictly "scientific" aspects of man and his environment. But regardless of the term used, these additional interactions must be included in any holistic and meaningful view of how man interacts with his environment.

As seen from Figure 3–3, the ecologist is concerned primarily with interactions between only five levels of organization of matter—*organisms, populations, communities, ecosystems,* and the *ecosphere* (Wiens 1972, Whittaker 1970). A group of individual organisms (pine trees, sheep, geese) of the same kind is called a *population* (grove, herd, flock). In nature we find a number of populations of different organisms living together in a particular area. This group of plant and animal populations occupying and functioning in a given locality is called a *natural community*. Any organism, population, or community also has an environment. It consists of two major categories: the *nonliving (abiotic) components* such as solar energy, air, water, soil, heat, wind, and various essential chemicals and the *living (biotic) components*—plants and animals. If we consider the living and nonliving environment together with the population or community we have an *ecosystem* or *ecological system,* a term first introduced by A. G. Tansley (1935).

Types of ecosystems   An ecosystem may be a planet, a forest, a pond (Deevey 1951), a fallen log, a garden, or a petri dish. It is any area with a boundary through which the input and output of energy and materials can be measured and related to some unifying environmental factor. The boundaries drawn around ecosystems are arbitrary and selected for convenience in studying them.

The large major aquatic ecosystems are lakes, ponds, rivers, springs, swamps, estuaries, coral reefs, seas, and oceans. On land the large major ecosystems—usually called *biomes*—are the forests, grasslands, savannas (combinations of grasslands with scattered trees or clumps of trees), chaparral (shrublands), tundra, and deserts (Jensen & Salisbury 1972, Krutch 1960, Reid 1970, Dasmann 1972). Each of these major types of ecosystems can be divided further. For example, colder regions have coniferous forests, dominated by cold-resisting evergreen trees; in temperate regions deciduous, or leaf-shedding, forests of oaks, maples, and beeches add to the beauty of our planetary home; tropical areas have luxuriant rain forests.

All of the various ecosystems on earth are connected to one another. Thus, if we group together all of the various ecosystems on the planet, we have the largest life unit, or planetary ecosystem, the *ecosphere*. The ecosphere can then be visualized as a vast graduation of diverse ecosystems all interconnected in a complex fabric of life. These connections help preserve the overall stability of an ecosystem. But disrupting or stressing an ecosystem in one place can have some complex, often unpredictable, and sometimes undesirable effect elsewhere. This ecological backlash effect has been eloquently stated by the English poet Francis Thompson: "Thou canst not stir a flower without troubling a star." The goal of ecology is to find out just how everything in the ecosphere is connected.

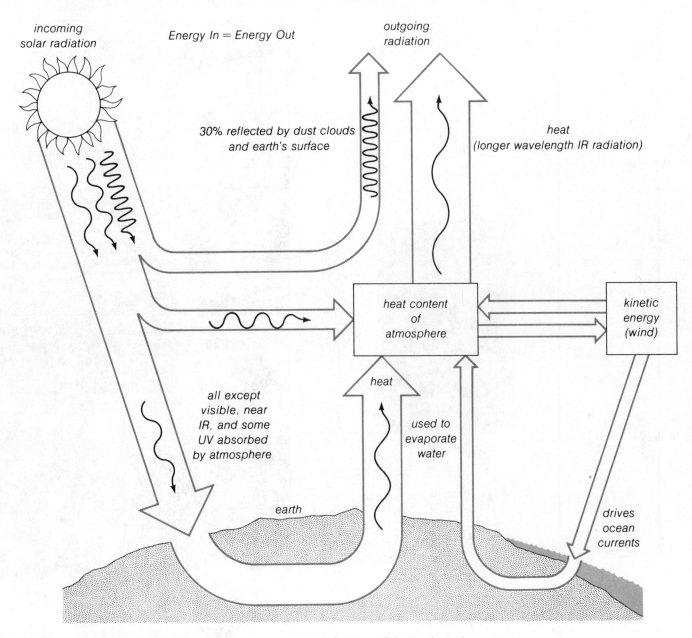

3–2   The atmospheric heat balance. In accordance with the first law of thermodynamics, energy in must equal energy out, but in accordance with the second law the energy leaving is degraded to longer wavelength infrared radiation (heat).

Ecosystem structure   An ecosystem has two major components, nonliving and living (Figure 3–4). The *nonliving,* or *abiotic, component* includes an outside energy source (usually the sun), various physical factors such as wind, and the chemicals necessary for life. The *living,* or *biotic, portion* consists of *producers* and *consumers.* Consumers are usually divided into *macroconsumers* (animals) and the *microconsumers* or *decomposers* (chiefly bacteria and fungi).

Habitat and niche   How would you get to know an organism in a biotic community? You would want to know where it lives and how it lives, what its occupation, function, and role in the community are, how it gets energy and necessary chemicals, and what its impact on the ecosystem is.

Ecologists call the specific place where an organism can be found its *habitat.* A habitat can be as large as an ocean or a desert or as small as a fallen log or the intestine of a termite.

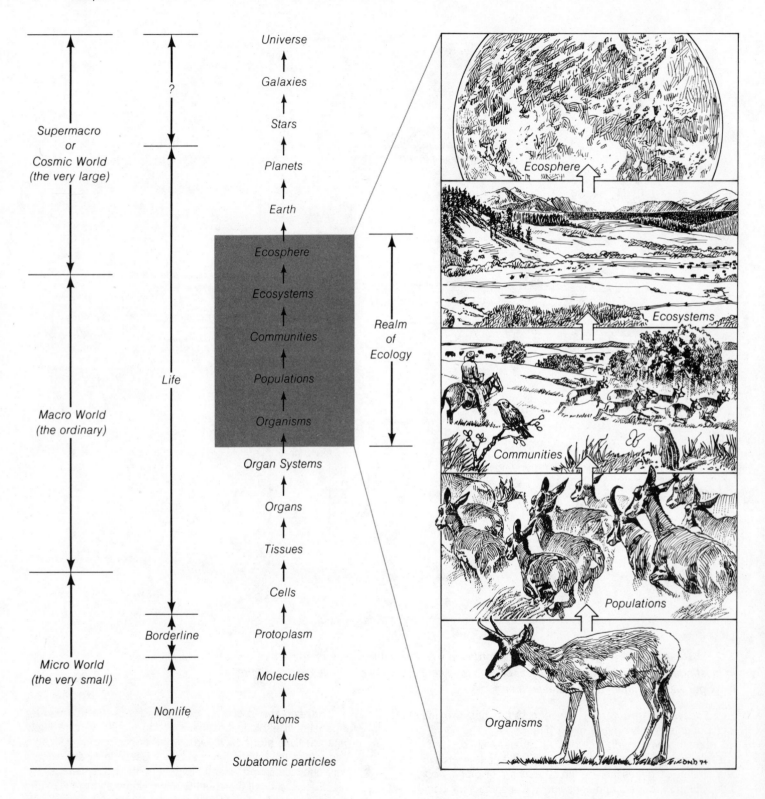

Supermacro
or
Cosmic World
(the very large)

Macro World
(the ordinary)

Micro World
(the very small)

Borderline

Nonlife

?

Life

Universe

Galaxies

Stars

Planets

Earth

Ecosphere

Ecosystems

Communities

Populations

Organisms

Organ Systems

Organs

Tissues

Cells

Protoplasm

Molecules

Atoms

Subatomic particles

Realm
of
Ecology

Ecosphere

Ecosystems

Communities

Populations

Organisms

3–3   Levels of organization of matter.

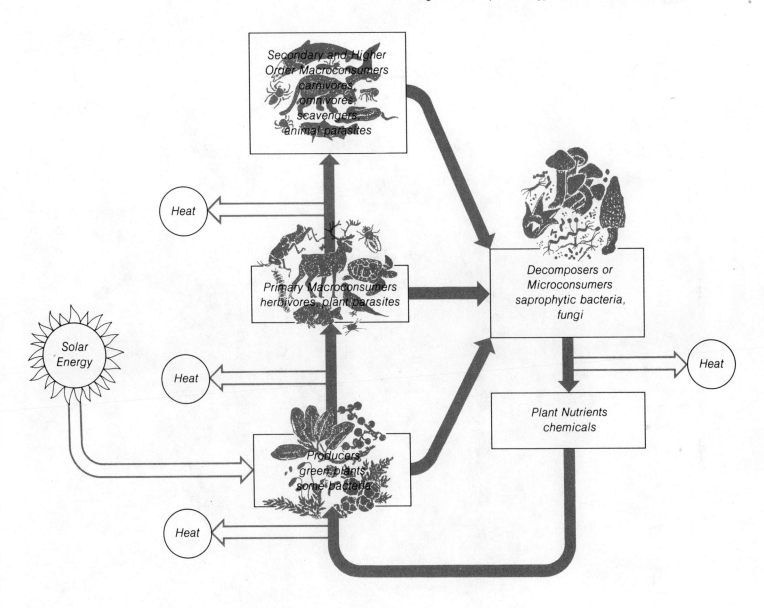

3-4   *The basic components of an ecosystem. Solid lines represent the cyclical movement of chemicals through the system and unshaded lines indicate energy flow.*

An organism's profession, or total role in a biotic community, is known as its *ecological niche*. The organisms on which it feeds, the organisms that feed on it, whether it is a producer, macroconsumer, or microconsumer, the chemicals it extracts from the environment, the chemicals it returns to the environment, its energy requirements and outputs are all facts that help establish the organism's precise niche. The ecological niche then includes all of the chemical, physical, and biological factors that represent the position and function of an organism or population of organisms within the community structure.

Man's ecological niche   What niche does man occupy (Darling & Dasmann 1969)? Most plants and animals are limited to specific habitats in the ecosphere because of their intolerance to a wide range of climatic and other environmental conditions. Some species such as flies, cockroaches, mice, and man are very adaptable and can live over much of the planet. Man's dominant position has resulted from his occupation of a new energy niche, never before occupied by any species. By learning how to use the stored solar energy of fossil fuels and more recently of atomic energy, we have ceased to depend directly on solar energy. We draw on solar

Solar Energy

Altered Air

Air

Feedback

Solid and Liquid Waste

Altered Water

Fossil Fuel and
Nuclear Energy

Feedback

Food

Water

Jobs
Manufacturing
Habitats

Heat

Entertainment, Ideas,
Information, Education,
Technology

Heat

Noise

Materials

Noise

Goods

People

People

Services

3–5   *Some of the inputs and outputs for a city, showing why it is not an ecosystem. (Photo
from Department of Housing and Urban Development)*

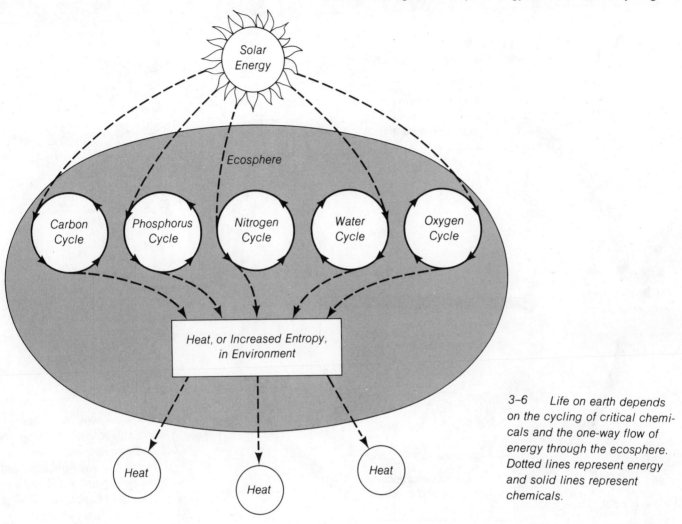

3–6 *Life on earth depends on the cycling of critical chemicals and the one-way flow of energy through the ecosphere. Dotted lines represent energy and solid lines represent chemicals.*

energy stored millions of years ago as chemical energy in coal, oil, and natural gas.

With this energy subsidy man has been able to alter major portions of the earth's land surface. Now with man's large population and growing thirst for affluence, competition and conflict over limited energy and other resources have increased. In effect less than one-third of the world's people occupies a high energy niche, with the remaining two-thirds in a lower energy niche. This is why the environmental crisis is basically an energy crisis.

Is a city or urban region an ecosystem? To be classified as a self-sustaining ecosystem an area must have producers, consumers, decomposers, energy, and chemicals (Figure 3–4). Cities, urban areas, and megalopolises are not complete ecosystems. They lack sufficient producers or green plants to support their human and vertebrate animal population. The limiting factor is lack of soil. To survive, these areas must depend on plant-growing areas outside their boundaries

—sometimes ranging over the entire world (Darling & Dasmann 1969, Strange 1969, Mines 1971). Besides food, they import fresh air, water, materials, and energy resources. Simultaneously they must export their solid, liquid, and gaseous waste products and heat to outside areas (Marquis 1968, Wolman 1965). In exchange for such life support, cities provide a number of important benefits including jobs and habitats for its inhabitants, goods, services, information, manufacturing, technology, and entertainment for society as a whole (Figure 3–5). In the words of Theodore Roszak (1972):

The supercity . . . stretches out tentacles of influence that reach thousands of miles beyond its already sprawling perimeters. It sucks every hinterland and wilderness into its technological metabolism. It forces rural populations off the land and replaces them with vast agrindustrial combines. Its investments and technicians bring the roar of the bulldozer and oil derrick into the most uncharted quarters. It runs its conduits of transport and communication, its lines of supply and distribution through the wildest landscapes. It flushes

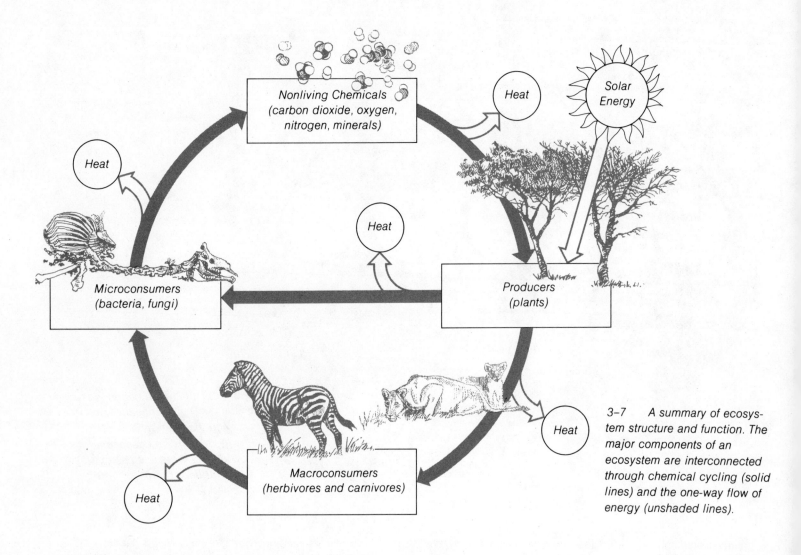

3-7   A summary of ecosystem structure and function. The major components of an ecosystem are interconnected through chemical cycling (solid lines) and the one-way flow of energy (unshaded lines).

its waste into every river, lake, and ocean or trucks them away into desert areas. The world becomes its garbage can.

Cities, urban areas, and megalopolises can be classified as self-sustaining ecosystems only if we include (1) the agricultural, mining, transportation, and other areas throughout the world that provide their input materials and (2) the air, rivers, oceans, and soil that serve as receptacles for their massive output of wastes. In earlier times cities were part of local or regional ecosystems, but today's urban areas are global ecosystems, all attempting to occupy the same global niche and exploit the same finite resources and the same air, water, and soil purification systems. As such areas grow, we must remember that *none of them can sustain themselves.*

3-4   Ecosystem Function: What Happens in Them?

For all practical purposes the total amount of matter on our planet is fixed. The earth is a closed system (Section 2-3) with no matter entering or leaving. (The amounts of matter represented by incoming meteors and other materials from space and the spaceships and satellites we have launched are negligible.) So the chemicals necessary for life must be continuously cycled and recycled throughout the ecosphere. Vital chemicals such as carbon, oxygen, nitrogen, water, and phosphorus are recycled with the sun's energy being used to drive and sustain these *biogeochemical* cycles (*bio* for living, *geo* for water, rocks, and soil, and *chemical* for the processes

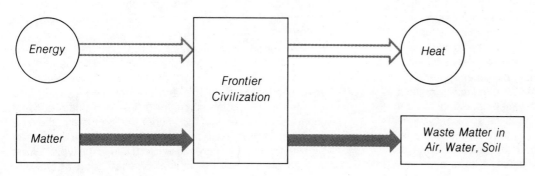

3-8   Today's obsolete frontier or linear civilization is based on a high rate of energy and matter flow.

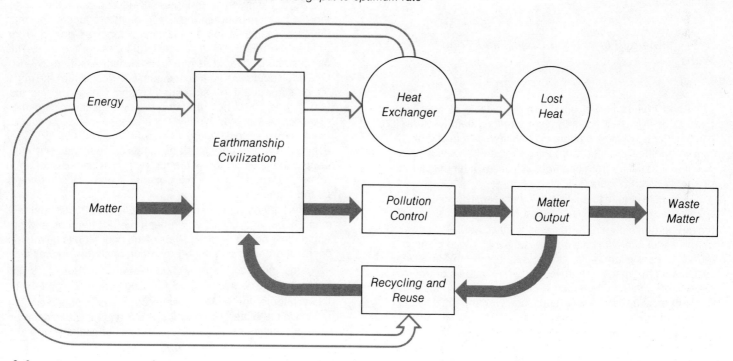

3-9   An earthmanship civilization would be based on energy flow and matter recycling in order to reduce waste and pollution.

involved). Note, however, that although some chemicals are cycled, energy is not; it *flows* in one direction through the ecosphere back into space (Figure 3-6).

Thus, an ecosystem functions through the two important processes of *chemical cycling* and *energy flow*. These two processes connect the various structural parts of an ecosystem together so that life is maintained (Figure 3-7). A study of ecosystem function involves an analysis of the rates and regulation of energy flow through the system and of chemical cycling within the system.

Two major processes in any ecosystem are

1. *Chemical cycling*
2. *One-way flow of energy*

These two processes are a major theme throughout this book. Indeed, the major problem with our present "frontier" approach is that it is a linear system based on *energy flow and matter flow* (Figure 3–8). The affluent nations are attempting to use more and more energy to convert more and more matter to waste as fast as possible. We are attempting to maximize the rate of throughput of matter and energy.

The basic meaning of earthmanship is that we must discard this wasteful and eventually self-defeating system and adopt one that more closely mimics the cyclical systems found in nature that are based on energy flow and matter cycling (Figure 3–9). By recycling many resources and at least partially reusing some energy before it flows back into the environment, we can reduce the throughput of matter and energy to an optimum rather than maximum rate. Figures 3–8 and 3–9 summarize one of the most important messages of this book.

3–5   Energy Flow: Food Chains and Food Webs

Food chains   Let us look more closely at what happens to energy as it flows through an ecosystem (Woodwell 1970a). Each link where energy is transferred from one organism to another is called a *trophic level,* and a particular sequence of transfers from one trophic level to another is a *food* or *energy chain* (Figure 3–10).

It is convenient to distinguish between two major food chains in an ecosystem. The *grazing food chain,* represented by the top portion of Figure 3–10, is the familiar *plant → animal → animal* sequence. We think of this as the major food chain in a terrestrial ecosystem (such as a forest), but in most terrestrial systems more energy is transferred by the *detritus* or *decomposer food chain,* represented by the lower portion of Figure 3–10. In most aquatic ecosystems, however, the grazing food chain is dominant. In any ecosystem both chains are present and they are usually interconnected, as the double arrows between decomposers and primary and secondary consumers in Figure 3–10 indicate.

Food chains and the second energy law: why most people in the world don't eat meat   As energy flows through a food chain about 80 to 90 percent[5] is lost or degraded to useless heat at each step in the chain (Odum 1971,

Phillipson 1966) (Figure 3–11). The second law of thermodynamics (Section 2–2) explains this phenomenon, which has far-reaching implications for the overpopulation and food problems.

Two important principles emerge from the food chain concept. First, the concept shows why all life begins with sunlight and green plants. All of our food can eventually be traced back to green plants and the statement that "all flesh is grass" is a concise summary of the food chain concept. Second, we can see that the shorter the food chain, the more efficient it is. For example, in the typical Asian food chain *rice → man,* far less energy is wasted than in the typical Western food chains that are animal oriented such as *grain → steer → man.* Thus, the ultimate size of the human (or other) population that can be supported is related to the number of steps in the food chain.

As is clearly seen in Figures 3–11 and 3–12, the shorter the food chain between the green plant producers and man the less energy is lost to the environment as heat and the greater the relative energy value (calories) of the food. This can also be illustrated as a pyramid of numbers (Figure 3–12). One adult could live for a year eating 600 trout. If they ate frogs, 30 persons could be supported. Going further we find that 900 people could be supported if they consumed 54 million grasshoppers a year. Finally, if we shorten the food chain as much as possible 2,000 people could be supported for a year eating 2,000 tons of grass. It becomes obvious then why most people in the world today are forced to live on a diet of grain rather than meat. It takes 5 pounds of grains to produce 1 pound of meat.

The typical North American diet contains about 31 percent meat, eggs, and fish, the European diet 22 percent, and the Asian diet about 3 percent. Diets of the poor tend to be monotonous and based on a high proportion of starchy foods, such as yams, rice, and wheat. Cereal grains provide 70 to 80 percent of the calories and 65 to 70 percent of the protein for these people. In 1969 per capita egg consumption was 314 in the United States and only 8 in India, and for young children in poor families it was far less than this national average.

Other implications of the second law   We read in the newspaper about some agricultural or other technological breakthrough, not realizing the thermodynamic and economic differences between discovering something in the laboratory and carrying it out on a world-wide scale. The first law—the conservation of energy—tells us that we can't get something for nothing. A man-made process on a world-wide scale always requires a massive input of energy, money, and time. The second law tells us that however we impose order on our system—by growing more food, mining materials, making cars, tractors, planes, plastics, building houses, factories, and cities, producing more fertilizer and pesticides—there will always be a net increase in disorder, or entropy, in our environment.

---

[5] Actually the figures vary with different species. Typically, only 10 percent of the energy entering the plant population is available to herbivores as food. For warm-blooded carnivores the conversion efficiency is likely to be lower than 10 percent while for cold-blooded predators it may be as high as 20 and in some cases 30 percent. Some sulfur bacteria have an energy transfer of only 2 percent. In any case, the efficiency of energy transfer is low and 10 percent is representative.

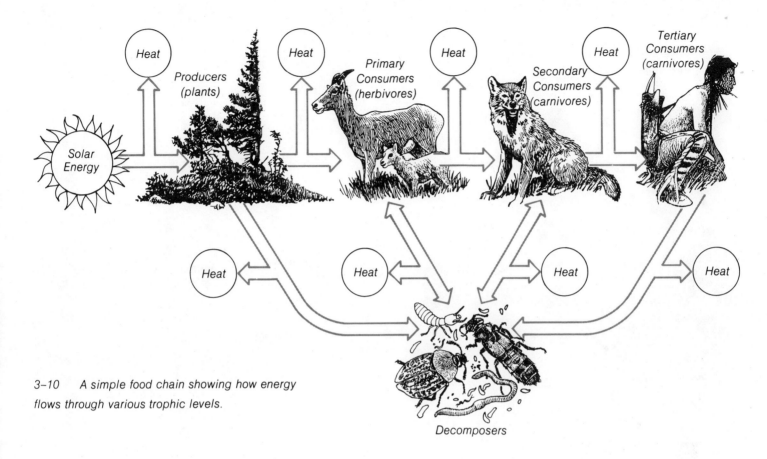

3–10   *A simple food chain showing how energy flows through various trophic levels.*

Man's quest for more food is based on using three levels of energy input to supplement the solar energy used by plants in photosynthesis. These three levels are (1) human muscle power, (2) human muscle power plus animal power, and (3) human muscle power plus fossil fuel power. As we move to the higher levels of energy input, yields per acre rise sharply, but so do the side effects of increased disorder (Section 2–2) and ecosystem oversimplification. Increased yields in modern agriculture are based on four fossil fuel powered technologies: mechanization, irrigation, fertilizers, and pesticides and herbicides. Modern agriculture does not use solar energy any more efficiently than unindustrialized agriculture but merely supplements it with fossil fuel energy. It is a mechanism for exchanging calories in fossil fuels for calories in food (Odum 1971) (Figure 3–13).

The production of 1 million tons of fertilizer not only adds to air and water pollution but requires 1 million tons of steel and about 5 million tons of fuel, mostly fossil fuels (McHale 1970, p. 103). World fertilizer production is doubling every 10 years and is projected to increase from 60 to 250 million tons between 1972 and 2000. Fertilizers increase crop yields and replace plant nutrients lost from the soil as a result of natural or man-induced processes. But they are also a major source of water pollution.

We have also greatly increased the output and efficiency of raising hogs, steers, and poultry for our meat-based diet, primarily by raising them in feedlots. Again, however, the practice of concentrating hundreds to thousands of animals in a small area leads to water pollution from the manure that accumulates.

Increases in the efficiency of production with modern agriculture are impressive. But growing most food requires an expenditure of fossil fuel energy greater than the energy contained in the food. We are being fed at the expense of rapidly depleting our fossil fuel energy. If the soaring maintenance costs are removed the entire system can collapse. Without fossil or other fuels the industrialized monoculture agriculture of countries like the United States would almost totally collapse. We would have to ask farmers in underdeveloped nations to show us how to survive using unindustrialized agriculture. Of course, our population, our level of food consumption, or both would drop sharply.

Crop and animal yields can and must be increased significantly, but many agricultural optimists have forgotten

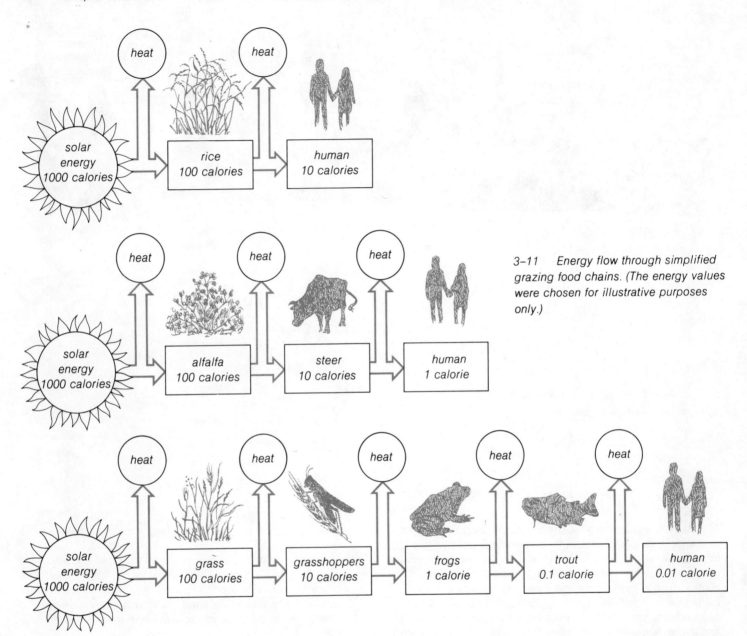

3–11 Energy flow through simplified grazing food chains. (The energy values were chosen for illustrative purposes only.)

or do not understand the environmental penalty exacted by the second law. As agricultural expert Lester R. Brown (1970) said, "The central question is no longer 'Can we produce enough food?' but 'What are the environmental consequences of attempting to do so?' "

Food webs   Although the concept of a simple food chain is very important and useful, such isolated linear food chains rarely exist in nature. Many animals feed on a number of different species and generalists or omnivores such as man, bears, and rats can eat plants and animals at several different trophic levels. As a result, many different food chains crosslink and intertwine to form a complex system called a *food web*.

3-6   What Can Go Wrong in an Ecosystem?

Many persons familiar with the term "balance of nature" interpret it to mean that ecosystems do not change with time.

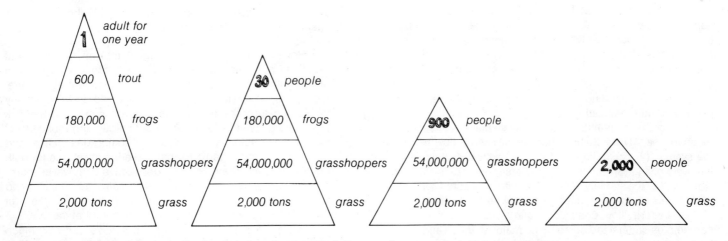

3-12   By eating further down the food chain a larger population can be supported. (Peterson 1970)

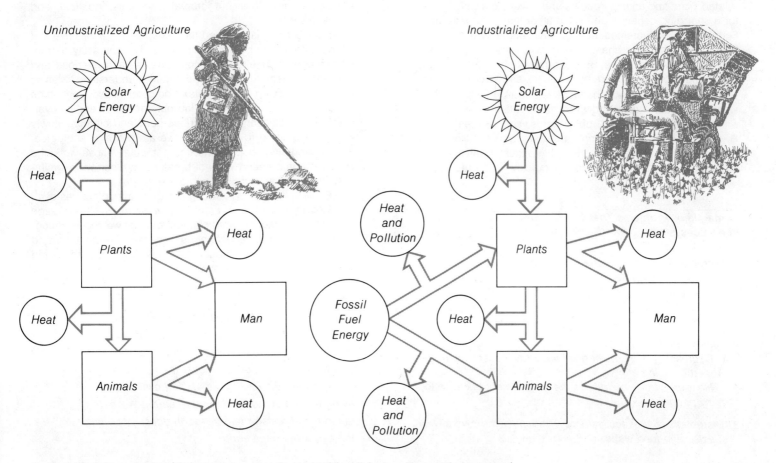

3-13   Modern agriculture is based on extensive use of fossil fuels with greatly increased disorder or entropy in the environment, as required by the second law of thermodynamics.

Nothing could be further from the truth. Ecosystems are dynamic not static. By their very presence organisms, and particularly man, continually alter local conditions. The biotic communities that make up an ecosystem are continually changing in response to environmental changes caused either by the communities themselves or by external stresses such as fires, flooding, erosion, farming, industrialization, pollution, and urbanization.

An ecosystem maintains its overall stability by three major mechanisms: (1) controlling the rate of energy flow through the system, (2) controlling the rate of chemical cycling within the system, and (3) maintaining a diversity of species and food webs so that the stability of the system is not affected seriously by the loss of some species or food web links. These principles of energy flow, chemical cycling, and species diversity can help us understand some of the major changes and problems that can arise in local, regional, or global ecosystems.

Without realizing it, we may have linked much of our productive technological society to features that are incompatible with preserving the stability of our life-support system. We bulldoze fields and forests containing thousands of interrelated plant and animal species and cover them with asphalt for a shopping center, highway, or other form of urbanization. Farming, once diversified, now consists primarily of monocultures, single crops of wheat, rice, or corn covering vast areas as far as the eye can see. Because they lack diversity, single crops must be supported by massive and ever-increasing use of fossil fuels and chemical fertilizers, much of which washes into our lakes and streams threatening to overload and disrupt the nitrogen, phosphorus, and oxygen cycles. Because a monoculture crop can easily be wiped out by a single species of insect, we attempt to protect it with more and stronger pesticides. As the insects quickly breed resistance,

---

Some Major Problems That Can Occur in an Ecosystem

1. *Disruption of essential chemical cycles*
   a. *Breaking the cycle*
   b. *Changing the rate of cycling by chemical overloads or leaks in the cycle*
   c. *Introducing man-made chemicals into the cycle*

2. *Disruption of energy flow*
   a. *Decreasing or increasing solar energy input by changing properties of the atmosphere*
   b. *Heat or entropy buildup in the environment because too many people are using too much energy*

3. *Disruption of the ecosystem by reducing the diversity of species and food webs.*

---

some of these same poisons are magnified higher in the food chain until they accumulate in high concentrations in our bodies.

However, this is not to suggest that all technological practices are bad. We should and will continue to simplify and regulate ecosystems. If we gave up modern agriculture, most of us would starve. And the world could do without many facets of nature. There is no useful purpose in rats that attack slum babies, yellow-fever- and malaria-carrying mosquitoes, tsetse flies, ticks, and myriads of other destructive and disease-carrying organisms that make life miserable for both man and beast. There are also destructive tidal waves, hurricanes, earthquakes, and other natural disasters. Finally and most important, there is the continuing lethal savagery of man. The world would be better off without all of these.

We must simplify sometimes to survive. But how much simplification is possible or desirable and by whom? What parts of the ecosphere are the most vulnerable? What levels of world and regional populations can we support? Do people in the developed nations have a moral obligation to reduce their consumption and population growth? These are not merely ecological questions but crucial economic, political, and ethical issues.

Paul Ehrlich has likened the ecosphere to a massive and intricate computer built by cross-linking a vast array of transistors and other electrical components—a mysterious and amazing system that we do not really understand. Man is rapidly simplifying the complex computer network on which life depends by randomly pulling out transistors and by overloading and disconnecting various parts and circuits. Slowly we are beginning to realize that we are playing "ecological Russian roulette," hoping that the computer whose workings we don't comprehend will not break down when we oversimplify its essential complexity to our purposes.

Ecology forces us to recognize three major features of all life: *interdependence, diversity,* and *vulnerability*. Its message is not that we should avoid change, but that we should recognize that man-induced changes can have far-reaching and often unpredictable consequences. It is a call for wisdom and care as we alter the ecosphere.

What has gone wrong, probably, is that we have failed to see ourselves as part of a large and indivisible whole. For too long we have based our lives on a primitive feeling that man's "god-given" role was to have "dominion over the fish of the sea and over the fowl of the air and over every living thing that moveth upon the earth." We have failed to understand that the earth does not belong to us, but we to the earth.

Rolf Edberg

Discussion Topics

1. If you had a choice would you rather be exposed to electromagnetic radiation with a short or long wavelength? High or low frequency? Explain why people who spend a lot of time getting suntans may be more susceptible to skin cancer.

2. Draw a diagram showing the major features of the heat or energy budget of the earth. List the major human activities that can upset this balance. Relate the basic features of this diagram to the first and second laws of thermodynamics.

3. List the major components of all ecosystems. How would you set up a self-sustaining aquarium for tropical fish? Suppose you had a balanced aquarium with a transparent glass top used to seal it. Can life continue in the aquarium indefinitely as long as the sun shines regularly on the aquarium? Which of the following will probably be the limiting factor—the oxygen supply in the air above the water, the original oxygen supply dissolved in the water, or the supply of nitrogen in soil at the bottom.

4. A friend cleans out your aquarium and removes all of the soil and plants, leaving only the fish and water. What will happen?

5. A popular ecological slogan seen on bumper stickers is "Have you thanked a green plant today?" Give two reasons for thanking a green plant. Trace the materials in the sticker back and see if the sticker itself represents a sound application of the slogan.

6. Discuss the idea that the city is not a local ecosystem but is a part of a global ecosystem. How does this affect the stability of the city? Of the ecosphere? What would happen to population size, industrialization, and land use patterns if a city depended only on its surrounding land for food supply and waste disposal?

Further Reading

Billings, W. D. 1970. Plants, Man, and the Ecosystem, 2nd Ed. Belmont, Calif.: Wadsworth. See especially the discussion of biomes in Chapter 7.

Clapham, W. B., Jr. 1973. Natural Ecosystems. New York: Macmillan. Excellent introduction to ecology at a slightly higher level.

Colinvaux, Paul A. 1973. Introduction to Ecology. New York: Wiley. Good basic text.

Commoner, Barry. 1970. "The Ecological Facts of Life," in H. D. Johnson, ed., No Deposit—No Return. Reading, Mass.: Addison-Wesley, pp. 18–35. Excellent simplified summary of ecological principles.

Darling, Lois, and Louis Darling. 1968. A Place in the Sun. New York: William Morrow. Beautifully done, simple introduction to ecology.

Darnell, Rezneat M. 1973. Ecology and Man. Dubuque, Iowa: Wm. C. Brown. Outstanding introduction to ecological principles. Highly recommended.

Ehrlich, Paul R., and Anne H. Ehrlich. 1972. Population, Resources and Environment, 2nd Ed. San Francisco: W. H. Freeman. Superb introduction to human ecological problems. See especially Chapter 7.

Emmel, Thomas C. 1973. An Introduction to Ecology and Population Biology. New York: W. W. Norton. Superb introduction.

Kormondy, Edward J. 1969. Concepts of Ecology. Englewood Cliffs, N.J.: Prentice-Hall. First-rate introduction.

McHale, John. 1970. The Ecological Context. New York: George Braziller. Highly recommended. Superb diagrams and summaries of ecosphere data.

Metillo, Jerry M. 1972. Ecology Primer. West Haven, Conn.: Pendulum Press. Very readable introduction.

Miller, G. Tyler, Jr. 1972. Replenish the Earth—A Primer in Human Ecology. Belmont, Calif.: Wadsworth. My own greatly abbreviated version of some of the key material in this book.

Odum, Eugene P. 1971. Fundamentals of Ecology, 3rd Ed. Philadelphia: W. B. Saunders. Probably the outstanding textbook on ecology by one of our most prominent ecologists.

Reid, Keith. 1970. Nature's Network. Garden City, N.Y.: Natural History Press. Beautifully done introduction to ecology. See Chapter 8 on succession and Appendix 1 on biomes.

Scientific American Editors. 1970. The Biosphere. San Francisco: W. H. Freeman. Excellent introduction to chemical cycling and energy flow.

Smith, Robert L. 1974. Ecology and Field Biology, 2nd Ed. New York: Harper & Row. An excellent basic text in ecology.

Smith, Robert L. 1972. The Ecology of Man: An Ecosystem Approach. New York: Harper & Row. Probably the best collection of selected ecological articles with excellent introductory commentaries.

Southwick, Charles H. 1972. Ecology and the Quality of the Environment. New York: Van Nostrand Reinhold. Very readable introduction to human ecology.

Watt, Kenneth E. F. 1973. Principles of Environmental Science. New York: McGraw-Hill. Outstanding discussion of ecological principles at a higher level.

We are born as wasteful and unremorseful as tigers; we are obliged to be thrifty, or starve, or freeze.

William Bolitho

4

Present and Future Energy Options: An Overview

4-1 Applying Energy Principles: Energy Quality, Energy Efficiency, and Net Energy

Energy quality and efficiency Different forms of energy such as heat, electrical energy, and the chemical potential energy available from fossil fuels vary in their *energy quality* or ability to perform useful work (Berg 1974a). Because of the second law of energy or thermodynamics (Section 2-2), each time we transform or transfer energy from one form or system to another *energy quality* is degraded (Figure 4-1), with much of the initial input lost as waste heat to the environment.

We have already seen that in food energy chains (Section 3-5) only 10 to 20 percent of the initial energy input can be used by the organism at the next link in the chain. When food is in short supply or is too expensive, survival depends on making the food chain as short as possible, that is, *grain → human*, in contrast to the longer and more wasteful *grain → animal → human*.

This energy chain concept can also be applied to the use of fossil fuels and other energy sources (Figures 4-1 and 4-2). The more links in the energy transfer chain the greater the waste of energy. We can never escape the consequences of the second energy law, but we can minimize energy waste by three basic approaches. First, where practical, we can decrease waste by keeping the energy transfer chain as short as possible (Figure 4-2).

Second, we can increase *energy efficiency*, the ratio of useful energy output to the total energy input (Section 2-2). In an energy transfer process with 30 percent efficiency, for every 100 calories of energy put into the system only 30 calories are available to perform useful work. Various energy transfer and transformation processes have widely different efficiencies and many of our most widely used processes have very low efficiencies (Table 4-1 and Figure 4-3). However, we can reduce energy waste by using more efficient processes or by improving processes so that they approach the maximum allowable efficiency.[1]

A careful study of Table 4-1 can reveal the source of many of our energy problems as well as a number of possible

[1] The maximum allowable efficiency for a particular motor or energy transfer process is determined by the second law of thermodynamics (Section 3-2), but the actual working efficiency is frequently below this limit.

improvements. For example, the efficiency of comparable air conditioners varies by a factor of 3 (Hirst & Moyers 1973). More efficient units will in the long run save energy and money because their electricity consumption is reduced threefold. This also demonstrates the need for a "truth in energy" labeling of energy efficiency appliances. Automobile efficiency could be more than doubled if an economically feasible steam turbine engine could be developed, and im-

Table 4-1 The energy efficiencies of common individual systems

Conversion system	Percent efficiency
Processing of natural gas	97
Mining of nuclear fuel (uranium)	95
Processing of coal	92
Processing of oil	88
Home natural gas furnace	85
Electric car storage battery	80
Surface mining of coal	78
Extraction of natural gas	73
Propeller driven wind turbine	70
Home oil furnace	65
Fuel cell	60
Processing of nuclear fuel	57
Deep mining of coal	55
Fossil fuel power plant with proposed MHD topping cycle	50
Steam turbine engine	45
Offshore oil well	40
Fossil fuel power plant and proposed nuclear breeder plant	38
Diesel engine	35
Today's nuclear power plant	31
Onshore oil well	30
Proposed solar power plant	28
Internal combustion engine	22
Fluorescent lamp	20
Wankel engine	18
Advanced solar cells (if developed)	15
Today's solar cells	10
Incandescent lamp	5

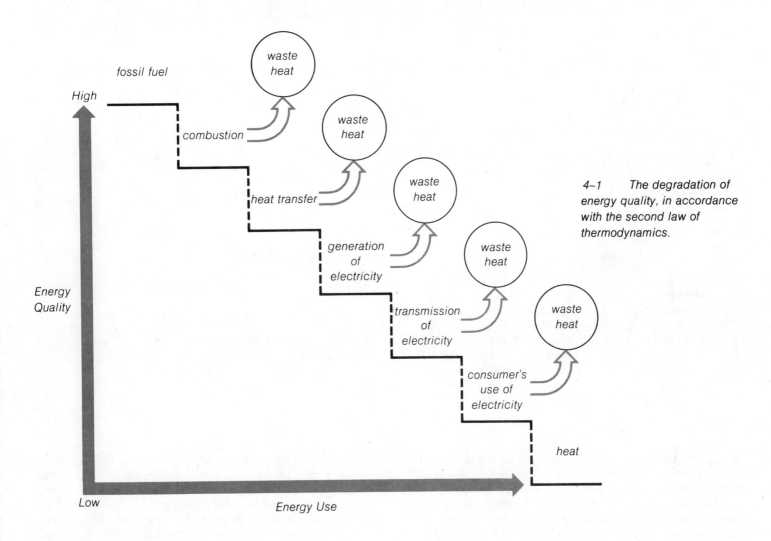

4–1   *The degradation of energy quality, in accordance with the second law of thermodynamics.*

proved even more with a shift toward mass transit. From Table 4–1 you might expect that an electric car storage battery, with an efficiency of almost 80 percent, would be the best choice to power an automobile. But the energy chain concept shows why this is not the case. When you subtract the large amount of energy used to produce the electricity for refueling or recharging the battery, overall efficiency drops to only 16 percent, considerably less than diesel and steam turbine powered cars (Figure 4–4).

The third method for reducing energy waste involves such well-known and simple architectural design techniques as increased insulation, use of natural ventilation, reduced lighting levels, and aligning buildings to take advantage of sunlight (see Chapter 7 for more details). Our most visible symbol of energy waste, the all glass office building, with windows that cannot be opened, massively heated and cooled by blowers rather than nature, and ablaze with light throughout the night, is now recognized as an ecological disaster and an economic liability as energy prices rise.

Net energy: it takes energy to get energy   Because of the first law of energy or thermodynamics (Section 2–1) we can't get something for nothing, and because of the second energy law (Section 2–2) we can't even break even. The true value of any energy source is the *net energy available*—the total energy available minus the energy used to find, concentrate, and deliver the energy to the user (Odum 1971, 1973). Many energy resources are of low quality because we have to use large amounts of energy to dig or pump them from the earth or sea, and then concentrate, refine, and transport them to the point of use. If it takes 9 units of energy to deliver 10 units of energy then there is little net energy gain.

As we drill and dig further and use more dilute energy resources, more and more of our remaining high grade fossil fuel energy (and money) is being used to find and provide energy. For example, only 30 to 35 percent of the oil in an average reservoir is now recovered. Some talk of recovering 50 to 60 percent, but the energy needed to produce the steam injected in the borehole to increase recovery exceeds the

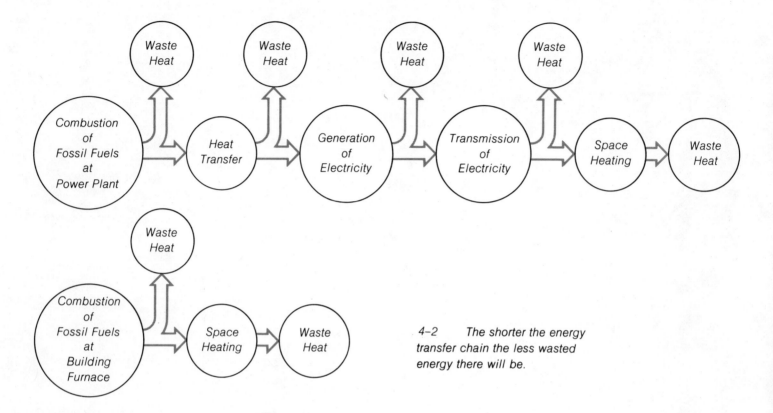

4–2   *The shorter the energy transfer chain the less wasted energy there will be.*

energy recovered as oil. As a result, although total energy consumption is increasing (Figure 1–3), net energy production is declining or at least not rising (Odum 1973).

The supply of most energy resources such as oil, natural gas, geothermal power, oil shale, uranium, and others are calculated as proven or expected total resource reserves—not net energy reserves. Thus, the years of supply may be much less than our present total energy estimates indicate.

For example, conventional nuclear energy is now subsidized heavily with fossil fuels. When we add the high energy costs of mining and processing uranium fuels, building costly nuclear plants, transporting and storing nuclear fuels and wastes, meeting complex safety and environmental concerns, and operating government atomic energy agencies, we find that conventional nuclear fuel barely yields any net energy (Odum 1973, Lovins 1974). Whether the nuclear breeder reactor, which generates additional fuel in the reactor (Chapter 6), or nuclear fusion (Chapter 7) will yield net energy is unknown.

The concept of net energy also explains why the widespread use of solar energy may not be feasible (Chapter 7). Even though solar energy is abundant and free, it is so widely dispersed that it may take more energy to collect and concentrate it than the energy it provides. Again the net energy yield

is unknown, but the widespread use of solar energy also appears to be tied to fossil fuel supplies needed to make solar panels, pipes, power plants, and energy transmission systems.

Perhaps the best example of the net energy concept is in the food production of an industrialized nation (Pimentel et al. 1973, Hirst 1974, Steinhart & Steinhart 1974a). As we have seen (Figure 3–13), modern high yield agriculture is possible only by a tremendous outside energy supplement from fossil fuels. The food "system" used about 13 percent of the total energy consumed in the United States during 1970 (Steinhart & Steinhart 1974a). If we consider the fossil fuel energy cost for growing, processing, packaging, transporting, refrigerating, and cooking food in the United States, then *it takes 5 to 10 calories of fossil fuel energy to yield only 1 calorie of food energy* (Steinhart & Steinhart 1974a), a net energy loss of 9 calories for each calorie of food that ends up on our table. This is in contrast to "primitive" cultures that obtained 5 to 50 food calories for each calorie of energy put into the system.

Technological optimists talk of exporting energy intensive agriculture to underdeveloped nations as a solution to the world food crisis. Feeding the entire world with a U.S. type food system, however, would require 80 percent of the world's annual energy consumption (Steinhart & Steinhart 1974a). As fuel prices increase, the entire energy intensive food

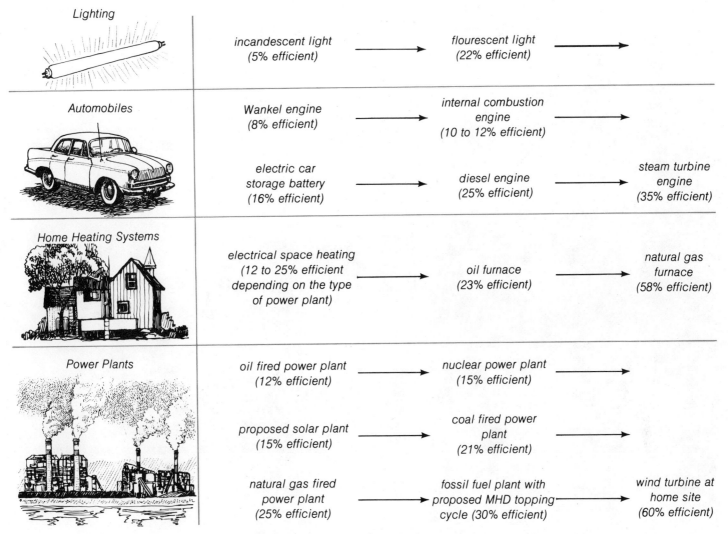

Lighting

incandescent light (5% efficient) → flourescent light (22% efficient) →

Automobiles

Wankel engine (8% efficient) → internal combustion engine (10 to 12% efficient) →

electric car storage battery (16% efficient) → diesel engine (25% efficient) → steam turbine engine (35% efficient)

Home Heating Systems

electrical space heating (12 to 25% efficient depending on the type of power plant) → oil furnace (23% efficient) → natural gas furnace (58% efficient)

Power Plants

oil fired power plant (12% efficient) → nuclear power plant (15% efficient) →

proposed solar plant (15% efficient) → coal fired power plant (21% efficient) →

natural gas fired power plant (25% efficient) → fossil fuel plant with proposed MHD topping cycle (30% efficient) → wind turbine at home site (60% efficient)

4–3   The net energy efficiencies of some of our most widely used energy transformation systems are very low but we could shift to alternates that are much more efficient.

system in the United States and other industrialized nations could collapse or at least be forced to a lower and less wasteful level.

4–2   What Are Our Energy Options?

In sorting out our energy options we have to think and plan in three time frames: the near future (today to 1985), the intermediate future (1985 to 2000), and the distant future (beyond 2000). For each time period we have to ask:

1. What are the realistic options?
2. What fraction of the demand can each potential source supply as net energy?
3. What are the environmental side effects in using each energy source?

Table 4–2 summarizes the major energy options for the United States. (See Chapters 5 and 6 for more detailed evaluation of fossil fuels and nuclear fission and Chapter 7 for the fusion, geothermal, wind, solar, and conservation alternatives.)

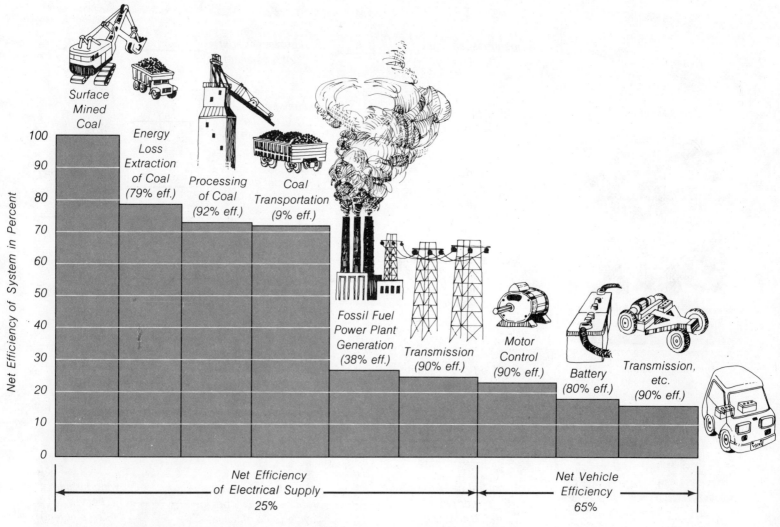

4-4   *In spite of the high efficiency of its batteries, the net energy efficiency of an electric car is only about 16 percent, because 75 percent of the energy in coal is lost in producing the electricity needed to recharge the car's storage batteries. (The effect of each individual process is shown in parentheses.)*

Environmental impact options: choosing the lesser of several evils   In accordance with the second law of thermodynamics the use of any form of energy has some environmental impact (Figure 4–5), and the faster the rate of energy flow or throughput the greater the impact (Figure 3–8). This is why energy use permeates almost every phase of the environmental crisis, and is directly or indirectly responsible for most of the pollution of our air, land, and water. Recent environmental restrictions to contain and reduce these threats had relatively little to do with the availability of energy supplies in the 1973–74 energy policy crisis (Hirst 1973, Train 1973), despite claims by energy companies and utility companies. But this may not be the case in the future as rising

energy demands and the accompanying environmental effects come into direct conflict. Table 4–3 provides more details about the potential environmental effects of the mining, processing, transportation, and use of various energy options (see also Council on Environmental Quality 1973a, Mills et al. 1971, Cambel 1970, Perry & Berkson 1971, Commoner et al. 1974, vols. 1 & 2, Berkowitz & Squires 1971).

4-3   Overall Evaluation of Options

From Tables 4–2 and 4–3 we can see that our best option, considering net energy and environmental impact, is energy

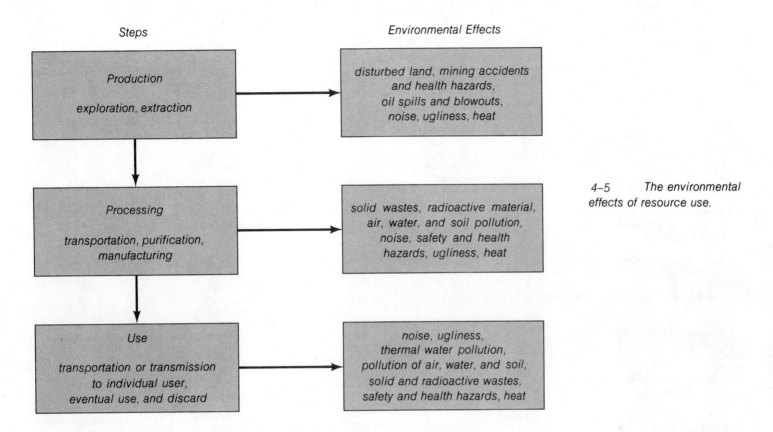

Steps	Environmental Effects
Production *exploration, extraction*	*disturbed land, mining accidents and health hazards, oil spills and blowouts, noise, ugliness, heat*
Processing *transportation, purification, manufacturing*	*solid wastes, radioactive material, air, water, and soil pollution, noise, safety and health hazards, ugliness, heat*
Use *transportation or transmission to individual user, eventual use, and discard*	*noise, ugliness, thermal water pollution, pollution of air, water, and soil, solid and radioactive wastes, safety and health hazards, heat*

4–5   *The environmental effects of resource use.*

conservation. Unfortunately, this option has very low priority in our present energy strategy in terms of specific laws, actions, and funding (Chapter 7). It takes about ten years to achieve major energy savings by phasing out low gas mileage cars, shifting to mass transit, requiring increased insulation on all new and most existing buildings, building energy conserving buildings, and changing to less energy intensive manufacturing and farming processes. Thus, energy conservation can have only a moderate impact for the short term but a major impact for the intermediate and long term. But because a 10 year lead time is needed, these crucial savings won't be realized unless a stringent and mandatory conservation program is put into effect now.

Natural gas, oil, hydroelectric, and tidal power also offer good combinations of moderate to high net energy and low to moderate environmental impact. But natural gas and oil will probably be available only for a few decades at rapidly escalating prices. Hydroelectric power now provides only about 4 percent of our total energy and 10 percent of our electricity, and these percentages are expected to decline in the future because most of the rivers with sufficient flow have already been dammed. Tidal power can be tapped only in the very few places where a major drop between low and high tide exists and can thus supply only a miniscule amount of U.S. energy needs and probably no more than 1 percent of world energy needs (Bengelsdorf 1971).

The burning of trash as fuel or its conversion to synthetic natural gas or oil by chemical processes or microorganisms (Kasper 1974, Hammond et al. 1973, Commoner et al. 1974, vol. 2) will be of great help in conserving metal resources through recycling (since metals and other resources must be removed before burning), saving energy by shifting from more energy intensive virgin resources to recycled materials, and reducing solid waste disposal problems. But even with extensive use and improved technology the U.S. Bureau of Mines estimates that trash burning can never provide more than 10 to 15 percent of our electricity and no more than 1 to 2 percent of our total energy needs (Maugh 1972b).

Coal can provide adequate supplies, but with greatly increased risks from air pollution and strip mining (see Chapter 5). We may be able to decrease pollution from sulfur oxides and particulates (Chapter 5), find commercially feasible ways to convert coal to less polluting natural gas, and pass strict laws for reclaiming strip mined land—but only at greatly increased energy costs.

Geothermal, solar, wind, and nuclear fusion energy are clean and essentially infinite energy resources (Chapter 7) that represent major hopes for the long term when supplies of oil and natural gas are depleted. Because we have yet to put significant amounts of money in their development (except for fusion), there is still much uncertainty and disagreement over their potential net energy yield and overall feasibility.

Table 4–2   Evaluation of energy options for the United States

Option	Short term (present to 1985)	Estimated availability* Intermediate term (1985 to 2000)	Long term (2000 to 2020)	Estimated net energy	Potential environmental impact†
Conservation	Fair	Good	Good	Very high	Decreases impact of other sources
Natural gas	Good (with imports)	Fair (with imports)	Poor	High but decreasing‡	Low
Oil					
Conventional	Good (with imports)	Fair (with imports)	Poor	High but decreasing‡	Moderate
Shale	Poor	Moderate to good?	Moderate to good?	Probably very low	Serious
Tar sands	Poor	Moderate? (imports only)	Good? (imports only)	Probably very low	Moderate
Coal					
Conventional	Good	Good	Good	High but decreasing‡	Very serious
Gasification (conversion to synthetic natural gas)	Poor	Good?	Good?	Moderate to low	Very serious
Liquification (conversion to synthetic oil)	Very poor	Poor to moderate?	Good?	Moderate to low	Serious
Wastes					
Direct burning	Poor to fair	Fair to poor	Fair	Moderate (space heating) to low (electricity)	Fairly low
Conversion to oil	Poor	Fair to poor	Fair	Moderate to low	Low to moderate
Hydroelectric	Poor	Poor	Very poor	High	Low to moderate
Tidal	Very poor	Very poor	Very poor	Unknown (moderate?)	Low
Nuclear					
Conventional fission	Poor	Good	Good to poor	Probably very low	Very serious
Breeder fission	None	None to low	Good?	Probably low	Extremely serious
Fusion	Poor	Moderate to low?	Moderate to low	Unknown (could be low)	Unknown (probably moderate to low)
Geothermal	Poor	Moderate to low?	Moderate to low	Unknown (probably moderate to low)	Moderate to low
Solar	Poor (except for space and water heating)	Low to moderate?	Moderate to high?	Unknown (probably low)	Low
Wind	Poor	Poor to moderate?	Moderate to high?	Unknown (probably moderate to low)	Low
Hydrogen	Negligible	Poor	Unknown§	Unknown (probably moderate to low)	Unknown§
Fuel cells	Negligible	Poor	Unknown§	Unknown (probably moderate to low)	Unknown§

* Based on estimated supply as a fraction of total energy use and on technological and economic feasibility.

† If stringent safety and environmental controls are not required and enforced.

‡ As high grade deposits decrease, more and more energy must be used to mine and process lower grade deposits, thus decreasing net energy.

§ Depends on whether an essentially infinite source of electricity (such as solar, fusion, wind, or breeder) is available to convert water to hydrogen and oxygen gas by electrolysis or direct heating. Impact will vary depending on the source of electricity.

Controlled nuclear fusion is the most difficult scientific and engineering problem man has ever faced, and it may never become feasible on a commercial scale in terms of net energy. To some (U.S. Atomic Energy Commission 1973a) geothermal, wind, and solar energy will never provide more than a few percent of our total energy needs. But to others (Heronemus 1971, see Inglis editorial) they could be key sources for the intermediate and long term with massive research and development over the next 2 to 3 decades.

The technology for many forms of solar energy is already available, and a panel of distinguished scientists (NSF/NASA Solar Energy Panel 1973) project that it could be available for space heating of buildings and homes within 5 to 10 years and for large scale electric power generation within 10 to 15 years (Chapter 7).

Estimates of the potential for geothermal energy vary from only 0.5 percent to all of our projected energy needs by the year 2000. But net energy availability is largely unknown.

A National Science Foundation and National Aeronautics and Space Administration panel and a prominent expert (Heronemus 1972, 1972a) suggest that by 2000 a major development program in wind power could provide electricity equivalent to all that produced in 1970. Wind turbines could be quickly added to supplement power, and a band of 100,000

Table 4–3   *Comparative environmental impacts of energy options*

Energy option	Air pollution	Water pollution	Solid waste	Land use impact	Occupational health	Possible large scale disasters
Conservation	Decreased	Decreased	Decreased	Decreased	Less	None
Natural gas	Low	Low	Negligible	Low	Low	Pipeline explosion; earthquakes if nuclear blasts used for stimulating wells
Oil						
Offshore wells	Moderate	Serious	Very low	Very low	Low	Massive spill on water from blowout or pipeline rupture
Onshore wells	Moderate	Serious	Very low	Low	Low	Massive spill on land from blowout or pipeline rupture
Imports	Low to moderate	Serious	Very low	Very low	Low	Massive spill from tanker accident
Shale	Moderate	Moderate to serious	Serious	Serious	Low	Massive spill on land from blowout or pipeline rupture; earthquakes if nuclear blasts used for production in wells
Tar sands	Moderate	Moderate to serious	Serious	Moderate	Low	Massive spill on land from blowout or pipeline rupture
Coal						
Deep mined	Very serious	Very serious	Moderate	Moderate	Very serious	Mine accidents
Surface mined	Very serious	Very serious	Very serious	Very serious	Serious	Landslides
Gasification	Low	Very serious (more coal mined)	Very serious (more coal mined)	Very serious (more coal mined)	Very serious	Mine accidents; landslides; pipeline explosion
Liquification	Low	Very serious (more coal mined)	Very serious (more coal mined)	Very serious (more coal mined)	Very serious	Mine accidents; landslides; spills from pipeline rupture
Wastes						
Direct burning	Moderate	Very low	Decrease	Decrease	Low	Fire or explosion in furnace
Conversion to oil	Moderate	Low	Decrease	Decrease	Low	Fire or explosion in furnace
Hydroelectric	Negligible	Negligible	Negligible	Serious	Low	Rupture of dam
Tidal	Negligible	Negligible	Negligible	Low to moderate	Low	None
Nuclear						
Conventional fission	Negligible for normal pollutants but serious for radioactive releases	Low for normal sources but serious for radioactive releases	Low but very serious for radioactive releases	Low but very serious for radioactive releases	Low but very serious for radioactive releases	Meltdown of reactor core; sabotage of plants; shipping accidents; highjacking of shipments for use in nuclear bombs or for release into environment
Breeder	Negligible for normal pollutants but serious for radioactive releases	Low for normal sources but serious for radioactive releases	Low but extremely serious for radioactive releases	Low but extremely serious for radioactive releases	Low but extremely serious for radioactive releases	Meltdown of reactor core; sabotage of plants, shipping accidents, highjacking of shipments for use in nuclear bombs or for release into environment (radioactivity more dangerous than from conventional reactors)
Fusion	Negligible for normal pollutants but moderate for radioactive releases	Low?	Low?	Low	Low	Meltdown or explosion of reactor with release of gaseous radioisotopes
Geothermal	Moderate	Moderate to serious	Very low	Low to moderate	Low	None
Solar	Negligible	Negligible	Negligible	Low to moderate	Low	None
Wind	Negligible	Negligible	Negligible	Low to moderate	Low	None
Hydrogen*	Variable	Variable	Variable	Variable	Variable	Variable
Fuel cells*	Variable	Variable	Variable	Variable	Variable	Variable

  * The systems themselves have low environmental impacts in all phases, but the environmental impact of the systems of electricity used to generate these fuels must be added.

to 300,000 giant wind turbines stretching from Texas to the Dakotas and about 50,000 floating off the East Coast might provide half the country's electrical needs (Chapter 7). But because the fuel for wind and solar power are free, these options are not being pushed by energy companies in the business of selling fuel.

Hydrogen gas as an energy source   There may be a number of possible options for producing electricity at power plants. But how will cars and other vehicles be powered when petroleum becomes too scarce and expensive? Electric cars are a possibility, but they are extremely wasteful of energy (Figure 4–4). At present they also lack the range and speed to effectively replace internal combustion vehicles.

One of the most frequent suggestions for the fuel of the future is hydrogen gas (H_2) (Bockris 1972, Gregory 1973, Maugh 1972a, 1972d, Winsche et al. 1973) and methanol (Reed & Lerner 1973). As a fuel, hydrogen has a number of advantages. It is lightweight, easily transportable, colorless, and odorless. It can be burned cleanly in a fuel cell (Maugh 1972d), power plant, or automobile to produce water. By producing fog not smog it eliminates most of the serious air pollution problems associated with the gasoline burning internal combustion engine.

Besides its use as a fuel for vehicles, hydrogen can also be used as a convenient means of storing energy from other sources. For example, the energy from a wind turbine or from a solar, nuclear, or geothermal power plant could be stored by using it to produce hydrogen gas by the electrolysis of water. Because seawater could be used as the basic source of hydrogen, our supply would be cheap, readily available, and almost infinite, in sharp contrast to fossil fuels. The hydrogen could be stored in tanks like compressed air) and shipped or transported via pipelines (probably existing natural gas pipelines) to households, industries, or hydrogen fueling stations (the old "gas" station).

But there is a major catch to this glowing hydrogen energy future. We must not forget the net energy concept. Because hydrogen is not available in large quantities we would have to use some other form of electrical or thermal power to convert water to hydrogen. In other words, it takes a lot of energy to get this energy, and a hydrogen fuel system is feasible only if we already have an essentially limitless and cheap energy source such as nuclear fission, nuclear fusion, solar, geothermal, or wind energy.

The nuclear fission option: should we accept the risks? One of the most important, complex, and controversial decisions now facing mankind is whether to provide most of our electrical energy in coming decades by controlled use of nuclear fission (see Chapter 6). Today nuclear energy provides only a small percentage of the electrical energy of the United States (7 percent in 1974). But after 25 years of research and development and billions of dollars the nuclear power industry is poised for an explosive growth over the next 30 to 50 years.

At the end of 1973 some 42 nuclear plants were licensed to operate in the United States, 56 were being built, and 101 had been ordered. By 1980 a total of 155 nuclear plants in the United States and 401 in the world are projected for commercial operation. The Atomic Energy Commission projects that nuclear power will provide 20 percent of our electricity by 1980 and approximately 50 percent by 2000. By the year 2000 the AEC projects 1,000 nuclear power plants in the United States, with 400 of these being the highly controversial and potentially much more dangerous breeder reactors.

There is almost unanimous agreement that nuclear fission is *potentially* the most hazardous of all sources of energy and must be operated with no technological or human failures. Because a serious nuclear accident could release extremely hazardous radioactive materials that might contaminate large areas for perhaps hundreds of thousands of years, it is not in the same category as a dam collapse, explosion of a chemical plant, oil spill, rupture of a railroad car carrying poisonous chemicals, or other nonnuclear accidents.

Humans could be exposed to deadly and long-lived radioactive materials released accidentally or intentionally to the environment through (1) a serious nuclear plant accident (meltdown); (2) destruction or damage to a nuclear plant by an earthquake, act of war, or sabotage; (3) accidents during the shipping of nuclear fuels and wastes; (4) highjacking of nuclear shipments to produce nuclear bombs or for use in nuclear blackmail by terrorist groups; and (5) failure of the storage facilities for nuclear wastes, which must be absolutely safe for periods up to 250,000 years. In addition, there is still no clear evidence that nuclear fission provides any significant net energy when all of the energy inputs for building, operating, and delivering the power are included (Lovins 1974).

The debate centers on the probability that these enormous dangers will ever be realized and the risks of using nuclear energy compared to other energy sources with adequate supplies such as coal (Chapter 5). With about 30 commercial reactors operating for a few years the nuclear industry has had an excellent safety record. But some experts (Chapter 6) seriously question whether this record can be maintained for 1,000 nuclear plants by the year 2000 and with over 100,000 shipments of nuclear material moving around the country each year. Although much concern has been expressed about nuclear plant safety, the two most vulnerable points in the system may be the shipments, which could easily be highjacked for conversion to nuclear bombs or for use as a form of unpreventable blackmail (see Chapter 6) and the radioactive waste storage facilities (which must be safe for hundreds of centuries).

Glenn T. Seaborg (1972), Nobel laureate and former Chairman of the Atomic Energy Commission (see his editorial in Chapter 1), and Dr. Alvin M. Weinberg, former director of the Oak Ridge National Laboratory and now director of research and development for the Federal Energy Administration, are two of the strongest proponents of nuclear power (see his editorial in Chapter 6). Dr. Weinberg (1972) projects a future world with 15 billion human beings using 24,000 giant nuclear reactors in 3,000 nuclear parks to give everyone an average energy consumption equal to twice today's U.S. per capita average. He envisions the creation of a permanent nuclear priesthood of responsible technologists to guard and protect all nuclear plants, shipments, and waste deposits:

It is clear that major changes will be needed in the methods we undertake to construct power stations. To attain the assumed level of 24,000 reactors of 5,000 megawatts electrical each means that the world will have to add more than four reactors a week on the average for the next 100 years. In addition, if the reactors last 30 years, we shall have to build two reactors per day, simply to replace those that have worn out. To meet this kind of need, present-day methods will have to be refined into assembly lines which resemble those which now turn out automobiles; in the process savings in cost and time should be achievable.

In spite of his strong belief that nuclear power can be made safe, he has also been one of the few proponents of nuclear power to emphasize that such a decision is the greatest single risk ever taken by mankind, one that should be accepted only after intensive public education and debate.

Guest Editorial: Energy and Environment

John Holdren is an outstanding example of the new breed of scientists who are young, talented, and sensitive to human needs and concerns. He has been a physicist in the controlled nuclear fusion program at Lawrence Livermore Laboratory (University of California), and a research fellow with the Environmental Quality Laboratory and Caltech Population Program at the California Institute of Technology. Presently, he is an assistant professor of physics with the Energy and Resources Program at University of California, Berkeley. Since 1970 he has been a member of the Committee on International Environmental Programs of the National Academy of Sciences.

*Besides technical papers on plasma theory and fusion fuels, he has authored or coauthored more than thirty chapters, papers, and articles on the interrelations among population, environment, and technology. He has coedited two books (*Global Ecology, *with Paul R. Ehrlich, 1971; and* Man and the Ecosphere, *with Paul R. Ehrlich and Richard W. Holm, 1971) and coauthored two others (*Energy, *with Phil Herrera, 1971; and* Human Ecology, *with Paul R. Ehrlich and Anne H. Ehrlich, 1973).*

John P. Holdren

The rapid increase of energy use, electrical and otherwise, has intensified a long-standing dichotomy: on the one hand, energy is the prime mover of technology and an essential ingredient in fashioning a decent standard of living; on the other hand, it is a major ingredient of man's growing detrimental impact on his environment. Thus, the nature of the "energy crisis" depends on whom one asks. Industry and many branches of government, including the Federal Power Commission, apparently regard the present growth rates as inviolable. They view the crisis as the problem of mobilizing resources and technology quickly enough—in the face of growing opposition from environmentalists—to maintain these rates indefinitely. To the environmentalists, the crisis is the possibility that growth rates will indeed be maintained, accompanied by a degree of environmental deterioration barely hinted at today.

No means of producing energy is completely free of environmental liabilities, and most have other drawbacks as well. The use of fossil fuels entails oil spills, ravaged landscapes from the mining of coal, and air pollution. Burning these fuels also depletes a limited resource that may ultimately be needed for lubrication and the synthesis of petrochemicals. Hydroelectric sites are in limited supply, and their development may have adverse effects on wildlife, flood fertile land, and compromise esthetic values. Present-day nuclear fission reactors use fuel inefficiently and burden us with radioactive wastes that must be handled with extreme care and must be safely interred for thousands of years.

Potential sources of energy for the future look better, but they will not be panaceas. Fission breeder reactors effectively "burn" abundant uranium-238 and thorium rather than relatively scarce uranium-235, but the radioactive waste and safety problems remain. Fusion reactors have not yet been demonstrated to be scientifically feasible, although few experts doubt that they will be. The environmental aspects of fusion cannot be precisely evaluated at this preliminary stage of development; it seems safe to say that they will be cleaner and less hazardous than fission reactors, although some radioactivity will have to be contained. Solar energy is abundant, and it is almost certainly the best option available in environmental terms. It will be used increasingly in the United States in the 1970s to supplant electricity and natural gas in home heating and air conditioning. How soon we might have large scale solar power stations producing electricity is more difficult to say.

Of course, all sources of energy—present and future—involve the dissipation of heat. Technology can ameliorate this problem by providing higher efficiencies, but the laws of thermodynamics tell us we cannot eliminate it. If nothing else limited the growth of energy consumption, the effect of waste heat on climate eventually would.

What then, should be our energy strategy? In the short term, money must be spent to minimize the environmental damage done by our present energy sources, particularly fossil fuels. Research to reduce the uncertain risks of

fission power is also essential. It is clear, too, that the growth rate of the demand for energy must be slowed. Rational planning will include increasing the price of energy (with the joint effect of paying for environmental controls and discouraging wasteful consumption) and changing the rate structure for electricity, to avoid a heavy burden on the poor. A premium will be placed on goods of greater durability, on recycling, on energetically efficient transportation systems.

Money must also be spent now to broaden the array of energy options for the future. Geothermal energy, wind energy, solar energy, controlled fusion—none will be available later unless work is done now. For even the achievement of zero growth in energy consumption, an eventual certainty, will not eliminate the question of how best to meet the stabilized demand. Increased research and development on energy sources of all kinds is needed if rational choices that maximize efficiency and minimize environmental degradation are to be possible.

Discussion

1. Debate each of the following statements:

a. We must meet the growing energy demands of our customers, the American public.

b. We must slow the growth rate of energy use by sharply increasing the price of all forms of energy.

2. Summarize the environmental problems associated with present and future alternatives for supplying our energy needs.

3. What implications will Dr. Holdren's proposed solutions have on your life style? On the poor in the United States? On the poor in underdeveloped countries?

An increasing number of prominent nuclear physicists, other scientists, economists, some industrialists,[2] and at least one former AEC official[3] are expressing serious doubts about our commitment to nuclear fission power (especially the

[2] Philip Sporn, prominent industrialist and former head of American Electric Power in The New York Times, July 20, 1969, suggests: "We ought to slow down. We ought to get some experience out of the nuclear plants ordered before we go ahead with more. . . . We're going to have some accidents with atomic plants. We don't want to have any, but we're going to. Let's get our experience now before we take more chances with more plants."

[3] David E. Lilienthal, the first chairman of the Atomic Energy Commission warned as early as 1968 (Forbes, Nov. 15, p. 58) that "Once a bright hope shared by all mankind, including myself, the rash proliferation of atomic power plants has become one of the ugliest clouds overhanging America."

breeder) as the major electrical energy source for the intermediate and long term future. They urge a slowdown (and in some cases an absolute moratorium) in the construction and operation of nuclear plants until we can get a clearer picture of the hazards, attempt to solve the shipping and waste storage problems, determine whether nuclear power will yield net energy compared to other options, and institute a long overdue research and development program to evaluate other energy options. The dimensions of this nuclear dilemma are discussed in Chapter 6.

Although it depends on a high flow rate of energy (Figures 1–1 and 3–10), the United States has yet to formulate a comprehensive national energy plan for the short term (next 10 years), intermediate term (next 25 years), and long term (next 50 years). After evaluating our major energy options in more detail I will use the energy principles discussed in this book to outline a proposed energy plan for the United States (Section 9-3).

We are witness to the end of an era. As much as we hate to face up to it, the joyride of cheap energy is really over. But that does not mean that we are on the road to a Spartan life, nor does it mean that we cannot in coming years develop transportation systems, cities, and indeed life styles that are superior to what we must leave behind. To fashion a new America will involve a whole lot more than an energy policy. But since energy is the life blood of modern society, it might provide the focal point.

S. David Freeman

Discussion Topics

1. Trace your own direct and indirect energy consumption each day and show how it probably averages 230,000,000 calories per day (Figure 1-1). Contrast this with that of a Mississippi farm laborer, a peasant in India, a slum resident in Chicago.

2. Explain how the use of nonfuel mineral resources such as copper and iron depends on the availability of energy resources. What energy conditions are necessary for having a truly recycling society?

3. List the relative advantages and disadvantages of each of the following energy resources and options: (a) coal, (b) petroleum, (c) natural gas, (d) conventional nuclear fission reactors, (e) nuclear breeder reactors, (f) oil shale, (g) natural gas, (h) geothermal deposits, (i) wind, (j) solar energy, (k) coal gasification, (l) nuclear fusion, (m) conservation.

4. Why has the United States in recent years shifted from coal to natural gas and oil even though coal is our most abundant fossil fuel (Figure 1-4)?

5. List the major energy options we have for the short run (now to 1985), intermediate term (1985 to 2000), and long term (2000 to 2020).

6. List our energy options in decreasing order with respect to environmental impact. Now list them in decreasing order with respect to potential total supply and net energy potential. Which ones offer us the best compromise between available supply and environmental impact?

7. Criticize the following statements:

a. Clean hydroelectric power can solve our energy problems.

b. Tidal energy is a clean, untapped source that can solve our problems.

c. Fuel cells are the solution.

d. Using hydrogen as a fuel will save us.

e. We can solve the energy crisis by converting human and animal wastes to fossil fuels.

Further Reading

Cambel, Ali B. 1970. "Impact of Energy Demands," *Physics Today,* December, pp. 38-45. Excellent presentation of environmental impact of energy use.

Cheney, Eric S. 1974. "U.S. Energy Resources: Limits and Future Outlook," *American Scientist,* vol. 62, Jan.-Feb., pp. 14-22. Excellent overview of options.

Clark, Wilson. 1974. *Energy for Survival: The Alternative to Extinction.* New York: Anchor/Doubleday. Very useful analysis of energy use and evaluation of alternative energy resources.

Commoner, Barry, Howard Boksenbaum, and Michael Corr, eds. 1974. *Energy and Human Welfare: A Critical Analysis,* 3 vols. New York: Macmillan. A comprehensive evaluation of the scientific and social aspects of energy alternatives.

Cook, Earl. 1972. "Energy for Millenium Three," *Technology Review,* December, pp. 16-23. Superb summary of depletion curves and the energy crisis.

Energy Policy Project. 1974. *Exploring Energy Choices— A Preliminary Report.* Washington, D.C.: Ford Foundation Energy Policy Project. Superb overview by a high level task force. Highly recommended.

Fisher, John C. 1974. *Energy Crises in Perspective.* New York: Wiley. Highly optimistic view by an industrial scientist that the fossil fuel era will not be over as soon as most other experts predict.

Hammond, Allen L., William D. Metz, and Thomas H. Maugh II. 1973. *Energy and the Future.* Washington, D.C.: American Association for the Advancement of Science. One of the best evaluations of our energy options. At a slightly higher level.

Healy, Timothy J. 1974. *Energy, Electric Power and Man.* San Francisco: Boyd and Fraser. Excellent introductory text on energy principles and options. At a slightly higher level.

Holdren, John, and Philip Herrera. 1971. *Energy.* San Francisco: Sierra Club. Superb summary of the scientific and political aspects of the energy crisis. Includes some brief case studies.

Inglis, David R. 1973. *Nuclear Energy: Its Physics and Social Challenge*. Reading, Mass.: Addison-Wesley. Probably the best introduction to nuclear energy available. At a slightly higher level.

Lovins, Amory B. 1974. "World Energy Strategies, Parts 1 and 2," *Science and Public Affairs*, May and June, pp. 14–37. One of the best overviews of energy options and policy. Highly recommended.

Marion, Jerry B. 1974. *Energy in Perspective*. New York: Academic Press. Good overview.

Odum, Howard T. 1971. *Environment, Power and Society*. New York: Wiley. Outstanding analysis of energy principles and energy use in society. At a slightly higher level.

Odum, Howard T. 1973. "Energy, Ecology and Economics." Paper invited by Royal Swedish Academy of Science. Available from the author, Dept. of Environmental Engineering Sciences, University of Florida, Gainesville, Fla. 32611. Highly recommended presentation of the net energy concept and its implications.

Peach, W. N. 1973. *The Energy Outlook for the 1980's*. Washington, D.C.: Government Printing Office. Stock No. 5270–02113. Very good overview prepared for the Joint Economic Committee of Congress.

Rocks, Lawrence, and Richard P. Runyon. 1972. *The Energy Crisis*. New York: Crown Publishers. Excellent overview, but very weak on serious evaluation of the nuclear option.

Rose, David J. 1974. "Energy Policy in the U.S.," *Scientific American*, 230:1, 20–29. Fine summary of energy options.

Schurr, Sam H. 1971. *Energy Research Needs*, Resources for the Future. Washington, D.C.: Government Printing Office. One of the most comprehensive and best overall presentations of the energy crises.

Scientific American. 1971. *Energy and Power*. September. Entire issue devoted to the energy crisis.

Shell Oil Company. 1973. "The National Energy Outlook." Available free from Shell Oil Company, Public Affairs, P.O. 2463, Houston, Texas 77001. Excellent overview of our energy future.

Weinberg, A. M. 1972. "Social Institutions and Nuclear Energy," *Science*, vol. 177, 27–34. Highly optimistic view based on widespread and safe use of nuclear energy.

Wilson, W., and R. Jones. 1974. *Energy, Ecology and the Environment*. New York: Academic Press. Useful overview at a slightly higher level.

Woodwell, G. M. 1974. "Success, Succession and Adam Smith," *Bioscience*, 24:2, 81–87. Outstanding overview of energy crisis and its ecological implications.

World Environment Newsletter. 1974. "New Energy Sources," *Saturday Review/World*, Feb. 9, 47–50. Superb and concise summary. Highly recommended.

World Environment Newsletter. 1974a. "Alternate Energy Sources," *Saturday Review/World*, Feb. 23, 29–32. Superb overview. Highly recommended.

Fossil Fuel Energy Resources

Modern man seems to believe he can get everything he needs from the supermarket and corner drugstore. He doesn't understand that everything has a source in the land or sea, and that he must respect these sources.

Thor Heyerdahl

5–1 Fossil Fuel Resources: Is the Joyride Over?

J curves again   Will the depletion of finite, nonrenewable resources such as iron, copper, zinc, and fossil fuels be the factor that limits the growth of population and affluence in the world?

Nowhere is the potential collision between resources, people, and pollution more probable than in the United States (Park 1968). In attaining our present standard of well-being, we have used more minerals and fossil fuels during the last 30 years than all of the peoples of the world have used since the beginning of history (McKelvey 1972).

On a per capita basis Americans use more natural resources than any other nationality. With only 6 percent of the world's population we consume about one-third of all the world's resources (Figure 5–1). During 1972 the United States used about 4.2 billion tons of mineral and fossil fuel resources. This means that each American indirectly or directly used an average of 42,500 pounds or almost 20 metric tons of resources. Approximately half, or 2.1 billion tons, of this ended up as solid waste. Much of the remaining half will remain in circulation for several years before becoming waste or ending up as air and water pollution. Only a tiny fraction of these valuable resources was recycled or reclaimed.

Depletion curves   How can we determine how long a given resource might last? Any projections are based on two major sets of assumptions. We must estimate the potentially available supply at existing (or future) acceptable prices and with existing (or improved) technology, and we must estimate the annual rate at which the resource may be used. Obviously, with different sets of assumptions we get quite different answers to our question.

The most useful approach is to use the best available data to project several alternative depletion patterns, each based on a clearly defined set of assumptions. M. King Hubbert (1962) has developed the very useful concept of *depletion curves* to represent various alternatives for the use and supply of a nonrenewable resource (Figure 5–2).

Actually *depletion* is a misleading word. No resource will ever be completely exhausted because as it becomes scarce the cost of mining marginal deposits and thus the cost to the consumer will become too high. In practice, depletion time is estimated as the time required to consume a certain fraction (typically 80 percent) of the estimated supply.

Each alternative depletion curve in Figure 5–2 represents different assumptions about the supply, rate of usage, and pattern of usage. Curve A represents our present course of mining, using, and throwing away a resource. The life of the resource can be lengthened by efficient recycling and improved mining techniques, as illustrated by curve B. A combination of extensive recycling, improved mining technology and exploration, and reduction in per capita consumption can prolong depletion time considerably, as shown by curve C. Of course finding a replacement for a resource negates all of these curves and requires another set for the new resource.

Depletion rate estimates   Thus, we can distinguish between several types of projections of the future supply of a resource.[1] One estimate, the *static reserve index,* is the number of years the known world reserves of a resource will last if we go on consuming it at the same rate as today. It is one calculation of the years to the endpoint of depletion curve A in Figure 5–2.

In most cases, however, consumption rates do not remain constant but increase rapidly, typically around 2 to 3 percent per year. A second and more realistic projection is the *exponential reserve index* — the estimated number of years known world reserves will last if they are consumed at a rate increasing by a given percentage each year. In effect it gives a narrower version of curve A.

Finally, we get a more optimistic estimate by combining the exponential reserve index, which produces rapid depletion, with an assumption that newly discovered deposits, mining technology, and some recycling will increase the presently known reserves by some factor, say five times. This yields a depletion rate curve similar to curve C.

---

[1] For summaries of resource supply estimates in the world and in the United States see Brown et al. 1957, Brown 1970a, Chourci 1972, Cameron 1973, Cloud 1968, 1969, Fisher & Potter 1971, Frischman & Landsberg 1972, Landsberg 1964, Lovering 1968, McKelvey 1972, 1974, Skinner 1969, U.S. Bureau of Mines 1970, U.S. Geological Survey 1973, National Academy of Sciences 1969b, 1973, Population Reference Bureau 1970.

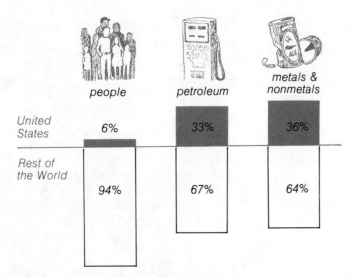

5-1   Can the world afford the United States?
The annual use of resources. (Data from U.S.
Bureau of Mines, Minerals Yearbook)

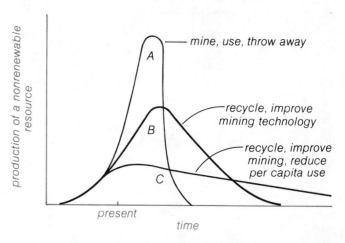

5-2   Alternate depletion patterns for a nonrenewable resource. (Modified after Hubbert 1962
and Cloud 1971)

None of these three depletion rate calculations takes into account large amounts of recycling, significant reduction in per capita demand, or substitution that shifts the problem to a new set of curves. These curves are, however, very important in indicating those resources for which crash programs of recycling, exploration, search for substitutes, and reduction of frivolous and wasteful demands should be instituted.

Estimates of fossil fuel supplies   How much longer can world and U.S. supplies of oil, natural gas, and coal last with energy demands escalating exponentially (Figures 1–2 and 1–3)? There are a number of possible answers depending on the accuracy of estimated reserves, the potential for finding new deposits, and our rate of usage.[2] However, there is one important difference. Metals and some other minerals can in principle be recycled but energy cannot, because it flows through the ecosphere (Section 3–4) and cannot be used again.

---

[2] For estimates of fossil fuel supplies and projected energy growth patterns see Hubbert 1962, 1969, 1971, Cheney 1974, Joint Committee on Atomic Energy 1973, Peach 1973, Committee on Interior and Insular Affairs 1973, Whittemore 1973, Williams 1972, Darmstadter 1971, 1972, Office of Scientific Technology 1972, National Petroleum Council 1971, Theobald et al. 1972, Woodwell 1974, Surrey & Bromley 1973, Averitt 1969, Cook 1972, Fisher 1974, Hendricks 1965, McLean 1972, Petersen 1971, U.S. Bureau of Mines (*Minerals Yearbook* and *Mineral Facts and Problems*), Commoner et al. 1974, vol. 2.

M. King Hubbert (1969) has projected depletion curves for world (Figure 5–3) and U.S. supplies (Figure 5–4) of oil, natural gas, and coal. Some other observers (Fisher 1974, Peach 1973, Theobald et al. 1972, Skinner 1969) take a more optimistic view of fossil fuel supplies. Yet, even Hubbert's estimates may be too optimistic because they consider total resource reserves and not net energy reserves. Major finds of new reserves or *reduced usage rates* merely shift the estimated depletion times a relatively short time into the future. For example, the big find of oil in Alaska will be depleted within 10 to 13 years once it reaches its maximum production rate (Cheney 1974).

Based on information we now have it seems clear that the epoch of readily available supplies of oil and natural gas will probably be over in the world around 2015 to 2030 and in the United States by 1990 to 2015, if not sooner (Hubbert 1969, Figures 5–3 and 5–4). Since it takes 20 to 50 years to develop and phase in a new energy system, we have no time to lose in seeking replacements.

Natural gas and especially oil exploration in the United States and the world was stimulated by a rapid rise in prices during the 1973-74 energy policy crisis. If these explorations are successful, we may have an oil (and perhaps a natural gas) glut for a few years (Macrae 1974). Regardless how real the 1973-74 energy situation was or whether by 1985 we have a real or contrived energy glut, we must not lose sight of the real severe shortages that seem destined to occur within a few decades. We cannot delay the institution of a massive energy conservation program and a crash program to develop alternate energy sources.

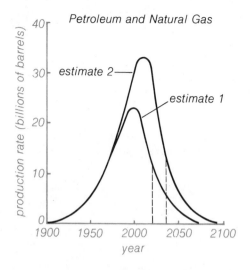

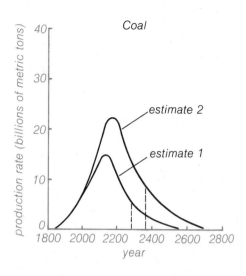

5–3 Estimated depletion curves for world supplies of fossil fuels. Dotted vertical lines indicate the approximate time at which 80 percent of the fuel will be depleted. (Modified after Hubbert 1969)

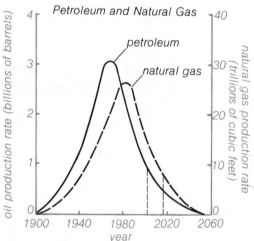

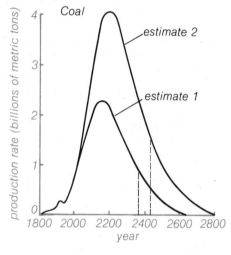

5–4 Estimated depletion curves for U.S. supplies of fossil fuels. Dotted vertical lines indicate the approximate time at which 80 percent of the fuel will be depleted. (Modified after Hubbert 1969)

Instead of getting all of our fossil fuels out of the ground as quickly as possible, a very strong case can be made for deliberately setting aside perhaps a third of our reserves of natural gas and petroleum as raw material to produce *petrochemicals* in future decades. These chemicals are used to produce most of the fertilizers, pesticides, detergents, synthetic fibers, inorganic and organic chemicals, plastics, and other products in modern society (Figure 5–5). A look at Figure 5–5 also reveals why the price of antifreeze, plastics, clothes, paint, tires, and many other products in an industrialized nation rises a few months after any shortage or price increase in crude oil or natural gas.

The use of petrochemicals is growing rapidly and already accounts for about 6 percent of all fossil fuels used in the United States. It seems unlikely that an entirely new chemical industry (one not based on fossil fuel raw materials) could be developed in the next few decades. As a result this may be the single most important use of these resources. On the other hand, Barry Commoner[3] argues that we should deliberately shift from the widespread use of petrochemicals, which are inherently incompatible with the environment, to more natural chemicals and products.

Another possibility: oil shale Oil shale is an underground rock formation that contains a hydrocarbon mixture known as kerogen. The shale rock could be strip mined or deep mined much like coal and transported to a nearby processing plant where it would be crushed and heated to yield low sulfur shale oil, which can then be refined to yield petroleum products. Vast oil shale deposits exist in a 16,000 to 17,000 square mile area of Colorado, Utah, and Wyoming,

[3] News report in *Chemical and Engineering News,* Nov. 26, 1973, p. 9.

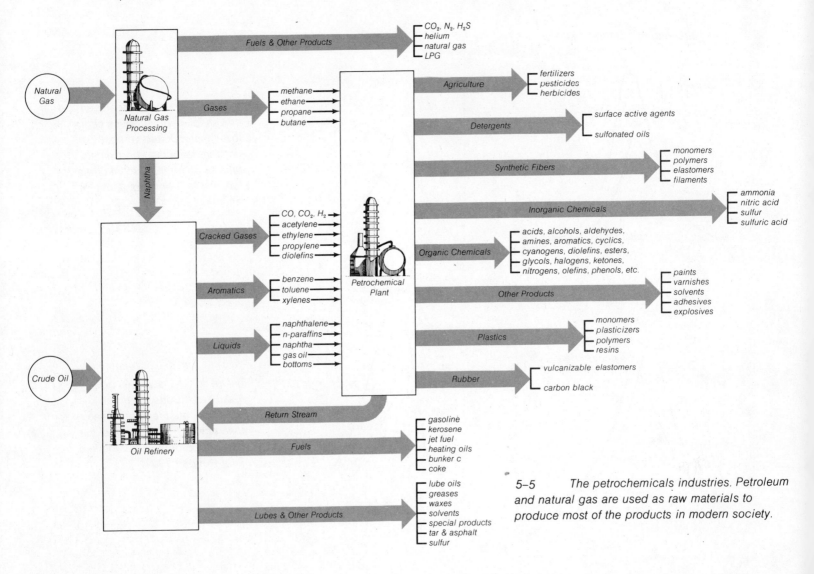

5-5   The petrochemicals industries. Petroleum and natural gas are used as raw materials to produce most of the products in modern society.

with 80 percent of the deposits on government owned land. Proved reserves in this area alone are estimated to be about 8 times our total petroleum reserves (Hammond et al. 1973) and greater than all the oil in the entire Middle East (Peach 1973).

But unfortunately there are some thermodynamic, economic, and environmental catches. Because the kerogen is so widely dispersed in the rock and because it must be heated to be converted to shale oil, more energy may be needed to mine, process, and ship it than the energy it contains. At best it may produce only a slight gain in net energy at a high cost. In addition, a 1973 environmental impact evaluation by the U.S. Department of Interior indicated that an oil shale industry would create serious environmental side effects including disruption of land, a decrease in air quality, destruction of vegetation and wildlife, lowering of water tables, and

a decrease of the quality of surface water in a region already experiencing serious water problems.

Another drawback is the staggering amount of solid waste produced, which would take up at least 12 percent more space than the original rock. The only obvious way to dispose of this powdered waste is to dump it into canyons and mountain valleys. The waste from strip mining a single oil shale tract (2,000 hectares) would fill six 700 acre (280 hectares) canyons to a depth of 25 feet (8 meters).

A suggestion for avoiding some of these problems is to distill the kerogen out of the rock below the surface either (1) by blasting underground chambers with conventional explosives and then injecting natural gas (the net energy problem again) into it and setting it afire, or (2) by exploding atomic bombs in deep layers of shale rock. But the J curve gets us again. Just to supply 10 percent of our projected oil needs by 1985 would require about 6 underground nuclear blasts per day,[4] with unknown geological and ecological hazards.

The Interior Department has leased six tracts of government owned land to private industry for an experimental oil shale program. But without strict environmental controls and a more favorable net energy gain, oil shale may have little to do with our energy future, despite its potential. Its most promising use may be as a source of raw materials for the petrochemicals industry (Hubbert 1969).

Coal and coal gasification   As seen from Figures 5–3 and 5–4, coal is our most abundant fossil fuel, constituting 80 percent of America's and 93 percent of the world's fossil fuel resources. World and U.S. supplies should last an estimated 200 to 400 years. Yet coal supplies only 18 percent of overall the U.S. energy demand and 55 percent of our electrical power. Even to maintain this percentage, coal production will have to increase 70 percent by 1985.

Some see a return to coal as a solution to shrinking oil and natural gas supplies (Osborn 1974, Nephew 1973), but there are a number of problems associated with such a shift. Coal is the fuel that produces the most air pollution, from the sulfur oxides and particulates that are emitted when it is burned. In addition, it can have a disastrous impact on the land from strip mining (Section 4–5), can pollute streams from acid mine drainage and runoff, and is dangerous to mine. Over 1,600 accidental mine deaths and some 75,000 injuries have occurred since 1966. Without very stringent air, water, and land environmental controls and mine safety regulations, it offers unacceptable threats to human health and to the environment. In 1974 the American Public Health Association estimated that 3,800 more people would die each year from heart and respiratory diseases if existing electric power plants burning natural gas or low-sulfur oil were converted to coal burning plants without additional air pollution controls.[5] Another problem is that much of our rich and low-sulfur coal deposits are in the West. Shipping the coal East would add significantly to the cost and decrease net energy yield.

Thus, substituting coal for much of our oil and natural gas during the next 2 to 3 decades is possible only if we are willing to pay 2 to 3 times the present cost to cover necessary air pollution controls,[6] land reclamation, improved mine safety practices, and increased shipping costs. With such controls, coal may well be a more desirable option than depletion of oil and natural gas or a major commitment to nuclear power. But we would still have to find other energy options by 2050, since if coal became our sole source of

energy our proven reserves would probably last only about 47 years and our total estimated reserves only 75 years (Perry 1974).[7]

Some feel that coal could be used most effectively, especially between 1980 and 2000, if it were converted into synthetic natural gas (SNG) (Hammond et al. 1973, Mills 1971, Perry 1974, Maugh 1972c). This processing eliminates the sulfur oxide and particulate air pollution problems along with the transportation problem, because SNG could be transported by pipeline. Gasification of coal has been carried out since the late eighteenth century and is widely used in parts of Europe today. But thermodynamics enters again because about 25 percent of the energy in the coal is lost in the conversion (Osborn 1974). In addition, with today's processes SNG is too low in energy value to substitute for natural gas and must be upgraded by an additional process, again adding to the cost and decreasing the net energy yield.

Several coal gasification demonstration plants are already operating successfully, and others are being constructed. Research into new processes is increasing (Perry 1974), including schemes for converting coal to synthetic crude oil, but again whether coal gasification or liquefaction become economically and thermodynamically feasible remains to be seen. Even with a crash program it could provide no more than 15 percent of our projected natural gas demand by 1985 (Maugh 1972c) and probably no more than 5 percent.[8] Because coal gasification is more wasteful of coal supplies, both strip and deep mining of coal would increase significantly and coal reserves might be used up within 25 to 50 years.

Fossil fuels and international politics   Competition for increasingly scarce fossil fuel and mineral resources will almost certainly form the power arena of international politics in coming decades. There appear to be several major future trends for the U.S. energy situation. *First,* energy prices (and thus all prices) will rise sharply. *Second,* despite talk of energy self-sufficiency, the United States may become increasingly dependent on foreign sources for oil and natural gas. In 1973 35 percent of the U.S. oil supply was imported. By 1985 the National Petroleum Council (1971) projects that we will be importing 60 percent of our oil and 28 percent of our natural gas supplies. The resulting imbalance of payments was already $9 billion in 1973 and could rise to $20 to $30 billion by 1980 (McLean 1972, White 1973). Even increased petroleum production from intensified offshore exploration and new oil fields will not eliminate import dependence unless refinery capacity can be increased enough to process the crude oil.

Third, to stimulate domestic production of oil, natural gas, and coal there will be increasing pressure to relax air pollu-

---

[4] This is based on the estimate by Cohen (1967a) that one 50 kiloton atomic bomb could pulverize about 1 million tons of rock and yield at best about 0.5 million barrels of oil.

[5] News item in *Environment*, 16: 4, 20 (May 1974).

[6] This assumes that reliable and economically feasible methods for removing sulfur from coal or sulfur oxides from stack emissions can be developed.

[7] This assumes a 3.5 percent rise in energy demand per year.

[8] Statement by energy expert Sam H. Schurr, quoted in *Technology Review*, February 1973, p. 58.

tion, strip mining, and other much needed environmental standards. *Fourth,* there will be increasing pressure to hasten the development of nuclear power despite its considerable risks (see Chapter 6). *Finally,* international tensions could heighten. The industrialized nations will be competing for oil and natural gas supplies, and famine will be increasing in poorer nations where higher energy prices make less fuel available for fertilizer production and for running irrigation pumps. By the year 2000, the USSR will be the only remaining superpower who is self-sufficient in most basic mineral (Petersen 1971, Wade 1974) and energy resources. The Soviet Union possesses an estimated 37 percent of the world's oil, 40 percent of the natural gas, 25 percent of global hydroelectric resources, and 54 percent of the coal, plus a rapidly expanding nuclear power base.

Although this economic and political situation can be viewed with alarm, it could also be beneficial for rich and poor nations alike. First, as prices rise the industrialized nations will be forced to stop squandering resources and to institute increasingly stringent programs for energy conservation, resource recycling, and less energy intensive products and habits. Second, the rich nations will be forced to accelerate research for new energy sources and better environmental control methods. Finally, the United States, Western Europe, and Japan may be forced to cooperate and more justly redistribute wealth with poorer nations in Asia, Africa, and Latin America, who possess rich deposits of the world's key mineral and energy resources.

Even if we greatly increase recycling (Figure 3–9), there are still two ultimate limitations on the level of population and affluence on the planet: the energy input and the heat output (Figures 3–8, 3–9, and Chapter 8). Without an infinite energy source such as solar, wind, or fusion energy, we do not have enough energy to mine resources, convert them to useful materials, and then recycle them at ever-growing rates. Even with an infinite energy source the ultimate limit becomes the ability of the ecosphere to absorb the heat automatically produced as energy flows through the system (the second law). Thus, in the long run our only serious energy option is reduced use of energy throughout (Figure 3–9) by a combination of energy conservation, less energy-intensive life styles, and a switch to energy sources that minimize environmental impact (Table 4–3).

5–2   Fossil Fuels and Air Pollution

Our finite air supply   Take a deep breath, push it into your lungs, and then release it. If the air you just took in was not polluted, you are in a small and rapidly shrinking minority. According to the Public Health Service over 43 million Americans live in 300 cities described as having "major" air pollu-

tion problems.[9] They also report that every city of over 50,000 population has an air pollution problem of some form. What might happen if our population increases by another 50 to 100 million and 9 out of 10 of us live in urban areas?

Air pollution, of course, is not new. Our early ancestors living in smoke filled caves had air pollution problems, as have most cities throughout history. Over 2,000 years ago Seneca complained of air pollution in Rome and the first known laws to control air pollution were enacted in London in 1273 when King Edward I passed a law prohibiting the use of one type of coal. In the Middle Ages one man was even hanged for burning coal (Griggin 1965). In 1300 King Richard III placed a heavy tax on coal to discourage its use. In the early 1800s Shelley wrote: "Hell is a city much like London, a populous and smoky city." In 1911, a great London air pollution disaster from the burning of coal killed 1,150 people. In his report on the episode, Dr. Harold Antoine Des Voeux first introduced the name *smog* to describe the mixture of smoke and fog that made up the air in the city of London.

Allowing a pollutant to be diluted or dispersed by air or water is a valid use of the spontaneous tendency for increased disorder as required by the second law of thermodynamics. But it is only valid as long as the supply of air or water is infinite and pollutants are not dumped in massive quantities in one place over a short period of time.

Contrary to popular belief we do not live at the bottom of a seemingly infinite sea of air. About 95 percent of the air on this planet is concentrated in a layer only 12 miles thick around the earth's crust (*Chemical & Engineering News* 1966). Furthermore, most of this air is contained in the lower part or *troposphere* of this 12 mile layer. In relative terms, our air supply is about as thick as the layer of varnish on a desk globe.

Most air pollutants are found in the troposphere where they mix vertically and horizontally, often reacting with each other or with other materials. Eventually, they are returned to the land or water by rainfall or fallout. This finite troposphere receives more than 770,000 metric tons of air pollutants *each day* from the United States alone. Each American is responsible for about 3.5 kilograms or 7.4 pounds of air pollutants each day or over 1 metric ton per year. Perhaps if our share was dumped at our doorstep we would become more aware of our effect on our finite air renewal system.

Types, sources, and effects of air pollutants   Where does all the pollution come from? The top five air pollutants in

[9] For general discussions of air pollution see American Chemical Society 1969, Section 1, Blaustein 1972, Brodine 1972a, 1973, Cole 1968, Council on Environmental Quality 1971, Hinch 1969, Hodges 1973, League of Women Voters 1970, Linton 1970, Chapters 2–4, Marshall 1968, Newell 1971, Pryde 1973, Stern 1968, Stoker & Seager 1972, Treshow 1971, Turk et al. 1972, Williamson 1973, Commoner et al. 1974, vol. 1.

terms of the tonnage emitted per year are in order (1) carbon monoxide, (2) hydrocarbons, (3) particulates, (4) sulfur oxides, and (5) oxides of nitrogen. By source the major contributors in decreasing order are (1) transportation, (2) fuel combustion from power plants, (3) industry, (4) forest and agricultural fires, and (5) incineration of solid wastes (U.S. Department of Health, Education, and Welfare 1970d, Robinson & Robbins 1970).

But should we base our pollution control programs on tonnage data alone? The effect of a specific pollutant is not based solely on its total tonnage per year but on its relative toxicity and the average length of time it remains in the air before it is rendered harmless by natural processes or chemical cycles. For example, 1 ton of fine particles reduces visibility 25 times as much as 1 ton of larger particles (Council on Environmental Quality 1972, p. 5). Fine particles also are more of a health hazard and harder to control .

A better evaluation of the air pollution problem can be obtained by considering both the total weight and the relative tolerance for each of the major pollutants (Babcock 1970). A crude tolerance level can be estimated for each pollutant and then converted to a relative tolerance weighting factor. The tonnage values are then multiplied by the various weighting factors to provide a tonnage–tolerance overview of air pollution. Figure 5–6 shows the different rankings of major sources and pollutants obtained by considering tonnage alone and by weighting pollutants according to tolerance.[10] Using the weighted index power plants, space heating, and industry supercede the automobile and other forms of transportation as the major source, although automobiles still remain important. An even more dramatic shift is seen in the relative importance of various pollutants. Carbon monoxide drops from first to fifth. Using the weighted index particulates, sulfur oxides, and nitrogen oxides are the most important pollutants. This is still an extremely crude estimate, however, since the values calculated vary considerably with different assumptions about complex and poorly understood health effects. But this and more sophisticated air pollution indices (see Council on Environmental Quality 1972, pp. 5–10, 31–47) provide a more realistic measure for air quality and pollution control priorities than simply using the total tonnage emitted for each pollutant.

Effects of air pollution   Although we have known for decades that ill health and sometimes even death is related to air pollution (Figure 5–7), the direct linkage between various diseases and specific pollutants has not been established and in most cases will probably never be established. (For more details and documentation see Waldbott 1973, Brodine 1972, Carnow 1970, Lave & Seskin 1970, National Tuberculosis and

[10] The weighted index used here is modified from Babcock's index (1970) to include the time of exposure and 1975 air pollution standards.

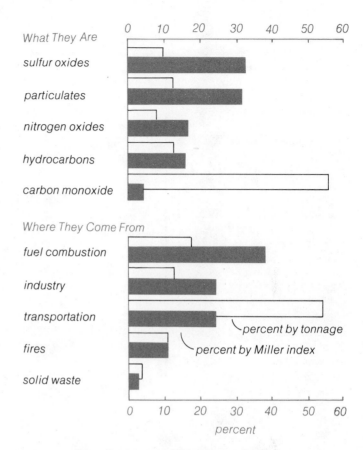

5–6   *Air pollutants and their sources for the United States in 1970. Two percentages are shown. One is based on tonnage of emissions (Council on Environmental Quality 1972), and the other is based on a weighted index that takes into account the relative health effects of each pollutant.*

Respiratory Disease Association 1969, Shy & Finklea 1973, Stokinger 1971, Resources for the Future 1974.) Officially almost no one ever dies of air pollution. Instead the death certificate reads chronic bronchitis, emphysema, lung cancer, stomach cancer, or heart disease. In recent years these non-infectious killers have replaced infectious diseases as the major health problem in developed countries.

Diseases of the heart and blood vessels were responsible for only 20 percent of the deaths in the early 1900s but now account for more than half of the deaths. Lung cancer, now the single largest killer from cancer among American males, has increased thirtyfold in this century, killing over 50,000 men and 10,000 women each year. Cigarette smoking appears to be a prime factor in this increase in lung cancer, but smoking alone apparently cannot account for the different rates of lung cancer in urban and rural areas (National Research Council 1972,

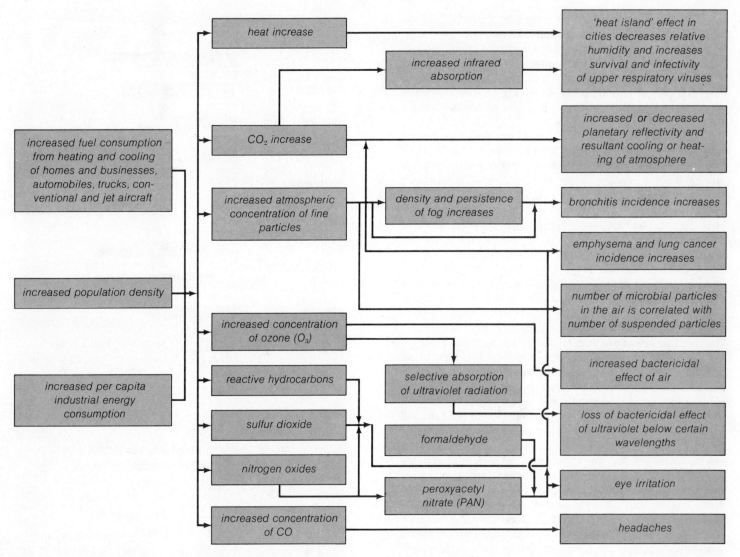

5–7   A crude model of air pollution and some human ecological effects. (Modified after Institute of Ecology 1969)

Lambert & Reid 1970). Although many factors are undoubtedly involved, the higher levels of air pollution and radioactive airborne dust in urban areas are probably contributing causes (Menck et al. 1974).

Emphysema, a killer and crippler, has increased over seventeenfold since 1950 (National Tuberculosis and Respiration Disease Association 1969, p. 71). An estimated 1.3 million persons suffer from emphysema in the United States, 55 percent of them younger than 65 (Figure 5–8). Chronic bronchitis now affects one out of five of all American men between 40 and 60 and has also been indirectly related to smoking and living in polluted urban areas. Investigators have shown cor-

relations between photochemical oxidants and respiratory distress, emphysema, and susceptibility to respiratory infection (Jaffe 1968). In Los Angeles, a correlation was shown between carbon monoxide levels and fatality rates in patients with heart trouble (Goldsmith & Landaw 1968). These same investigators found that automobile drivers thought to be responsible for accidents had elevated carbon monoxide levels in their blood.

The Environmental Protection Agency (see Council on Environmental Quality 1971, pp. 106–107) estimates that medical care and work loss costs in the United States from air pollution are around $6 billion per year. The EPA also esti-

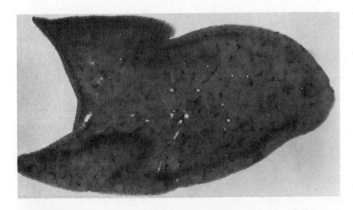

5–8   *The lung of a normal person (above) and the lung of a person suffering from pulmonary emphysema (below). (Webb-Waring Institute for Medical Research, Denver, courtesy of the Environmental Protection Agency)*

mates annual air pollution damage to materials and vegetation at $4.9 billion and lowered property values at $5.2 billion. Crop damage and reduction of yield is already a regional problem, especially in California, parts of the Midwest and eastern seaboard, and Europe.

Most damage to materials is caused by SO_2 and sulfuric acid, which attack metals, limestone or marble building or statue surfaces, rubber, plastic, and some types of clothing. In some cities women walking down the street have had their nylon stockings and blouses disintegrate. Fallout from particulates discolors and damages buildings, cars, and clothing, requiring greatly increased expenditures for cleaning. A 1969 staff study by Department of Health, Education, and Welfare analysts estimated that $16 million annually are spent just for extra lighting because of loss of visibility from air pollution —a vicious circle that worsens air pollution and the energy crisis by burning more fuels.

Brown air cities—photochemical smog   Large cities generally fall into one of two basic air pollution classes—the *brown air cities* and the *gray air cities* (Figure 5–9 and Table

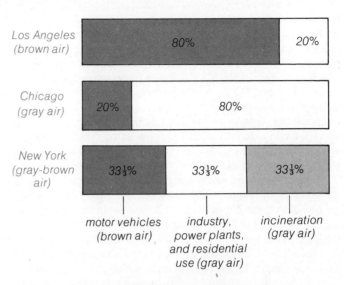

5–9   *Each city has unique air pollution problems. (The percentage values are crude estimates for illustrative purposes only.)*

5–1) (Berry 1970, p. 2). Brown air cities, like Los Angeles, Denver, Salt Lake City, Tokyo, Sydney, Mexico City, and Buenos Aires, are frequently young cities with warm, dry climates where the main source of air pollution is the internal combustion engine. Nitric oxide from automobile exhausts reacts with oxygen in the air to form nitrogen dioxide (NO_2), a yellow-brown gas that produces the brownish haze characteristic of automobile cities. When exposed to sunlight, the NO_2 and the accompanying hydrocarbons can react to form a new brew of secondary pollutants, such as ozone and PAN, known as *photochemical smog*. Brown air cities then are photochemical smog cities, with hydrocarbons, oxides of nitrogen, carbon monoxide, ozone, and PAN being the major pollutants.

The key to the photochemical smog problem then depends on what we do with the automobile or, more correctly, the internal combustion engine. There are four major ways of reducing auto emissions: (1) applying engineering changes and devices to the present internal combustion engine, (2) developing cleaner systems such as the gas turbine, electric, or steam engine, (3) providing alternative forms of mass transportation, and (4) reducing energy consumption and pollution by restricting the use of cars.

Gray air cities—industrial smog   The *gray air cities*[11] are older cities such as London, Chicago, New York, Baltimore,

---

[11] A well-matured photochemical smog can also appear gray. In southern California one frequently sees a gray haze caused by the particulates produced in photochemical smog, because the nitrogen dioxide concentration has been reduced to the point where its brownish color can't be seen.

Birmingham, Philadelphia, or Pittsburgh, which depend heavily on the burning of coal or oil for heating, manufacturing, and electric power generation. This burning produces two major classes of pollutants—particulates (soot, fly ash, and dust), which give the air over such cities its gray cast, and the sulfur oxides (SO_2 and SO_3), which are produced by oxidation of the sulfur that contaminates most oil and coal. We might call this characteristic type of air pollution *industrial smog*. Thus, gray air cities can also be called industrial smog cities. Industrial smog occurs more in cold and wet weather when furnaces in residences, power plants, and factories are going full blast.

The particulates and sulfur dioxide in industrial smog are the most damaging to health. They are associated with the big air pollution disasters of the past 25 years—in London during 1952 (3,500 to 4,000 deaths) and two episodes in 1956 (900 deaths), Danora, Pennsylvania, in 1948 (20 deaths, 6,000 sick), and New York in 1965 (400 deaths), when prolonged temperature inversions allowed them to accumulate.

Globally, sulfur oxide gases disperse fairly rapidly, and rain eventually washes out the sulfuric acid and particulates. But locally, especially in the form of sulfuric acid and particulates, sulfur oxides are the most toxic and dangerous pollutants in the air. This is particularly true in densely populated cities with cold winters. An estimated 20 million tons of sulfur dioxide were emitted in the United States in 1970, a concentration that is expected to rise to almost 96 million tons by the year 2000 without very strict controls (Staff report 1970c). Sulfur oxide emissions can be reduced by (1) switching to more expensive low-sulfur fuels (less than 1 percent sulfur) or to nuclear power, (2) removing sulfur from fuels, (3) removing sulfur oxides from combustion gases, and (4) reducing energy consumption and waste.

5-3   Oceans and Oil Spills: The Ultimate Sink

The ocean is truly the "ultimate sink" for most natural and man-made by-products of life (Olson & Burgess 1967, SCEP 1970). Everything we "throw away" in liquid form or in a form that can be dissolved or flushed from the land eventually reaches the sea, except for a few substances that decompose rapidly. All the rivers and lakes of the world with their loads of debris from cities, sewers, and farmlands eventually empty into the sea. But the sea has no outlets.

We naively believe that the ocean will continue to absorb all the waste we pump into it while providing all the food we need for a protein starved population and bursting forth with oil, minerals, and riches to sustain our J curve age. Evidence is accumulating from all parts of the globe that man is already having a serious impact on the oceans. This is occurring when only a third of the world is industrialized and when industrial capacity is doubling every 15 to 20 years.

Table 5-1   Comparison of "gray air" and "brown air" cities

Characteristic	Industrial or gray smog	Photochemical or brown smog
Typical city	London, Chicago	Tokyo, Los Angeles
Chief pollutants	Sulfur oxides, particulates	Ozone, PAN, aldehydes, oxides of nitrogen, carbon monoxide
Principal sources	Industrial and household burning of oil and coal	Motor vehicle gasoline combustion
Major effects on humans	Irritation of lungs and throat	Eye irritation
Time of occurrence of worst episodes	Winter months (especially in the early morning)	Summer months (especially around noontime)

Oil spills and leaks   Oil pollution of the seas from natural leaks has probably always been a problem, but in recent years man has matched nature's input.[12] It is estimated that at present about half of oil pollution is natural and half is man-induced (Steinhart & Steinhart 1972). Over 360 billion gallons of oil are transported over the seas each year by gigantic tankers—enough to cover the entire world with a paper thin layer of oil.

Despite publicity about offshore blowouts, pipeline breaks, and tanker accidents, these sources probably contribute less than 20 percent of the oil introduced into the oceans by man (Schurr 1971). A 1972 survey by the U.S. Geological Survey and the Environmental Protection Agency showed that *more than two-thirds* of the oil polluting our waters comes from the disposal of billions of quarts of waste oils from automobile crankcases and machines.[13] With the recent energy crisis and without extremely strict regulation, the drive to open thousands of new offshore wells and to pipe oil from Alaska could change this ratio. In 1970, 17 percent of the world's oil came from offshore wells. By 1980 between 3,000 and 5,000 new offshore wells are expected to be drilled *each year*. In any event, both crude and refined[14] oil can be introduced by man into the ecosphere from a number of sources (Figure 5-10).

[12] For more details on oil pollution see Battelle Memorial Institute 1967, Blumer 1971, Devanney 1974, Coan 1970, Fay 1970, Holcomb 1969, Lehr 1973, McCaull 1969, Potter 1973, Radcliffe & Murphy 1969, Smith 1968, Steinhart & Steinhart 1972, Wilson et al. 1974, Commoner et al. 1974, vol. 1.

[13] News item in *Scientific American*, February 1973, p. 48.

[14] *Crude oil* is oil as it comes out of the ground. *Refined oil* is obtained by distillation and chemical processing of various components from crude oil.

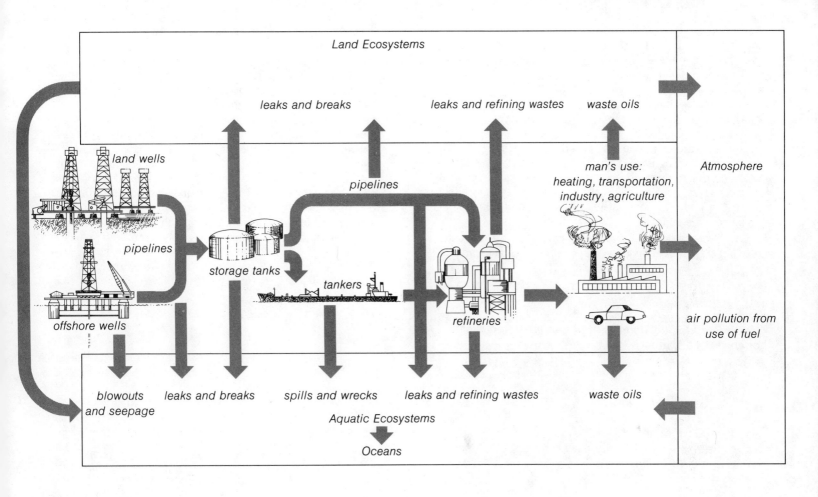

5–10   *Major ways that oil can pollute the hydrosphere, lithosphere, and atmosphere.*

Effect of oil in the marine ecosystem   The amount of harm that oil does is not really known. The problems are complex and vary with the type of oil (refined or crude) and the size, location, duration, and type of spill, blowout, or leak. But research is beginning to reveal some tentative conclusions. Crude oil is not a single chemical but a collection of hundreds of substances of widely different properties. These include low-boiling, lighter, and highly toxic aromatic hydrocarbons that are the primary cause of immediate kills of a number of aquatic organisms, especially bottom dwelling shellfish. Most of these chemicals vaporize into the atmosphere within a day or two.

Some higher boiling hydrocarbons remain on the water surface, and some sink to the bottom to form tar-like globs and chunks as big as tennis balls. A number of these hydrocarbons are degraded by various bacteria, but this may be an extremely slow process in very cold (Arctic or Antarctic) waters or in oxygen-depleted waters. Thus, oil production in the Alaskan

North Slope may pose especially persistent oil pollution problems in the Arctic Ocean.

Other oil hydrocarbons find their way into the fatty tissues of some marine organisms and in some cases can be biologically magnified up the food chain to man. Although little is known about the nature and extent of this phenomenon, there is some evidence (Carruthers et al. 1967, Graef & Winter 1968) that among these chemicals are well-known carcinogenic (cancer causing) chemicals such as 3,4-benzopyrene.

The toxicities of the numerous petroleum compounds and the thresholds for damage to different forms of sea life are not known quantitatively in most cases, and existing data often present a conflicting picture of potential damage. There is general agreement, however, that many of these substances may be especially damaging to the larval forms of marine life. Even if the concentration of oil is not sufficient to kill marine organisms, it may reduce their resistance to infections and other stresses. Extremely low concentrations may also block smell and taste receptors or mimic natural stimuli and thus interfere with the ability to find food, select a habitat, or escape from predators. For example, lobsters are attracted to some crude oil compounds, especially kerosene. An oil spill may attract them away from their normal food sources and into a spill area where they can be contaminated or killed.

Crude oil compounds may also interact synergistically with sewage, chlorinated hydrocarbon pesticides, and other hydrocarbons to cause more serious damage than that of each pollutant acting by itself. Chlorinated hydrocarbons such as DDT and dieldrin can be concentrated in oil slicks because they are very soluble in oil. Such poisons can seriously affect larval fish and plankton that tend to spend part of the night hours near the surface.

Most of the publicity and outcry against oil pollution has resulted from its economic, recreational, and esthetic damage to coastal resort areas and pleasure boats and to the thousands of sea birds killed. Although these are important concerns, they are potentially the least of our worries.

There is considerable dispute, uncertainty, and conflicting evidence over the extent and seriousness of oil spills (Devanney 1974). For example, some very large tanker spills of crude oil (the Torrey Canyon disaster and the Santa Barbara blowouts) have apparently (but not necessarily) had less serious effects on marine life than some smaller spills of refined oil such as those off Baja California and Falmouth, Massachusetts. Extensive research at the Woods Hole Oceanographic Institution has revealed that the effects of refined oil in shallow water near the coast may be much more widespread and longer lasting than originally suspected (Blumer 1971). Whether these results also apply to crude oil spills is still unknown.

Guest Editorial: Pollution Control—An Input Approach or an Output Approach?

Kenneth E. F. Watt

Kenneth E. F. Watt is a professor of zoology at the University of California at Davis and one of the foremost scholars applying systems analysis to ecological problems. At present, he is the principal investigator in a 30-person team engaged in building computer simulation models of human society. He has done research in 24 countries and has been awarded the Fisheries Ecology and Management Award of the Wildlife Society and the Gold Medal of the Entomological Society of Canada. Professor Watt combines research talents with the ability to communicate complex ideas to others. He has lectured at 80 institutions and among his 75 publications are five important books: Mathematical Models for Use in Insect Pest Control, Environmental Realities and Economic Revolution, Ecology and Resource Management, Principles of Environmental Science, and The Titanic Effect.

There are two possible approaches to solving the pollution problem, an input approach and an output approach. Remarkably, almost all the attention has been focused on the latter, yet it is far less useful and effective. We can think of all industrial and transportation activity as the systems analysts black box, into which useful energy and matter flow, and out of which pollutant solid, liquid, and gaseous end products emerge. The current philosophy of pollution control is to ask, "Given the amount of matter and energy flowing into the black box, what can we do to get rid of the output?" Even recycling is an output approach to this problem, albeit a sophisticated one.

A more useful approach is to question why so much matter and energy flow into the system in the first place. If, for example, all the goods, services, and transportation now available in our society could be available with 5 percent of the present expenditure of matter and energy, then we would have 5 percent as much pollution, without even trying to control it.

When we inspect the relevant figures, it appears that the central reason we use so much matter and energy is not our demand for goods, services, and transportation, but rather the fantastically inefficient way in which we are now using matter and energy. For example, consider transportation.

Cars, with the typical load of 1.3 passengers, deliver only 18.3 passenger miles of transportation per gallon of fuel. Jet aircraft on average carry 54 passengers and deliver only 13 passenger miles of transportation per gallon of fuel. These are the twin backbones of the current U.S. transportation system. Buses, amazingly, can deliver about 270 passenger miles of transportation per gallon of fuel, and electric trains can deliver about 1,130 passenger miles of transportation per gallon of fuel. Thus, we have drifted into a social system that makes profligately wasteful use of matter and energy and develops a totally unnecessary amount of pollution per passenger mile.

But this is only the beginning. Cars and aircraft also make fantastically inefficient use of the space around cities. Trains and buses use a small fraction of the band width of right-of-way to move a given number of passengers per hour: a train can move about 100 times the number of people per foot-width of right-of-way per hour as a car–freeway system.

Some readers will argue that the reason for traveling by car and aircraft is to save time. An analysis of the portal-to-portal times on a series of sample trips between various pairs of points will show how fallacious this argument is. On some short jet trips mean velocity, portal-to-portal, can be as little as 24 miles per hour. We in North America forget about the Tokkaido High Speed Express train in Japan that runs at 175 miles per hour. Hitachi has been advertising a proposed train service to run at 310 miles per hour.

Personal experience makes these numbers very real. I grew up in Toronto and remember vividly the unimaginable traffic jams created by cars before the advent of the rail subway system. The Toronto rail system has made travel so much more rapid and pleasant that masses of people now return downtown at night for entertainment because of the speed and ease with which this is possible; the result has

been a renaissance of the urban core. Recently, I was traveling by rail in Switzerland. I noticed that between Geneva and Lausanne, where the highway parallels the railway, the train passed every car I could see on the highway. We all know how fast European highway driving is! The North American traveler is always amazed at the ease with which one can move around in much of Europe, because of their integrated transportation system.

The same type of analysis that one could apply to transportation can be applied to most areas of our lives. We have unwittingly drifted into a life style in which we pay a tremendous price in matter, energy, pollution, and sickness caused by pollution for goods, services, and transportation that are not as useful or of such high quality as those we could buy with less pollution and resource depletion, if we reconsidered the aims of our society. It would appear that the true aim is to provide a high-quality existence for people. We somehow seem to have lost sight of this aim. We should now use our best scientific and engineering know-how to get back on a rational track.

Discussion

1. Why has the input approach to pollution control been so neglected in the United States?

2. What other pollution problems might be controlled by an input approach? Are there any that would not lend themselves to this approach?

3. What are the economic, political, and ecological consequences of shifting to an input approach for pollution control? How would it affect your lifestyle?

Much can be done to reduce the amount of man-made oil pollution entering the ocean (input approaches) and to remove it or minimize its effects once it has been introduced (output approaches). Some of these approaches are still in developmental or testing stages.

Some Approaches to Oil Pollution Control

Input Approaches

1. Reduce our extravagant and wasteful use of oil as we reduce population growth.

2. Strictly regulate the building of supertankers and the construction of superports (Marcus 1973, Lehr 1973).

3. Use "load on top" (LOT) procedures for loading and emptying all oil tankers (already done on 80 percent of all tankers).

4. Develop better bilge pumping and cleaning operations and strictly enforce regulations for tankers. Eighty percent of the world's tankers now separate oil from the water used for ballast or for cleaning unfilled compartments instead of emptying this oily water into the ocean.

5. Reduce the potential for tanker accidents by improved training of tanker crews, establishment of shipping lanes, and improved navigation aids.

6. *Strictly enforce safety regulations for all offshore wells.*

7. *Strictly enforce safety and disposal regulations for refineries and industrial plants.*

8. *Collect used oils and greases from service stations and other sources (possibly by a payment incentive plan) and reprocess them for reuse.*

9. *Strengthen existing international agreements on oil spills and establish a strong international control authority for the oceans.*

Output Approaches

1. *"Corral" the oil to hold it at sea and pick it up mechanically with straw. One engineer said this is like trying to get smoke back into a smokestack (the second law again).*

2. *Treat oil chemically (usually with detergents) so it will emulsify, dissolve, or sink. The detergents used to help clean up the Torrey Canyon spill probably killed more marine life than the oil. Even though advances have been made in producing less toxic dispersants, most ecologists do not favor the use of chemicals (Blumer 1971).*

3. *Ship oil in a solid state much like a gel, so that it could be picked up quickly and easily if an accident occurs.*

4. *Use air delivered antipollution systems (ADAPT) based on transfer of oil from a stricken tanker to large rubber bladders.*

5. *Improve mechanical barrier devices to contain oil until it can be picked up.*

6. *Develop special bacteria to biologically degrade the oil. (This approach may not be useful for the deep ocean because of low temperatures and lack of the nutrients needed to keep bacteria alive but could prove useful on land and along the coasts.)*

7. *Use oil-soluble ferrofluids. Iron-containing material soluble in oil is added to the spill and an electromagnet can then be used to remove the oil.*

5–4   Strip Mining: A Land–Energy Tradeoff

Types and extent of surface mining   Imagine a gargantuan shovel 32 stories high with a boom as long as a football field, capable of gouging out 200 cubic yards of land every 55 seconds and dropping this 325 ton load a block away. This is a description of Big Muskie, a $25 million power shovel now used for strip mining coal in the United States (National Coal Association 1968, p. 28).

Surface mining (of which strip mining is one form) is the process of removing the earth's crust (overburden) of topsoil, rock and other strata to obtain coal, sand, gravel, stone, phosphate, iron, copper, and other mineral resources. There are several types of surface mining (Figure 5–11): (1) *open pit mining,* used primarily for stone, sand and gravel, iron, and copper; (2) *area strip mining,* in which 30 to 40 foot deep trenches are cut out of flat or rolling terrain (used primarily for coal and phosphate); (3) *contour strip mining,* used on hilly or mountainous terrain by cutting out a series of contour bands (used primarily for coal); and (4) *dredging* of sea beds, used primarily for sand and gravel. Of these types contour strip mining is probably the most destructive of land.

Since World War II, an estimated 4 million acres or 6,200 square miles have been disrupted by surface mining, mostly in Appalachia (U.S. Department of Interior 1967). Estimates vary, depending on whether they come from the coal mining industry or from government and environmental groups, but only between one-third and one-half of these 4 million acres have been reclaimed to any extent. The unreclaimed land is at least equivalent to the land area of Connecticut or to a barren swath of land more than one mile wide stretching from New York to San Francisco.

Most people associate the strip mining of coal with West Virginia and Pennsylvania, but it already affects nearly half of our states. The newest and largest battleground over strip mining is in the northern Great Plains—primarily the coal rich states of Montana, South Dakota, North Dakota, Wyoming, Colorado, and New Mexico. Under these vast grasslands and high plateaus lie more than 40 percent of the nation's coal supply and 77 percent of the "economically strippable" reserves. These delicate ecosystems could be subject to permanent damage from strip mining. But the more severe drawback may be a lack of water to support simultaneously strip mining operations, the necessary land reclamation, and the increase in population associated with the industry. Mining operations in many of these arid regions could destroy aquifers and interrupt the flow of vital ground water.

Land disruption by surface mining is already a serious problem but because our use of resources is increasing on a J curve, worse disruption is ahead. Between 1970 and 2000, a total of 15 million additional acres of disrupted land will be added to the present 2.8 million acres of unreclaimed land (Karsch 1970, Weisz 1970). Approximately 5 million acres will result from the surface mining of coal, and 10 million acres from the mining of phosphate, sand, and gravel to provide fertilizer and urban building and transportation for the next 70 million Americans. If we include existing unreclaimed acres the total of almost 18 million disturbed acres or about 23,400 square miles is equivalent to the total land areas of Connecticut, Delaware, New Hampshire, Rhode Island, New Jersey, and our nation's capital.

Another environmental controversy   The biggest use of surface mining (accounting for almost 45 percent of the

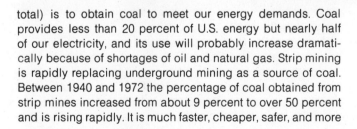

5-11   (a) Open pit mining of copper in Butte, Montana. (b) Area strip mining of coal in Colstrip, Montana. (c) Contour strip mining of coal in Kemmerer, Wyoming. (Photos from U.S. Department of Interior, Bureau of Reclamation and USDA, Soil Conservation Service)

total) is to obtain coal to meet our energy demands. Coal provides less than 20 percent of U.S. energy but nearly half of our electricity, and its use will probably increase dramatically because of shortages of oil and natural gas. Strip mining is rapidly replacing underground mining as a source of coal. Between 1940 and 1972 the percentage of coal obtained from strip mines increased from about 9 percent to over 50 percent and is rising rapidly. It is much faster, cheaper, safer, and more

efficient than underground mining. Environmentalists argue, however, that the only reason surface mining appears cheaper is that mining companies are not being required to pay the true environmental and social costs of this massive ecological disruption of land and water (Caudhill 1971, Surface Mining Research Library 1972, Commoner et al. 1974, vol. 1). Again we have a highly controversial issue, as summarized in Table 5–2.

Table 5–2   The strip mining controversy

Arguments for	Arguments against
Strip mining produces short term environmental damage, but it can be repaired with available technology. Surface mining and reclamation often improve the land.	Surface mining should be abolished because it destroys irreplaceable natural resources such as land, forests, soil, and water. It leaves hideous scars on the denuded landscape, disrupts wildlife habitats (about 1.7 million acres have already been destroyed), can cause landslides and soil erosion, and may pollute nearby rivers and streams with silt and acid runoff (some 11,000 miles of U.S. waterways are polluted from strip and underground mining). Surface mining actually destroys outdoor recreational resources valued at $35 million.*
Surface coal is the lowest-coal source of fuel available in large supply to meet energy demands. A ban on strip mining would disrupt energy supplies and damage the economy.	All the nation's energy needs could be met by development of underground coal reserves. Government figures show that deep mine reserves outweigh surface reserves by a ratio of 34 to 1.
Electric generating plants depend on surface-mined coal. More than one-fourth of all electric power is generated by surface coal; indeed, this is its main use.	Surface coal should be reserved as an emergency supply to be used after underground reserves are exhausted.
Coal companies could not convert to deep mining quickly enough to replace the surface coal that is now used for electric power generation.	More than 1,500 deep mines have been closed since 1969. Many of these mines still contain coal that could replace the supplies lost due to a ban on strip mining.
It takes five years to bring an underground mine to full production.	New underground mines could start production within 18 months.
Surface mining recovers nearly 100 percent of the coal, compared to 55 percent for underground mining. New technology that permits a higher recovery of underground coal cannot be used in all mines.	Coal recovery in deep mines could be increased from 55 percent to nearly 100 percent by using new technology.
Underground miners who have been laid off are either too old to return to the mines, or their skills are outdated because of new technology.	Sufficient manpower exists to man the deep mines. More than 19,000 underground miners lost their jobs in Appalachia alone between 1966 and 1971.
Surface mining is safer than underground mining by a ratio of 2 to 1.	Underground mining can be made as safe as surface mining. The safety record in some large underground mines is far superior to that in some surface mines.
Deep-mined coal is too expensive. Deep-mined coal costs about 63 percent more to produce than coal from surface mines.	Conversion to deep mining would increase the cost of coal, but the price of all fuels is rising as supplies dwindle.

*Statement by Rep. Ken Hechler (D., W.Va.) before the Senate Interior and Insular Affairs Committee, March 13, 1973.

Some solutions   It is not surprising then that concern is rising in Congress over this national land use problem. In effect we are trading land for energy. As we become increasingly gripped in energy crises there will be even greater needs to strip coal, our only plentiful fossil fuel, from the ground. Although some call for a total ban on strip mining, much of the argument between environmentalists and coal company officials is based on what constitutes adequate rec-

lamation, who sets and regulates the standards, and who should pay the costs.

In principle, reclamation of strip-mined land is simple—after the coal is removed, the removed material (overburden) is put back into place and replanted with fast growing vegetation or trees as needed. The costs for effective reclamation, however, are high. In Great Britain, where strip mining regulations are very strict, reclamation costs range from $1,350 to

$7,542 an acre (Greenburg 1973). Estimated costs in the United States for adequate restoration vary from a minimum of $500 to several thousand dollars per acre, depending on local conditions. Under growing pressure and new laws in Illinois, Kentucky, Arkansas, South Dakota, North Carolina, and Montana, some companies are increasing reclamation efforts, but they rarely spend more than $300 to $400 per acre. Satisfactory reclamation of contour-mined land (Figure 5–11c) on relatively steep slopes is difficult if not impossible, and in some areas soil type and light rainfall can rule out prompt revegetation.

Mining companies proudly point to showcase strip mining reclamation projects such as the Lonesome Pine Airport and Norton Elementary School in Wise County, Virginia, a park in Jellico, Tennessee, and the Fairground State Park in DuQuoin, Illinois. But these projects represent only a tiny fraction of the disrupted land, and most of the costs were borne by the state, federal, and local governments (Greenburg 1973).

A wholesale ban on all strip mining then is probably not necessary, desirable, or even possible considering the need for coal and other resources. But very strict regulations for all surface mining should be adopted at the federal and state level and should include:

1. Strictly enforced federal regulations for surface mining in all states. (This proposal is opposed by the mining industry, who finds it easier to prevent, soften, or get around most state regulations.) States, however, must be allowed to impose stricter regulations than federal guidelines.

2. Prohibition of contour mining on steep slopes with moderate to heavy rainfall and in areas where soil types and climate prevent prompt revegetation.

3. Permits to be obtained from state officials before any strip mining is allowed, with adequate time for public hearings.

4. Surveying and photography of all land before it is disturbed. A detailed reclamation plan must be submitted and approved by the state agency before the project begins.

5. Rapid restoration of all land to its original contour, dressed with topsoil, seeded with grass and, where needed, planted with trees.

6. All restoration costs for disturbed land and water resources to be borne by the mining company with a minimum requirement of $500 per acre to be guaranteed by the posting of bonds before operations can start. Higher values may be required by a state, depending on the nature of the land. For example, reclamation costs in Pennsylvania, which is generally considered to have the most stringent and best enforced strip mining laws, may cost the company up to $5,000 per acre.

7. Restoration of past damage (at an estimated cost of $1 billion) by federal, state, and local governments because of the difficulties in requiring mining companies to do so now.

There are no ecological sanctuaries.

Lester R. Brown

Discussion Topics

1. Debate the resolution: The United States uses far too many of the world's resources relative to our population and should deliberately cut back on consumption.

2. Is the increasing dependence of the United States on foreign imports of critical resources such as fossil fuels a desirable trend in relation to world peace?

3. What, if any, are the surface mining laws in your state? Why have state and local governments failed to enact and enforce effective surface mining laws? Why do mining companies generally oppose federal laws on strip mining?

4. Evaluate the pros and cons of the statement that "since we have not proven absolutely that anyone has died or suffered serious disease from air pollution, automobile manufacturers should not be required to meet the 1976 air pollution standards."

5. Simulate an air pollution hearing at which the automobile manufacturers request a delay in meeting the 1976 air pollution standards until 1981. Assign three members of the class as members of a decision-making board and other members as the president of an auto manufacturing company, two lawyers for that company, William Lear who is hoping to build a steam car, the president of General Electric who hopes to build electric cars, two government attorneys representing the Environmental Protection Agency, the chief engineer for an auto manufacturer, a public health official, and two citizens (with one opposing and one favoring the proposal). Have a class discussion of the final ruling of the board.

6. The provost of MIT has stated that "each automobile costs the public at large about one dollar per mile." Make an estimate of direct and indirect costs to verify or dispute this figure. At this rate how much are you paying per year?

7. Have a class debate on the relative advantages and disadvantages of banning the internal combustion engine by 1990.

8. What are the major effects of oil on the ocean ecosystem? Explain why the killing of sea birds and esthetic and economic damage to recreational areas are not necessarily the most serious consequences of oil pollution.

9. *Should we ban all offshore oil wells? Why or why not? What might be the consequences of this to the nation? For our foreign policy? For our security? For your town? For you? What might be the consequences of not doing this?*

Further Reading

See also references for Chapter 4.

American Chemical Society. 1969. *Cleaning Our Environment: The Chemical Basis for Action.* Washington, D.C. American Chemical Society. Superb summary of pollution problems and solutions.

Barnett, Harold J. 1967. "The Myth of Our Vanishing Resources," *Transactions—Social Sciences & Modern Society,* June, pp. 7–10. Fine statement of the optimistic view of our resource situation. Compare with the article by Preston Cloud.

Berry, R. Stephen. 1970. "Perspectives on Polluted Air—1970," *Bulletin of the Atomic Scientists,* April, pp. 33–42. Superb overview.

Blumer, Max. 1971. "Scientific Aspects of the Oil Spill Problems," *Environmental Affairs,* vol. 1, 54–73. One of the best summaries of the sources and effects of oil spills by a prominent expert.

Brodine, Virginia. 1973. *Air Pollution.* New York: Harcourt Brace Jovanovich. Very good nontechnical survey. Good bibliography.

Brubaker, Sterling. 1971. *To Live on Earth.* Baltimore: Johns Hopkins Press for Resources for the Future. (Also available in paperback, New York: New American Library, 1972.) One of the most authoritative and balanced views of all types of pollution and their causes.

Chourci, Nazli. 1972. "Population, Resources and Technology: Political Implications of the Environmental Crisis," in D. Kay and E. B. Skolnikoff, eds., *World Eco-Crisis.* Madison: University of Wisconsin Press. Pp. 9–47. Good overview of present and future resource supplies.

Cloud, Preston E., Jr. 1968. "Realities of Mineral Distribution," *Texas Quarterly,* vol. 11, 103–126. Probably the best summary of the view that our resource supplies will soon be in jeopardy. Compare with the article by Harold Barnett.

Ewell, Raymond. 1970. "U.S. Will Lag U.S.S.R. in Raw Materials," *Chemical and Engineering News,* vol. 48, August 24, pp. 42–46. Good comparison of the two countries.

Lehr, William E. 1973. "Marine Oil Pollution Control," *Technology Review,* February, pp. 13–22. Good overview of methods for preventing and cleaning up oil spills by an expert.

Meadows, Donnella H., Dennis L. Meadows, Jørgen Randers, and William W. Behrens, III. 1972. *The Limits to Growth.* New York: Universe Books for Potomac Associates. Very important and controversial book giving the results of a computer simulation of the world ecosystem.

National Research Council, National Academy of Sciences. 1969. *Resources and Man.* San Francisco: W. H. Freeman. One of the most authoritative sources on our resources. See especially Chapters 6 and 7 on mineral resources from the land and sea and Chapter 8 on energy resources.

Steinhart, Carol E., and John S. Steinhart. 1972. *Blowout. A Case Study of the Santa Barbara Oil Spill.* North Scituate, Mass.: Duxbury. Superb case study.

Stoker, H. S., and Spencer L. Seager. 1972. *Environmental Chemistry: Air and Water Pollution.* Glenview, Ill.: Scott, Foresman. Probably the best summary of air and water pollution at a slightly higher level than this book.

Surface Mining Research Library. 1972. *Energy and the Environment: What's the Strip Mining Controversy All About?* 1218 Quarrier St., Charleston, W. Va. 25301. Balanced analysis and pictures showing both sides of the strip mining controversy.

Waldbott, George L. 1973. *Health Effects of Environmental Pollutants.* St. Louis: C. V. Mosby. Superb overview at a slightly higher level. Detailed bibliography.

Williamson, Samuel J. 1973. *Fundamentals of Air Pollution.* Reading, Mass.: Addison-Wesley. Magnificent discussion at a slightly higher level. Highly recommended.

We nuclear people have made a Faustian
compact with society; we offer . . . an
inexhaustible energy source . . . tainted with
political side effects that if not controlled could
spell disaster.

Alvin M. Weinberg

6

The Nuclear Energy Dilemma

One of the most important, complex, and controversial decisions facing mankind is whether to use nuclear fission as our major source of electrical power in coming decades. There is general agreement that nuclear fission is potentially the most hazardous of all energy sources. But the debate centers on the probability of these potential dangers ever being realized and the comparison of the risks and benefits of using nuclear energy with those of using other energy sources (see Chapter 4).[1] Before accepting or rejecting nuclear fission as the major source of electrical energy, the public should know the answers to the following questions: (1) How safe are nuclear power plants? (2) What might be the consequences if radioactive fuel escapes? (3) What are the problems and risks in shipping nuclear materials and storing nuclear wastes for long periods of time? (4) What are the short and long term risks and benefits from nuclear fission energy as compared to other energy sources (see Chapter 4)? (5) Do we have an adequately funded energy policy to develop other potential energy sources so that we can have a real choice among several options? (6) Will nuclear power provide a net energy yield (Section 4–1)? It is useful to begin with some understanding of how a nuclear power plant works.

6–1   How Nuclear Power Plants Work

Comparison of fossil fuel and nuclear power plants
In a fossil fuel power plant (Figure 6–1), coal, oil, or natural gas is burned in a firebox to produce superheated steam in a boiler. The high pressure steam is used to spin a huge turbine

whose shaft is coupled to a larger generator that produces electricity. The steam is then condensed and cooled before being pumped back into the boiler for reuse. A modern fossil fuel plant that produces 1,000 megawatts of electricity consumes about 240 metric tons of coal (or 53,000 barrels[2] of oil, or 790,000 cubic feet of natural gas) each hour (Hull 1971), or about 200 railroad cars full of coal per day. Without pollution controls a coal fired plant of that size would emit over 340,000 metric tons of sulfur oxides, nitrogen oxides, and particulates per year as air pollutants (Chapter 5) along with small amounts of radioactive radium (Hull 1971).[3] In accordance with the second law of thermodynamics (Section 2–2), about 60 percent of the energy released ends up as heat in the air or in a nearby body of water used to cool the condensed steam before it is pumped back to the boiler for reuse (Figure 6–1).

In a nuclear power plant a nuclear fission reactor is substituted for the fossil fuel fire box (Figure 6–2). Inside the reactor energy is released when the nucleus of a heavy atom such as uranium-235 is split apart by a slowly moving neutron into lighter fission fragments plus two or three neutrons (Figure 6–3).[4] If these new neutrons can be slowed down sufficiently by passage through a moderator (Figure 6–2) such as graphite or water, they can be used to split other uranium-235 atoms, which release more energy and more neutrons. If repeated and controlled the result is a self-sustaining nuclear chain reaction that continually releases enormous amounts of energy (U.S. Atomic Energy Commission 1967a). The fission

---

[1] *Arguments against* nuclear power are found in Abrahamson 1970, 1972, Ackerman 1972, Commoner 1970b, Curtis & Hogan 1970, Gofman & Tamplin 1971, Tamplin & Gofman 1970, Alfven 1974, Novick 1969, 1973a, Lewis 1972, Metzger 1972, Speth et al. 1974, Clark et al. 1974, Holdren 1974. For pro arguments see Hammond 1974b, Ramey 1970, Rocks & Runyon 1972, Seaborg & Corliss 1971, Weinberg & Hammond 1972, Weinberg 1973, Cohen 1974, Commoner et al. 1974, vol. 1, and the Understanding the Atom series published by the U.S. Atomic Energy Commission. For more balanced discussions of the pros and cons see Bryerton 1970, Inglis 1973, Foreman 1971, Lapp 1971a, 1973, Sagan 1972, Rabinovitch 1973, Kneese 1973, Rose 1974a, Sagan & Eliassen 1974, Geesman & Abrahamson 1974.

[2] A barrel contains about 42 gallons of oil.

[3] An uncontrolled oil fired power plant would release about 105,000 metric tons per year of these air pollutants, and a plant using natural gas would release about 30,400 metric tons per year.

[4] The nucleus of an atom contains uncharged neutrons and positively charged protons, each with a relative mass of 1. The *mass number* is the mass of the neutrons and protons in the nucleus. Each atom of uranium-235 has 235 neutrons plus protons in its nucleus; its mass number is 235. A sample of uranium ore contains only about 0.7 percent of fissionable uranium-235. The remaining 99.3 percent exists as slightly heavier, nonfissionable uranium-238 with three more neutrons in its nucleus. Two forms of the same chemical element with different mass numbers or numbers of neutrons in their nucleus are known as *isotopes*. Some isotopes of an element are stable while others are unstable, or radioactive, and emit radiation in the form of alpha particles (a helium nucleus with two protons and two neutrons), beta particles (an electron), or high energy gamma rays.

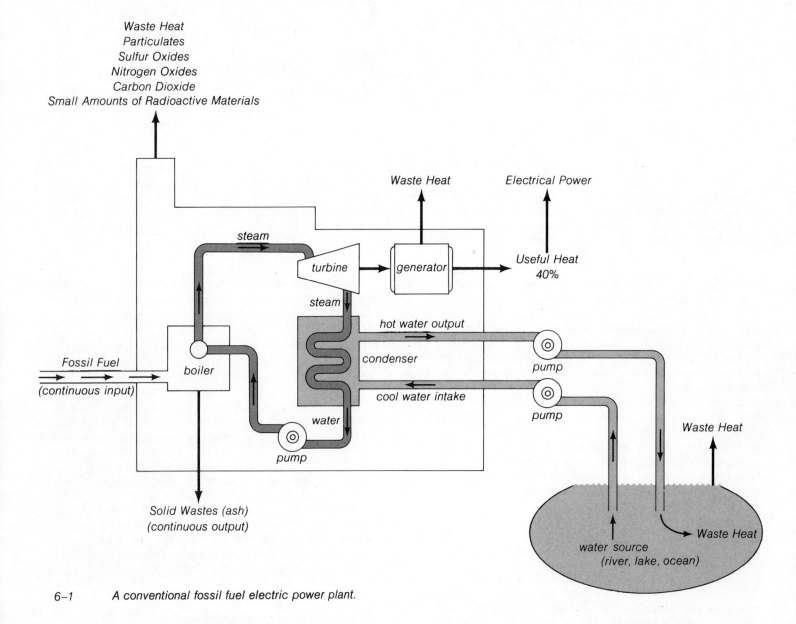

Waste Heat
Particulates
Sulfur Oxides
Nitrogen Oxides
Carbon Dioxide
Small Amounts of Radioactive Materials

steam

Waste Heat   Electrical Power

turbine   generator   Useful Heat
                                   40%

steam

hot water output

Fossil Fuel   boiler   condenser   pump

(continuous input)

cool water intake

water   pump

pump

Waste Heat

Solid Wastes (ash)
(continuous output)

Waste Heat

water source
(river, lake, ocean)

6–1   A conventional fossil fuel electric power plant.

rate of uranium-235 is controlled by moving neutron-absorbing control rods (Figure 6–2) in or out of the fuel core. A coolant —water, heavy water, gas, or a liquid metal such as sodium— is then passed through the reactor to absorb heat. The heat is used directly or indirectly to convert water into superheated steam. It is used to drive the blades of a turbine, which in turn runs an electrical generator as with fossil fuel plants.

The three major types of fission converter reactors are the *boiling water reactor* (BWR), the *pressurized water reactor*

(PWR), and the *high temperature gas cooled reactor* (HTGR).[5]

[5] In the boiling water reactor (BWR), water is used as the reactor coolant and moderator and is converted directly to steam inside the reactor core. In the pressurized water reactor (PWR) (Figure 6–2), water is used as the coolant and moderator but is kept under pressure to prevent it from being converted directly to steam. Water in a second circuit, not under such high pressure, is then converted to steam to drive the turbine. High temperature gas reactors (HTGR) use a gas such as helium as the coolant. The superheated gas is passed through a heat exchanger and used to convert water to steam in a second heat transfer loop.

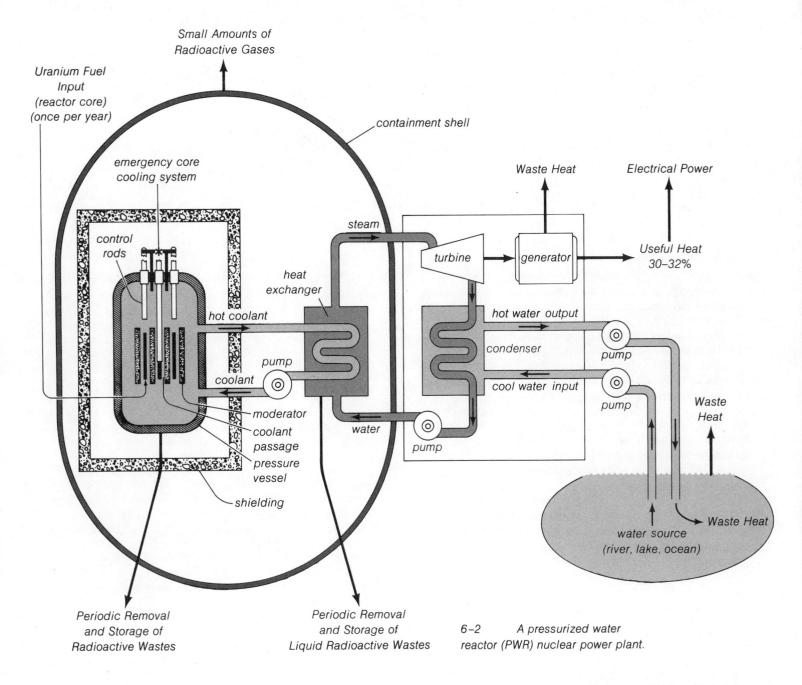

6–2   *A pressurized water reactor (PWR) nuclear power plant.*

Most reactors in the United States are either boiling water or pressurized water reactors and are known collectively as *light water reactors.*

A 1,000 megawatt fossil fuel plant consumes over 2 million metric tons of coal (or 460 million barrels of oil) per year on a continuous basis, but a nuclear fission reactor is loaded only about once a year with about 100 metric tons of uranium oxide pellets. Because about 99.3 percent of natural uranium is nonfissionable uranium-238, large amounts of

uranium ore must be processed and enriched to a higher percentage of fissionable uranium-235 at high cost. This enriched mixture is molded into thimble sized pellets (Figure 6–4) and about 10 million of these tiny pellets are inserted in a series of 12-foot tubes, or fuel rods. Precisely arranged bundles of these rods (Figure 6–5) are then lowered into the huge steel pressure vessel with 6-inch walls. Once a year the spent fuel is replaced and accumulated radioactive wastes are removed. The pressure vessel is surrounded by a massive

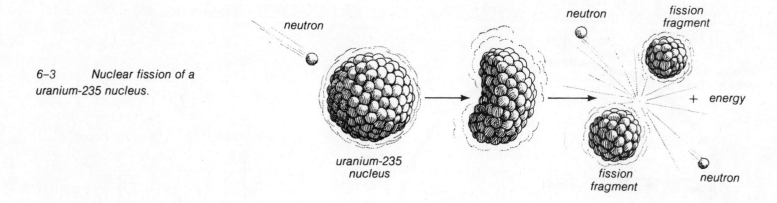

6–3   *Nuclear fission of a uranium-235 nucleus.*

shield, and the entire system is then surrounded by a containment shell to add another level of safety should the reactor core vessel be ruptured (Figure 6–2).

Unlike fossil fuel plants, nuclear plants in their normal operation do not emit any air pollutants and emit less radiation than that found in the smokestack outputs of coal fired plants. In addition, the mining of the much smaller amounts of uranium puts considerably less stress on the land and on water systems than coal mining (Section 5–4) or the production and refining of oil and natural gas. Nuclear plants, however, produce considerable amounts of high and low level radioactive materials as wastes and as spent fuel. These wastes must not be accidentally released to the environment and must be periodically removed and safely transported to fuel reprocessing plants or waste disposal sites. Compared to fossil fuel plants, the light water reactor nuclear plants now in use require much larger volumes of cooling water and emit about one and one-half times as much heat per unit of electricity generated, thus greatly increasing the potential for thermal water pollution (Section 8–5).[6]

Breeder reactors   A major disadvantage of the converter nuclear reactors now in operation or planned for the future is that they consume our limited supply of uranium-235 fuel. Estimates of available uranium supplies vary. But most experts agree that the supply of relatively low cost uranium at $8 to $15 per pound (as uranium oxide) is very limited, while there are relatively large amounts at $50 to $200 per pound (U.S. Atomic Energy Commission 1973b).

This argument that U.S. supplies of uranium will be depleted within 30 to 50 years has been used to promote our present crash program for the *breeder reactor*. Converter reactors use slow neutrons to fission rare uranium-235. Breeder reactors use a mixture of abundant, nonfissionable uranium-238 and fissionable plutonium-239 which will be extracted and purified from present day converter reactor wastes. Under bombardment with *fast* neutrons plutonium-239 undergoes fission and uranium-238 is converted to fissionable plutonium-239. The net result is a hundredfold multiplication of our usable uranium reserves. Fast breeder reactors using only known U.S. uranium resources could provide all of our electricity needs for at least 64,000 years.

Most research in the United States is being devoted to the liquid metal fast breeder reactor (LMFBR) (Figure 6–6), which uses liquid sodium as a coolant, and the gas cooled fast breeder reactor (GCFR), which uses helium gas. Because fast neutrons are needed water cannot be used as a coolant, since it slows neutrons down. A third type, the molten salt breeder reactor (MSBR), uses thorium-232 rather than plutonium-239 as the fissionable isotope. Unfortunately, this approach is largely being ignored even though thorium is safer to handle and store than plutonium.

In a 1974 draft environmental impact statement[7] on the commercial use of LMFBRs, the Atomic Energy Commission projected that by 2020 the United States would have about 550 breeder reactors generating about 38 percent of its electricity. This projection is based on three important assumptions that: (1) workable large scale breeder reactors can be built and yield net energy (2) their cost will not be prohibitively high, and (3) the environmental costs will not be too great.

---

[6] High temperature gas cooled reactors (HTGR) and breeder reactors release about the same amount of waste heat per unit of electricity as fossil fuel plants. If we should eventually switch over to these the heat contribution of a nuclear power plant would not be any greater than that from a fossil fuel plant.

[7] Summarized in *Chemical and Engineering News*, March 25, 1974, pp. 21-22. For the case for breeder reactors see Seaborg & Bloom 1970, Vitti & Staker 1972, Commoner et al. 1974.

For the case against breeders see Cochran 1974, Alfven 1974, Lovins 1973, 1974, Gofman & Tamplin 1971, Kneese 1973, McPhee 1974, Willrich & Taylor 1974, Commoner et al. 1974, Clark et al. 1974.

6-4   *Fuel pellets of enriched uranium oxide.
Each pellet weighs less than one gram (one
thirtieth of an ounce) but has the energy equivalent
of 566 pounds of coal. (Hanford Engineering
Development Laboratory)*

6-5   *Bundles of fuel rods filled with enriched
uranium pellets serve as the fuel core for a nuclear
fission reactor. (Samuel A. Musgrave, Atomic
Industrial Forum)*

One of the difficult technical problems to be solved before large scale fast breeders become commercially feasible is that of finding a suitable metal to contain the core. Engineers must also solve the problem of precisely spacing the thousands of fuel rods in the reactor core. Unless the sodium coolant can flow freely around the rods the core can dangerously overheat and melt down, as demonstrated by the failure of a small experimental breeder near Detroit.

Liquid sodium has superb properties as a coolant, but presents some difficult engineering problems. If allowed to come in contact with air or water it explodes. Because it is highly corrosive (especially at high temperatures) finding metals, pumps, valves, and seals that will safely contain it is a difficult problem. Even if solutions to these problems are found, they may raise the price of building such plants to unacceptable levels and lower net energy yield.

A more serious drawback of the breeder, however, is the fact that each typical commercial reactor will contain over 1 metric ton of plutonium, as compared with the smaller, but still significant amounts produced in today's converter reactors. Plutonium from any type of reactor is extremely dangerous (Bair & Thompson 1974), but the breeder greatly

increases the amount of plutonium that must be safely handled so that even a single large accident would become disastrous (Rose 1974a, Novick 1973a, Lovins 1973). An ounce (29 grams) of plutonium is enough to kill every human being on earth if it could be widely dispersed. Even inhaling or absorbing a tiny speck can cause cancer or death.[8] Some experts (Tamplin & Cochran 1974) indicate that even the present maximum tolerance limits of about two-billionths of a gram of plutonium are 150,000 to 300,000 times too high. In addition, because its half-life is 24,000 years, plutonium must be stored for 250,000

---

[8] Plutonium-239 emits alpha particles, which have low penetration power. Thus, radiation from plutonium-239 cannot penetrate the skin but inhalation, ingestion, or absorption of only a few particles can eventually be fatal.

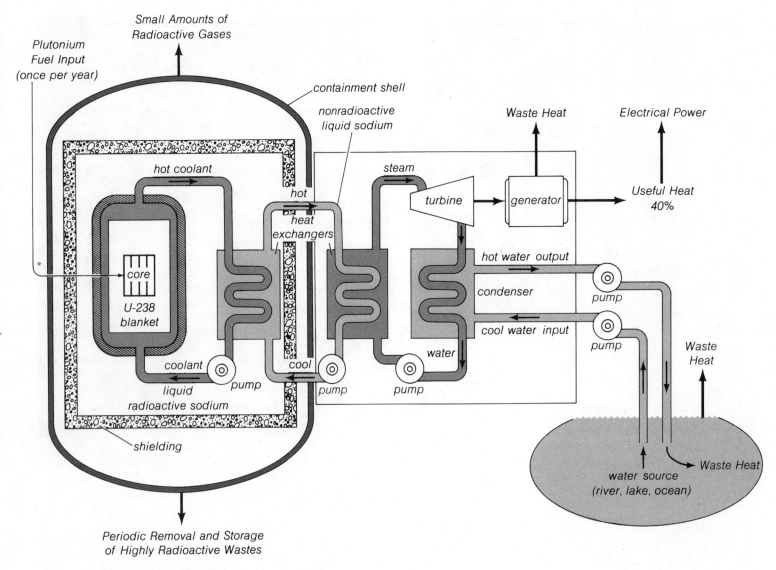

Plutonium
Fuel Input
(once per year)

Small Amounts of
Radioactive Gases

containment shell

nonradioactive
liquid sodium

Waste Heat   Electrical Power

hot coolant

steam

hot

turbine   generator

Useful Heat
40%

heat
exchangers

hot water output

core

condenser

U-238
blanket

pump

cool water input

water   pump

coolant   liquid
radioactive sodium

cool

pump

pump

pump   Waste
Heat

shielding

water source
(river, lake, ocean)   Waste Heat

Periodic Removal and Storage
of Highly Radioactive Wastes

6-6   *A liquid metal fast breeder reactor (LMFBR) power plant.*

years[9] before it decays enough to be released with safety to the environment.

The most serious threats may involve sabotage of a breeder plant and highjacking plutonium shipments (McPhee 1974, Willrich & Taylor 1974a). By 2020 the Atomic Energy Commission estimates that 100,000 plutonium shipments will be made annually in the United States. Only about 4.5 kilograms or 10 pounds (an amount about the size of a softball) of plutonium or 20 kilograms of uranium are needed to make an atomic bomb (Gillinsky 1971). Plutonium is an attractive target for highjacking at its present price of $10,000 per kilogram (2.2 pounds)—more than the value of heroin and ten times that of gold. Plans for easily constructed small atomic bombs have already been circulated among some underground groups in the United States. For these reasons it is not surprising that an increasing number of experts are seriously questioning our present commitment to the breeder reactor (Alfven 1974, Gofman & Tamplin 1971, Inglis 1973, Lapp 1973a, Kneese 1973, Cochran 1974, Lovins 1973).

The AEC argument that we must develop the breeder reactor quickly because we will run out of uranium for converter reactors within 30 to 50 years has also been seriously challenged. Rose (1974a) feels that potential uranium reserves

---

[9] As a general rule, any isotope must be stored for a period of at least ten times its half-life before it decays to a safe level. Recall that *half-life* is the time required for half of a given amount of a radioactive isotope to decay.

have been underestimated and does not feel the breeder will become economically attractive until well into the twenty-first century. Reducing our annual increase in use of electricity from 7 percent to 5 percent and doubling known reserves of uranium would extend U.S. uranium supplies to 65 years at today's price of $8 per pound and to 87 years if the price doubles to $16 per pound as expected. In other words, the present crash program may be unnecessary.

6-2 How Safe Are Nuclear Power Plants?

Reactor accidents Unfortunately, some who oppose the building of nuclear power plants have the mistaken idea that these plants can explode like an atomic bomb. The nuclear fuel is only 3 to 5 percent fissionable uranium-235 (30 times less concentrated than the fuel needed for bombs). This fissionable material is so spread out and interspersed with coolant and other nonfissionable material that a violent nuclear explosion cannot occur because a critical mass cannot develop.

The real danger arises from the highly improbable but possible simultaneous failure of a number of multiple safeguards which could cause overheating, meltdown, and the release of radioactive materials into the surrounding environment. In 1966, an experimental breeder reactor near Detroit went on what reactor engineers call a "grand excursion," a softened phrase for a runaway nuclear reactor. Fortunately, backup safety systems kept it from completing the trip. Had it done so, a University of Michigan study estimated that 10,000 people would have been killed, Detroit would have had to be evacuated, and an agricultural quarantine might have been necessary for a large area of the Midwest because of radiation contamination of crops and animals.

Commercial reactors have a multitude of design features to prevent such a loss of nuclear fuel and waste materials to the environment. First, fuel pellets are clad in metal to confine most of the fission products. Next, the primary reactor pressure vessel (Figure 6-2) provides very strong containment for radiation from any pellets that might leak or melt. Third, a sophisticated backup system automatically inserts control rods into the core to stop fission if certain emergencies occur. In addition, if temperatures begin to approach meltdown a system is designed to flood the reactor core with emergency cooling water within one minute.

Another line of defense for U.S. reactors (but not those in England and the Soviet Union) is the steel or steel and concrete outer containment shell that encloses the entire reactor and gives nuclear power plants their dome-shaped appearance. This shell is designed to contain the radioactive substances even if the primary reactor vessel is ruptured. It will also withstand explosions equivalent to several tons of TNT. The small nuclear or chemical explosions that could conceivably occur inside a nuclear reactor are on the order of no more than 1 ton of TNT.

The type of "grand excursion" that most concerns nuclear experts is the sudden loss of coolant water that flows through the boiling water and pressurized water reactors in wide use today in the United States. It would begin with a break in one of the heavy pipes that conduct cooling water and steam to and from the reactor core (Figure 6-2), as a result of faulty construction or maintenance, sabotage, or some catastrophic natural disaster. The first result of such a rupture would be a "blowdown," in which a mixture of steam and water would be expelled from the reactor core. The steam pressure could prevent emergency core cooling water from reaching the core. In the presence of the intense radioactivity in the core, steam could be converted into hydrogen and oxygen, which could then explode violently and rupture the reactor core. Radioactive materials and gases would be released, but if the strong containment shell did not rupture they would be prevented from entering the atmosphere. Meanwhile the reactor fuel core would be heating up rapidly. Although multiple backup systems would automatically move a large number of control rods (Figure 6-2) into place to stop nuclear fission, the residual heat from the radioactive materials in the core would still be sufficient to melt the fuel rods in a minute or less and cause a complete meltdown of the reactor core. Within a minute the molten core would begin to fall to the bottom of the reactor containment vessel, melt through its thick concrete slab, and burn itself into the earth, presumably in the general direction of Asia—explaining why nuclear engineers call this type of excursion the "Chinese syndrome." No one really knows what would happen. Depending on geological characteristics of the underlying strata it might sink to a depth of 20 to 30 feet and gradually burn itself out (Hammond 1974b) or it might burn itself deeply into the earth's crust. Hammond (1974b) feels that the underground ball of fuel would present little hazard and could be recovered, but this view is not widely held.

A melt-through is a nightmare for reactor engineers, but the most serious hazard would be the release of highly radioactive gases and particulates to the atmosphere that could occur from blowholes in the ground during the first hour or two. This cloud of radioactive materials would be at the mercy of the winds and weather. This worst, most credible accident is extremely improbable and depends on a chain of very unlikely events.

In 1957, the AEC commissioned the Brookhaven National Laboratory to project the deaths, injuries, and property loss from a "maximum credible accident" releasing 50 percent of all fission products 30 miles from a city of 1,000,000 with no evacuation. The resulting report, which has been disputed, estimated that the maximum possible accident (which is extremely unlikely) for plants much smaller than those being built today might result in as many as 3,400 persons dead, 43,000 injured, and property damages from $500,000 to $7 billion (Brookhaven National Laboratory 1957).

Some have put the probable death toll from an accident in today's better designed plants at 100 to 200 persons because the maximum credible accident could never occur.

Others point out that today's reactors have 6 times more power output than the one used for the 1957 study and that the breeder reactors projected for use in the 1990s will be 10 to 50 times larger in output. In 1965 the Brookhaven study was updated, but the results have never been made public.

Based on the Brookhaven report and their own assessment, insurance companies refused to insure a nuclear reactor for even $500 million. Because this meant that the fledgling nuclear industry could never get off the ground, Congress in 1957 passed the Price-Anderson Act, which makes you and me primarily responsible for nuclear liability payments. The liability for any single nuclear accident will not exceed $500 million, and of this amount up to only $82 million would be paid out by private insurance companies with the government (you and me) providing up to $418 million. Critics argue that it is only because of this immense government subsidy that the price of electricity from nuclear power is competitive with that from fossil fuel plants.

Do emergency core cooling systems work?   To prevent the possibility of meltdown all water cooled reactors are equipped with an emergency core cooling system (Figure 6–2), which is designed to instantaneously flood the reactor with large amounts of water to prevent meltdown. This system has multiple backup systems so that if one failed another would take over. However, these systems have never been actually tested, and scientists within the nuclear establishment sharply disagree over whether the system will work.[10] In 1972 and 1973 simulated tests by the Atomic Energy Commission on models of nuclear power plants showed that the emergency cooling systems did not work. As a result, the AEC ordered all reactors in operation to lower their maximum operating temperatures, to modernize their cooling backup systems, and to triple their inspections of pipes, pumps, and valves. The effectiveness of the emergency cooling system is still unknown, and the AEC is now carrying out extensive tests to determine its reliability and to ascertain the need for any improvements or design changes.

What are the chances of an accident?   Driving a car, smoking a cigarette, flying in a plane, or doing almost anything involves some degree of risk, but in deciding to do or not to do something there are three fundamental questions. What are the chances of an accident? What risks are we willing to take relative to the benefits? And who takes the risks—you, I, or future generations?

Probably no single industry in the history of mankind has such an outstanding record of safety as the nuclear industry.

Although there have been some accidents, these have all occurred in experimental reactors,[11] quite different from the commercial water-moderated reactors now in use. No identifiable loss of life has resulted from radiation releases in any commercial reactors in the United States, although some deaths have occurred by component failure within plants. This enviable record, while reassuring, does not really tell us much about the probability of future accidents. It is based on only 7 years of intermittent operation of about 30 reactors, all much smaller than the plants now going into operation and those projected for the future. Even with this small number of reactors a 1973 report by the AEC's top safety experts (U.S. Atomic Energy Commission 1973) revealed that between January 1, 1972, and May 30, 1973, "approximately 850 abnormal occurrences" in nuclear plant operations were reported to the AEC. Critics such as Ralph Nader (Mayo 1974) see this as proof of the unreliability of nuclear plants. But the Atomic Energy Commission cites these same figures as evidence of how tough regulatory practices are.

The real question is whether this safety record can be maintained with the building and operation of the 500 to 1,000 much larger reactors predicted by the year 2000. An average of 25 to 50 nuclear plants would have to be constructed *each year* between 1975 and 2000—a yearly average equal to the total number of plants now in operation. Despite a strict licensing procedure (U.S. Atomic Energy Commission 1967), supervising and monitoring all these plants with a zero tolerance for error is a formidable task. It is not encouraging that one of the first responses to the 1973 energy crisis was the AEC proposal to speed up licensing procedures by removing the requirement that a mandatory public hearing be held before a construction permit for a proposed plant is issued (U.S. Atomic Energy Commission 1973a).

6–3   Radiation Standards: Are There Any Safe Levels?

Genetic and somatic effects of radiation   Man has always been exposed to some radiation from cosmic rays, soil, rocks, and other natural sources, but since 1900 we have added to this background level from man-made sources. What average exposure of radiation do we receive from natural sources? Are there any safe levels of exposure to radiation? What are the maximum levels of radiation that we should tolerate from nuclear power plants, x-ray equipment, and other man-made sources? These important questions have been the source of considerable controversy among scientists.

Exposure to radiation can have two major effects on humans[12]: (1) *genetic damage* to reproductive cells, pro-

---

[10] For a discussion of this and other aspects of nuclear safety see the series of news reports in *Science,* vol. 176, May 5, 1972, pp. 492–498; vol. 177, September 1, 1972, pp. 771–775; September 8, 1972, pp. 867–873; September 13, 1972, pp. 970–973; September 22, 1972, pp. 1080–1082; vol. 178, November 3, 1972, pp. 482–483; and vol. 179, January 29, 1973, pp. 360–363. Other references include Forbes et al. 1972, Ford & Kendall 1972, Lapp 1971, Novick 1969, 1969a, Commoner et al. 1974, vol. 1.

[11] For a description of these accidents, see Novick 1969, Inglis 1973, pp. 111–123.

[12] Radiation causes damage because the high speed atomic particles emitted from the nuclei of radioactive atoms can physically damage molecules in a cell or ionize (remove electrons) from atoms in cellular molecules.

ducing mutations that can be passed on to future generations in the form of fetal and infant deaths, and physical and mental deformities (U.S. Atomic Energy Commission 1966); and (2) *somatic damage* to tissues other than reproductive cells, which can cause various forms of leukemia, cancer of the nervous system, bone, thyroid, or lung cancer, miscarriages, cataracts, shortening of life span, and damage to unborn children.

Most experts agree that *any exposure* to radiation, including natural sources, can cause some genetic alteration (curve A, Figure 6–7), although long term genetic changes are very difficult to measure for small doses. But there is considerable debate over whether exposure to very low radiation levels causes somatic damage such as cancer. Some scientists say that any dose of radiation is harmful (curve A, Figure 6–7). Others (curve B) hold that low doses of radiation are not necessarily harmful below a certain threshold level. Unfortunately the evidence is not clearcut in deciding between the two hypotheses. As a result, radiation exposure standards must be set as low as possible while balancing benefits (such as medical x-rays) against the probability of harm from low doses.

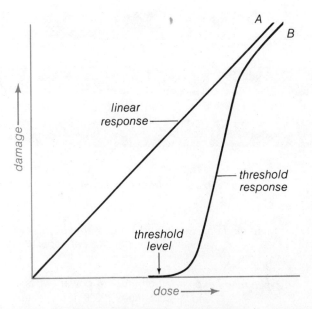

6–7   *Two hypotheses of radiation-dose damage: that no threshold level exists (curve A), and that there is a threshold dose before any damage occurs (curve B).*

Background and man-made radiation   All of us are exposed to a background of radiation from natural radioactive materials and from cosmic rays entering the earth's atmosphere. Until recently the natural background radiation in the United States was estimated at 100 to 200 millirems[13] per year with an average of about 130 millirems (Environmental Protection Agency 1971c). This was used as the basis for setting the U.S. maximum allowed radiation exposure from man-made sources at 170 millirems per year (Oakley 1972). But in 1972 the Environmental Protection Agency revealed that the average natural radiation may be only 88 millirems per year. If this new estimate is correct, then the presently allowed maximum annual exposure from man-made sources is *twice* the average natural background radiation, and newer and stricter standards may have to be set. The average per capita exposure to radiation from natural and man-made sources is shown in Figure 6–8.

In spite of wide publicity given to radiation from nuclear power plants, Figure 6–8 shows that most man-made radiation comes from medical x-rays, with only 0.15 percent coming from nuclear power plants. Most of this tiny fraction occurs in the 23 percent of our population living within 50 miles of a nuclear power plant, processing plant, or government nuclear facility.

Comparing the radiation from x-rays and from nuclear power is misleading, however. X-ray radiation comes from a short exposure to an energy source which has no half-life, does not remain in the environment, and requires no long term protection. The radioactive substances from nuclear plants must be isolated completely from the environment, in some cases for hundreds of thousands of years.

Controversy over radiation standards   The maximum permissible general radiation standards in this country have been systematically lowered as we have learned more and more about the subtle, frequently surprising, and unknown effects of radiation.[14] The present federal standard is that the general population should not receive more than 170 millirems of radiation per year from all combined man-made sources.

---

[13] The dosage received from a source of radiation can be expressed in rads, rems, millirems, or a newer unit called man-rems. For human tissue the *rad* (or *radiation-absorbed dosage*) and the *rem* (or *Roentgen equivalent, man*) are roughly equivalent and represent the radiation that delivers 100 ergs of energy to 1 gram of substance. A *millirem* is one-thousandth of a *rem*. The present maximum allowable U.S. standard exposure per year is 170 millirems or 0.170 rem. To obtain a more useful comparison of health risks from different radiation sources the new unit of *man-rems* is used. It is obtained by multiplying the exposure in rems by the number of people actually exposed each year (man-rems = exposure in rems × population exposed). If 214 million Americans are exposed to 100 millirems (or 0.100 rem) per year from some source, then this amounts to 0.100 rem × 214 million people = 21.4 million man-rems per year.

---

[14] For good summaries of the radiation standards controversy see Schurr 1971, pp. 98–127, Morgan 1971, Inglis 1973, pp. 128–138.

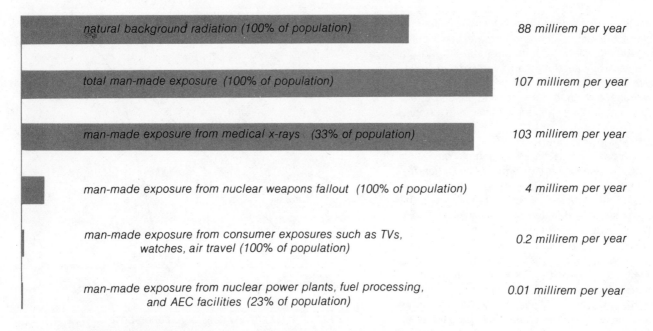

natural background radiation (100% of population)	88 millirem per year
total man-made exposure (100% of population)	107 millirem per year
man-made exposure from medical x-rays (33% of population)	103 millirem per year
man-made exposure from nuclear weapons fallout (100% of population)	4 millirem per year
man-made exposure from consumer exposures such as TVs, watches, air travel (100% of population)	0.2 millirem per year
man-made exposure from nuclear power plants, fuel processing, and AEC facilities (23% of population)	0.01 millirem per year

6–8   The average per capita exposure to radiation of the U.S. population in 1970 from natural and man-made sources. (Data from Environmental Protection Agency 1971c, Oakley 1972)

In 1970 we were below this level, and if exposure from medical x-rays were more carefully controlled we could reduce our exposure well below the legal maximum level.

But is the legal maximum level too high for human safety? In 1970 Dr. John W. Gofman and Dr. Arthur R. Tamplin, two highly respected scientists[15] working for the Atomic Energy Commission, calculated that if all Americans were exposed to the present maximum allowable limit of 170 millirems per year, the incidence of cancer would increase by about 10 percent (Gofman & Tamplin 1970, 1970a) and cancer deaths would increase by 32,000 per year. They recommended that the maximum permissible dose be reduced by a factor of 10 from 170 millirems to 17 millirems per year from man-made sources. Although Nobel laureate Linus Pauling (1970) supported their calculations, numerous AEC and other scientists attacked their assumptions (Holcomb 1970a, Lindop & Rotblat 1971).

Primarily as a result of the ensuing debate, several important things have happened. In 1970 the Federal Radiation Council, the advisory body that set U.S. radiation standards, commissioned the National Academy of Sciences to review the problem of radiation standards. Later that year the duties of the council were transferred to the newly formed Environmental Protection Agency. The National Academy of Sciences study (published in 1972)[16] concluded that some of Gofman and Tamplin's assumptions were questionable. But they still estimated that exposure of our entire population to 170 millirems would result in an estimated 3,000 to 15,000 extra deaths per year and would cause between 1,100 and 27,000 genetic defects and cancers per year, resulting in a 5 percent increase in the nation's ill health.

The strongest opposition to such tightening of the standards has come from the electrical power industry and the Atomic Energy Commission, even though their facilities contributed only 0.01 millirem in 1970 (Figure 6–8), a tiny fraction of proposed 17 millirems maximum. It is feared that the nuclear power industry doesn't want levels reduced because with 500 to 1,000 plants operating they might not be able to meet stricter standards in the future. Once the standards are reduced they would find it politically and scientifically difficult to have them raised again. Stricter controls might also raise the price of electricity from nuclear power so that it might not remain competitive with that from fossil fuels.

---

[15] At the time Gofman was the associate director of the Biomedical Division of the AEC's Lawrence Radiation Laboratory and Tamplin was a professor of medical physics at the University of California, Berkeley, and research associate at the Lawrence Radiation Laboratory.

[16] For the text see "Effects on Population of Exposure to Low Levels of Ionizing Radiation," Bulletin of the Atomic Scientists, March 1973, pp. 47–49. For a summary of their findings see Science, vol. 178, 966–968 (1972).

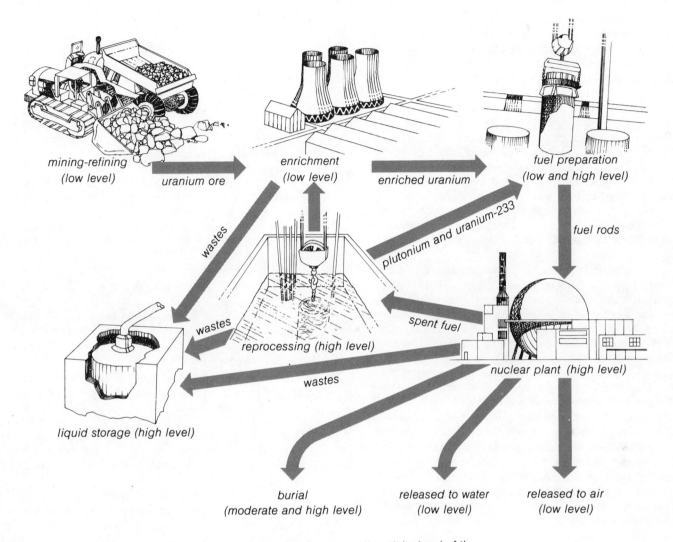

mining-refining
(low level)

uranium ore

enrichment
(low level)

enriched uranium

fuel preparation
(low and high level)

wastes

plutonium and uranium-233

fuel rods

wastes

reprocessing (high level)

spent fuel

nuclear plant (high level)

wastes

liquid storage (high level)

burial
(moderate and high level)

released to water
(low level)

released to air
(low level)

6–9   *The nuclear fuel cycle and nuclear wastes, showing the radioactivity level of the materials at each step.*

6–4   Transportation, Reprocessing, and Storage of Radioactive Materials

The nuclear fuel cycle   The nuclear fuel cycle involves the transportation, use, release, and storage of a wide variety of radioactive materials (Figure 6–9) (U.S. Atomic Energy Commission 1969). Unlike natural chemical cycles, this man-made chemical cycle must operate with absolute safety to insure that no major leaks occur at any point (Speth et al. 1974). As the rate and volume of materials being moved through this cycle accelerate the difficulty of the problem rises exponentially. The most vulnerable part of the cycle is the

transportation, reprocessing, and storage of increasing quantities of fuel materials and nuclear wastes. Nuclear plants have sophisticated multiple safety systems, and with continued public scrutiny and pressure they can be made even safer. But wastes and spent fuel elements are particularly open to accidents and highjacking. Even with strict security provisions, which do not presently exist, there can be no fail-safe system for these weak points in the nuclear fuel cycle (Holdren 1974).

Fuel reprocessing   Radioactive wastes are produced when the metal covering the nuclear fuel pellets becomes radioactive. In addition, the primary coolant (water) in today's reactors picks up neutrons, and the nonradioactive hydrogen-1 isotope in ordinary water is converted to radioactive hydrogen-3, or tritium. The resulting radioactive tritiated water is diluted with normal water and released to the ground near reactors, but this practice will not be possible as the number of plants increases.

About 20 percent of the radioactive fuel elements in a reactor are replaced each year. These spent elements are removed and allowed to cool for several months. They are then sealed in specially designed and heavily shielded casks and transported to reprocessing plants[17] where they are cut open, their contents dissolved in acid, and the uranium and plutonium recovered and shipped to fuel preparation plants to be reused (Figure 6–9). Large volumes of gaseous and liquid radioactive wastes from reprocessing must be stored permanently or released to the environment after temporary storage.

With present techniques, radioactive emissions are about 100 times greater at the reprocessing stage than at the power production stage. Existing commercial fuel reprocessing plants may discharge 100,000 to 500,000 gallons of low-level liquid wastes per day (Cook 1972) to the surrounding air or water. But the Atomic Energy Commission has specified that new reprocessing plants cannot discharge any radioactive liquid wastes (Berg 1973a). All industrial waste water must be recycled. Thus, during normal operation, the only radioactive discharges will be tritium and krypton-85. As the number of plants increases most experts feel that these gaseous emissions should also be controlled since effective dilution in the atmosphere will no longer be possible. The major hazards in such plants are the accidental release of airborne iodine-129 and plutonium dust (Berg 1973a) and the threat of highjacking or stealing of reprocessed fuel. Public scrutiny and pressure must be continually applied to insure that this point in the nuclear fuel cycle is as safe as humanly possible.

Shipping accidents and highjacking   By the year 2000 the AEC projects 111,300 shipments of radioactive materials per year, or an average of 305 en route somewhere in the United States every day by train or truck (Schurr 1971). If we shift to breeder reactors many shipments will contain

increasing amounts of plutonium, the most deadly radioactive material known to man.

Probably the major Achilles heel of the entire nuclear fuel cycle is the risk of highjacking and sabotage of shipments (DeNike 1974, Rose 1974a, Novick 1973a, Willrich & Taylor 1974a). A 1974 Atomic Energy Commission study team found AEC security precautions and regulations "entirely inadequate." An individual or group would find little difficulty sabotaging or taking over a nuclear plant (Gillette 1973) or highjacking a nuclear shipment.

For instance, a General Accounting Office investigation of three of the nearly 100 organizations possessing strategic or weapons grade nuclear materials revealed that security was lax and that stealing of such materials was relatively easy (Gillette 1973). Also, in March 1973 a guerilla band took temporary possession of a nuclear power plant in Argentina (DeNike 1974).

But the most serious threat is the highjacking of shipments of plutonium fuel elements (Lapp 1973a, Leachman & Althoff 1971, DeNike 1974, Willrich & Taylor 1974, Commoner et al. 1974, Geesman & Abrahamson 1974, Speth et al. 1974).[18] Although this plutonium is not of weapons grade, any competent physicist could upgrade it to the necessary quality with known techniques.

The real threat, however, may not be from nuclear bombs. Because of plutonium's extreme toxicity in producing lung cancer, the stolen plutonium need only be blown into the atmosphere by a conventional explosive charge set off on the top of any tall building. One pound (2.2 kilograms) of the metal dispersed in this manner could theoretically contaminate an area of 3 square miles with lethal radioactivity for 250,000 years (DeNike 1974).

Although plutonium-239 is deadly once inhaled or ingested, it is easy to steal with little danger to the thieves. Only a small amount need be taken and only lightweight shielding is needed for protection against the alpha particles it emits.[19] The chances for this ultimate form of blackmail by individuals or groups along the lines of airline highjackings are almost certain to occur and once sizeable quantities of nuclear materials have been diverted to the underworld its widespread criminal use is essentially impossible to prevent. Even with

---

[17] For details on fuel reprocessing techniques and problems see U.S. Atomic Energy Commission 1969, Berg 1973a, Murphy 1972. Until 1966 the AEC did all fuel reprocessing at its own plants in Richland, Washington, Idaho Falls, Idaho, and on the Savannah River near Aiken, South Carolina. Now a private reprocessing plant is in operation about 30 miles from Buffalo, New York (Berg 1973a), and a second one at Marion, Illinois, is nearing completion. At least two others now under construction in South Carolina should be in operation by 1980. By the year 2020 the Atomic Energy Commission projects 28 reprocessing plants and 28 fuel fabrication plants.

---

[18] Stealing the uranium fuel (in contrast to plutonium) used in present light water reactors is not a serious problem because it is more than 90 percent nonfissionable uranium-238. Enriching it to weapons grade uranium-235 would require a very expensive and sophisticated technology that would already be capable of making weapons material from natural uranium ore (Rose 1974a). This would not be true if we switched to high temperature gas cooled reactors (HTGR), which use weapons grade fuel that is 93 percent fissionable uranium-235.

[19] This is true only of plutonium-239 already reprocessed for fuel elements and not for the high-level radioactive plutonium and other wastes shipped as spent fuel to reprocessing plants.

the establishment of a highly trained federal nuclear protection and transportation service, as suggested by a 1974 AEC study panel, it would be essentially impossible to completely prevent highjacking, especially with over 100,000 shipments per year. For this reason alone the risks of nuclear energy and especially the breeder reactor appear to far outweigh the benefits.

Even Dr. Alvin M. Weinberg, former director of the Oak Ridge National Laboratory, one of the strongest and most optimistic advocates for nuclear energy, believes that the problem of shipping dangerous breeder fuel will be "difficult" and suggests that we develop nuclear parks as an alternative (Weinberg & Hammond 1972, p. 7). A cluster of eight nuclear plants, along with fuel preparation, fuel reprocessing, and waste storage plants, would be grouped in one complex to reduce the need and danger from shipments.

Nuclear wastes   If 1,000 grams of uranium-235 undergo fission, enormous amounts of energy are released. But some 999 grams of radioactive waste products are left over—a mixture of solids, liquids, and gases that must be stored until their radioactivity is no longer harmful. Some of these products are very short-lived and can be released to the environment after a few days or weeks, but others are dangerous for hundreds, thousands, and even tens of thousands of years.[20]

Table 6-1 shows some of the most hazardous isotopes produced in nuclear fission plants. All are dangerous (especially long-lived iodine-129 and plutonium-239), but iodine-131 and cesium-137 from power and reprocessing plants and strontium-90 from atomic bomb tests are particularly hazardous to man because of their biological magnification in food chains. Fortunately, most radioisotopes do not increase in concentration in passing through the food chain.

There are three methods used to dispose of radioactive wastes: (1) dilute and disperse; (2) delay and decay; and (3) concentrate and contain. Dilution and dispersion involves the discharge of low level wastes into the air, water, or ground to be diluted to safe levels. As wastes increase this already dangerous practice will begin to add significantly to man-made sources of radiation, particularly from hydrogen-3 (tritium) and krypton-85, which are difficult and fairly expensive to contain and remove.

Delay and decay applies to radioactive wastes with relatively short half-lives. They are stored as liquids or slurries

---

[20] For discussion of the problems of nuclear wastes see U.S. Atomic Energy Commission 1969a, Hambleton 1972, Starr & Hammond 1972, Kubo & Rose 1973, Micklin 1974, Dreschhoff et al. 1974, Farney 1974, Hammond 1974b, Commoner et al. 1974, vol. 1.

Table 6-1   Some isotopes produced in fission reactors that are particularly hazardous to man

Isotope	Half-life*	Critical organ
Iodine-129	17,000,000 years	Thyroid
Plutonium-239	24,000 years	Total body but especially lungs
Strontium-90	28 years	Bone
Cesium-137	27 years	Total body
Hydrogen-3 (tritium)	12 years	Total body
Krypton-85	11 years	Lungs, skin
Iodine-131	8 days	Thyroid

*Isotopes must be stored for periods of 10 to 20 times their half-life before they decay to safe levels. For a more complete listing of isotopes see U.S. Atomic Energy Commission 1969a, pp. 40–42.

in tanks for periods of 10 to 20 times their half-life (see Table 6-1) until they decay to harmless levels. At that time they are diluted and dispersed to the environment.

The most serious storage problem occurs for highly radioactive wastes with long half-lives. So far no method of permanent storage has been accepted, although a number of methods have been studied by the AEC for almost 20 years.

The AEC is temporarily storing about 90 million gallons of hot wastes in underground tanks at nuclear plants in Washington, Idaho, and South Carolina. Some wastes have been stored for 20 years, but they must be safely contained for at least 600 years. Although the AEC believes that tank storage "has proved both safe and practical" (U.S. Atomic Energy Commission 1969a), sixteen leaks (totaling nearly 350,000 gallons) have occurred over the past 16 years (General Accounting Office 1971, U.S. Atomic Energy Commission 1973b, Gillette 1973a).

Storage tanks must be very strong, corrosion resistant, protected in case of leaks, constantly stirred to prevent volcano-like eruptions, and provided with an uninterrupted source of power to run the stirring and cooling systems that must be used continuously to keep them from melting as their deadly contents boil vigorously for several years. The best tanks probably last no more than 20 years so that safe procedures for periodic transfer of wastes to new tanks must be available, as well as backup systems should leaks occur.

In 1965 the AEC began to solidify its military waste by evaporating it in the tank to an intensively radioactive "salt cake," which is less vulnerable to leakage and accidents. By 1980 the AEC hopes to have converted its liquid wastes to solid—leaving it with 380,000 tons of radioactive salt to store for 600 to 1000 years, and for several hundred thousand years where the wastes contain plutonium-239.

Guest Editorial: A Faustian Bargain We Snould Accept

Alvin M. Weinberg

Alvin M. Weinberg, former Director of the Oak Ridge National Laboratory, is now director of energy research and development for the Federal Energy Administration. From his early contributions to the theory of nuclear reactors to his current concern with the role of the national laboratories, he has been one of the leading spokesmen for nuclear energy. A member of the wartime team of theoretical physicists who designed the first large power reactors, he in 1960 received both the Atoms for Peace Award and the Atomic Energy Commission's E. O. Lawrence Memorial Award for his contributions to the theory and development of fission reactors. He has written extensively on some of the difficult problems of public policy posed by the growth of modern science. He coined the phrase "big science" to describe the new type of large-scale scientific enterprise exemplified by Oak Ridge. His awareness of various increasingly difficult socio-technological problems has been articulated in many articles and lectures.

There are two basically different views of the world's future. The one most popular these days is attributed to Malthus and holds that the resources of "Spaceship Earth" (Ward 1966) are limited. Nothing except drastic reduction in population, affluence, or technology can avoid the ultimate disaster predicted by Malthus and, more recently, by the Club of Rome (Meadows et al. 1972). The other, attributed sometimes to the economist David Ricardo, holds that as scarce materials are exhausted there will always be new, more expensive ones to take their place: Spaceship Earth is practically infinite, but it will cost more and more to stay where we are as we use up readily available materials.

The Ricardian view seems to me to be the more reasonable, especially since all of our past experience has shown that as one resource becomes scarce another takes its place. We do not use whale oil any longer, yet we have far better artificial lighting than did our lamp-lighting ancestors. And, in the very long run, mankind will have to depend on the most common, and almost infinitely abundant, elements: iron, sodium, carbon, nitrogen, aluminum, oxygen, silicon, and a few others. Glass, cement, and plastics will perform many more functions than they now do. Our standard of living will be diminished, but I cannot see this reduction as being by a factor of ten: more likely it would be, say, a factor of two.

Thus, in contrast to what seems to be the prevailing mood, I retain a certain basic optimism about the future. My optimism, however, is predicated on certain assumptions.

(1) I assume that technology can indeed deal with the effluents of this future society. Here I think I am on firm ground for, on the whole, where technology has been given the task, and given the time, it has come through with very important improvements. For example, many experts believe that the stringent emission standards imposed on cars by the Clean Air Act will indeed be met by 1980, if not before.

(2) Phosphorus, though essentially infinite (1,000 ppm in the earth's crust), has no substitute. Will we be able to so revolutionize agriculture that we can eventually use this "infinite" supply of residual phosphorus, at acceptable cost, for growing our food? This technological question is presently unresolved, though I cannot believe it to be unresolvable.

(3) All of this presupposes that man has at his disposal an inexhaustible, relatively cheap source of energy. As we now see the technological possibilities, there is only one that we can count on—and this is nuclear fission, based on fission breeders. This is not to say that fusion or geothermal or solar energy will never be economically available. It is merely that we do not know now that any of these will ever be successful, whereas we know that fission reactors are feasible.

In opting for fission breeders—and we hardly have a choice in the matter—we assume a moral and technological burden of serious proportion. A properly operating nuclear reactor and its subsystems is environmentally a very benign energy source. The issue hangs around the words "properly operating." Can we ensure that henceforth we shall be able to maintain the degree of intellectual responsibility and social commitment and stability necessary to manage this energy form so as not to cause serious harm? This is basically a moral and social question, though it does have strong technological components.

It is a Faustian bargain that we strike: in return for this inexhaustible energy source, which man must have if he is to maintain himself at anything like his present numbers and at his present state of affluence, we extract a commitment— essentially forever—that man will exercise the vigilance and discipline necessary to keep our nuclear fires well behaved. As a nuclear technologist who has devoted his career to this quest for an infinite energy source, I believe the bargain is a good one, and that it may even be an inevitable one. It is well that the full dimension and implication of the Faustian bargain be recognized, especially by the young people who will have to live with the choices that are being made on this vital issue.

Discussion

1 Do you agree that Spaceship Earth is practically infinite?

2. Dr. Weinberg bases his optimism on three assumptions. What evidence can you provide that would make these assumptions reasonable? Are there any other assumptions that should be added?

3. Who was Faust and what is a Faustian bargain?

4. Do you agree that we should accept the Faustian bargain of nuclear fission with conventional or breeder reactors? Why or why not? What are the consequences of not having this service and depleting our fossil fuels within the next 20 to 50 years? How will your life be affected?

Guest Editorial: The Energy Frontier

David Rittenhouse Inglis is a nuclear physicist and professor of physics at the University of Massachusetts. He was a senior physicist at Argonne National Laboratory between 1949 and 1969 and has also taught at Princeton, Johns Hopkins, Ohio State, and the University of Pittsburgh. He is on the editorial board of Science and Public Affairs and on the board of directors of the National Committee for Nuclear Responsibility. Dr. Inglis has written many articles and books on atomic and nuclear physics. His latest book, Nuclear Energy: Its Physics and Its Social Challenge (1973) is considered one of the best descriptions and evaluations of nuclear power for liberal arts students and educated laymen.

David R. Inglis

Among all possible future energy sources, nuclear energy from reactors has been the darling of government funding because it is a spin-off from the military nuclear adventure. The development of the first atomic bomb during World War II was an intense and dedicated exploration into the unknown with a spirit based on a sense of national urgency. The obstacles in the way of the achievement seemed enormous—the unprecedented separation of isotopes on a massive scale, the possibility of some unwanted isotopes gobbling up the neutrons without contributing to the chain reaction, and other such pitfalls. In spite of all the uncertainty and enormous obstacles, a brave decision was made by President Franklin D. Roosevelt. Two billion 1945 dollars were poured into the gamble and it paid off.

The first nuclear reactor was invented and built as a part of that wartime burst of enthusiasm and dedication. After the war, reactors were developed almost to the point of commercial practicability in the new national laboratories, with a contribution on the side to nuclear submarines. Then in the mid-fifties the decision was made to throw to industry the main task and opportunity of engineering development and building of commercial nuclear reactors, with the national laboratories retaining the back-up role of necessary research. Both government and industry have since poured billions into the project, and because of this there is strong vested interest and an inclination to scorn other energy alternatives.

The proponents of an enormous expansion of nuclear reactor deployment rightly point out that such a program can probably be kept reasonably safe if eternal vigilance and the meticulous care appropriate to so dangerous an enterprise can be maintained. But there are already abundant signs that with pressures to build a large number of reactors, this safety cannot be assured. An example is the firing of a welding inspector at a nuclear power plant at Virginia Beach, Virginia, for being too faithful in reporting faults in the welds that are vital to the safety of any nuclear plant. Recently two workmen were killed when a steam pipe burst in that same plant. Anyone who guesses that the probability of catastrophic accident in a large nuclear power plant is only one in ten thousand per year, or even less, is guessing about the performance of vessels with inadequately inspected welds and of much more intricate apparatus. Some proponents of the massive nuclear program accept the one-in-ten-thousand guess, but consider it is worth an average of one accident killing hundreds or thousands of people every ten years for the sake of the output of a thousand nuclear plants in the same way as it is worth thousands of highway deaths each year for the sake of getting around in automobiles and other vehicles.

With this crass moral judgment I do not concur, for the alternative choices are very different in the two cases. It would be much easier and less disruptive of our way of life to seek safe alternatives to nuclear power and even to fall far short of doubling our per capita electric consumption every decade than it would be to return to a minimal-transport civilization. Of all the reasons to seek alternate energy sources, the most important is avoiding the proliferation of nuclear materials that adds to the likelihood of nuclear war and blackmail.

What we need again today is a brave decision by national leaders to explore with vigor and dedication the unknown but real potential of new energy sources. True, some effort and some public funds are being devoted to developing exotic new energy sources, but they are miserably small compared to the need, aside from nuclear fusion, which is receiving perhaps half as much funding as it could right now usefully employ. Fusion is a noble gamble, a bit more than a gleam in the scientist's eye. It may work. It may not. If it does it will be several decades hence and it will have its troubles, including radioactive troubles less severe than those of fission reactors. It has the blessing of the vested interests because it could serve as a later-generation nuclear energy source.

Of the meager funds going into some of the other possibilities, it seems that more is going into paper studies and committee reports than into enthusiastic developmental work. Yet there are enthusiasts with ideas who cannot obtain funding.

Of the solar energy possibilities, the Meinels' worthy steam-turbine-in-the-desert scheme (Meinel & Meinel 1971, 1972) and the biological production of fuels are receiving some funding, but much too far below the Manhattan Project scale. Other solar schemes, such as direct production of hydrogen from water to produce a transportable and storable fuel are receiving no support at all.

As another example of inadequate effort, no one is building a giant windmill. One prototype was built on a limited experimental basis during World War II and fed a thousand kilowatts into the electric grid in Vermont. That experiment came just at the dawn of the atomic age and was not followed up, probably because of early rosy hopes for infinite and trouble-free nuclear power. Now that those early dreams have faded, it is high time to follow up on wind power development. The potential is enormous—almost limitless—and prototypes should be built to see how far modern engineering can reduce capital costs. Yet wind power is conventionally being written off as of little practical consequence, even as fission might have been in 1940 before there was a determined effort to develop it.

Senator Jackson has introduced a bill in Congress to promote many possible future energy sources. The bill has a yearly $2 billion price tag, appropriately reminiscent of the dedicated wartime A-bomb effort. Money alone will not do the job, but money in such abundance and properly administered could foster the surfacing and development of all sorts of brave new ideas. A wide gamut of such ideas should be explored so that we may have available the best options ten and twenty years from now, and, even more importantly, for the next century when the more serious crunch will come. Anything less is shunning the challenge of the energy frontier.

Discussion

1. Compare the viewpoint in this editorial with that of Weinberg in the previous editorial. Which position do you support? Why?

2. Should a massive commitment to the evaluation and development of solar, wind, geothermal, and other energy sources be undertaken simultaneously with the continuing development of nuclear power, or should the latter be slowed down or stopped for a period? Defend your answer.

3. Why do these alternate energy sources continue to receive so little funding compared to conventional and breeder reactors? (See Table 9–2.)

Long term storage   Assuming that solidification processes keep up with the mounting volume of wastes, the problem becomes one of storing relatively small volumes of deadly solid wastes for thousands of years with absolute safety. With solidification the amount of solid radioactive waste produced by each U.S. citizen per year in electricity consumption would be equivalent to the volume of one aspirin tablet (Starr & Hammond 1972). During a 70-year lifetime each of us would accumulate enough solidified radioactive wastes to fill a 16-ounce beer can. As a result the total wastes produced by the year 2000 could be stored in a building or vault about 200 feet long and wide and about 12.5 feet high — occupying space roughly equivalent to a football field (Hammond 1974b). Although this greatly simplifies the problem one should not be lulled into a false sense of security by such analogies. Remember that these wastes must be stored in absolute safety for much longer than the entire history of man on the planet.

The major alternatives[21] (besides slowdown or abandonment of nuclear power) under evaluation are (1) permanent burial in dry, earthquake-free geologic formations such as salt mines; (2) storage in surface warehouses, possibly until a better solution is found; (3) burial under Antarctic ice sheets; (4) burial in an underground hole created by a nuclear bomb until the wastes eventually melt with surrounding rock into a glassy ball; (5) disposal in deep ocean trenches; (6) shooting the wastes off into space; and (7) transmutation of harmful isotopes into harmless ones by high level neutron bombardment or by nuclear fusion.

Until 1972 the AEC talked optimistically of using an abandoned salt mine near Lyons, Kansas, as the National Radioactive Waste Repository for permanent storage of long-lived wastes. Salt mines are attractive because they are usually isolated from ground and underground waters. In addition, salt is a good conductor for the intense heat generated by nuclear wastes and is a good radioactive shield; because of its plasticity any fissures would seal or close rapidly. The long term safety of this approach depends on preventing the intrusion of water into the salt beds by any means. After 20 years of testing by the AEC this site was abandoned in 1972 because of a number of problems

Mostly because of the Kansas failure and the need for more time for research, the AEC announced in May 1972 that in 1979 it would begin building an interim surface storage facility for solidified commercial high level wastes. The safety of this facility, of course, depends on multiple engineering and security safeguards (Kubo & Rose 1973). The AEC contends that this presumably earthquake, tornado, and bomb proof shelter should provide safe management for at least 200 years, during which more suitable permanent disposal methods might be developed.

The suggestion that the wastes be stored under the Antarctic ice cap is being considered but the plan may have serious drawbacks (see letters in *Science and Public Affairs*, April 1973, pp. 2–3, 54–56, and Kubo & Rose 1973). These include the fact that the ice caps might not last the 500,000 years needed for plutonium storage, the possibility that the intense heat from the wastes might melt large portions of the ice and cause unpredictable geologic and climatic changes, and the hazards and difficulties of shipping wastes to the Antarctic.

Disposal of wastes in deep ocean trenches is considered extremely dangerous. Although transmutation into harmless isotopes is not presently feasible, if the technology could be developed it would be a very attractive method. Former AEC chairman Dr. James Schlesinger suggested shooting wastes in rockets to the sun where they would burn up. But a rocket that exploded prematurely or returned to the earth because of a minute miscalculation in the trajectory path would cause widespread death and contamination. By the year 2020 we would have to shoot off about 17,000 tons of waste per year.

Conceivably, one of these long term storage schemes may work. But any failure in this Faustian bargain will be borne by over 7,000 future generations, who will inherit the decision we are now making.   •

Fission energy is safe only if a number of critical devices work as they should, if a number of people in key positions follow all their instructions, if there is no sabotage, no highjacking of the transports, if no reactor fuel processing plant or reprocessing plant or repository anywhere in the world is situated in a region of riots or guerilla activity, and no revolution or war — even a "conventional one" — takes place in these regions. . . . No acts of God can be permitted.

Hannes Alfven

Discussion Topics

1. Compare the major parts and major environmental impacts of fossil fuel, normal fission, and breeder electric power plants. How does a breeder "breed" new fuel? Which type of plant do you prefer? Why?

---

[21] For a more detailed evaluation of these alternatives see Kubo & Rose 1973, Micklin 1974, Farney 1974.

2. *Debate the issue now before Congress: We should declare a moratorium on the licensing of all nuclear power plants until we can be more assured of their safety and of the feasibility of safe transportation and storage of nuclear wastes.*

3. *A nuclear power plant is proposed for your town or city. Respond to the following statements made at a public hearing.*

a. *Power plant executive: "The Atomic Energy Commission has assured us that our construction plans more than meet their rigid safety specifications."*

b. *Environmentalist: "The past record of the Atomic Energy Commission is not reassuring, and even so there is a finite possibility of a serious accident."*

c. *Power plant executive: "As you know fossil-fueled power plants are a major air pollution and health hazard. It would be better to build nuclear power plants, which have no air pollution emissions."*

d. *Environmentalist: "Air pollution wouldn't be a problem, but what about chances of a nuclear accident and the transportation and storage of wastes from the plant? Besides, we could easily add pollution control devices to fossil plants that would eliminate almost all air pollution. Does the power company intend to shut down their five fossil-fueled plants in this state because they are a health hazard?"*

4. *Explain why the "atomic bomb syndrome" frequently associated with nuclear power plants is not a valid fear or criticism. What is a "grand excursion"? Why is it sometimes called the "Chinese syndrome"? List the series of multiple safeguards in a nuclear reactor that make such an excursion extremely improbable.*

5. *Explain the fallacy in the statement that nuclear power plants are safer than driving your car, flying in an airplane, or engaging in most everyday activities. It is estimated by different sources that the chances of a serious nuclear accident are 1 in 10,000 to 1 in 1,000,000,000. Is this an acceptable risk for you? Explain.*

6. *Distinguish between genetic damage and somatic damage by radiation. What is "background radiation"? Does it cause cancer? Should we add to this natural background? Under what circumstances? Should the allowable radiation dose be reduced?*

7. *In May of 1995 the director of the National Nuclear Security Guard announced that one of the several thousand heavily guarded shipments of deadly plutonium made each year to breeder reactors had been highjacked by a small but well-organized terrorist group calling itself the Nuclear Liberation Army (NLA). About 50 pounds of plutonium was taken. Because plutonium is a weak emitter of alpha radiation, its presence is almost impossible to detect. The highjackers could break up the material into smaller pieces and carry it in their pockets, briefcases, or suitcases with only newspaper, aluminum foil, or any thin covering needed to protect themselves from the*

radiation. *The danger occurs only when plutonium is inhaled as dust particles into the lungs or ingested through water or food intake, with the inhalation of only one tiny speck enough to cause lung cancer. One week after the highjacking the president of the United States received an ultimatum from the NLA that within six weeks he is to shut down and dismantle all nuclear power plants and have the U.S. Treasury send checks for $15,000 to every person below the poverty level. Otherwise the NLA threatens to use conventional plastic explosives to blow up and inject plutonium particles into the air above 10 major U.S. cities, and to pour dissolved plutonium compounds into the water systems of these cities. If this occurred, tens of thousands and probably millions could contract lung or other cancers and large urban areas of the United States would be uninhabitable for centuries. As president of the United States, how would you respond (Lapp 1973a)? Check the feasibility of this scenario with a chemist, a physicist, and a security expert and see if you can conceive of a way to prevent such a possibility. A major feature of our present energy policy calls for the widespread phasing in of breeder reactors between 1985 and 2020. Do you favor this policy? Why or why not? What are the alternatives?*

8. *Debate the issue of whether we should accept the Faustian bargain of nuclear fission with conventional reactors. With breeder reactors. Either way, how might your life be affected? Your children's lives?*

Further Reading

Abrahamson, Dean E. 1972. "Ecological Hazards from Nuclear Power Plants," in M. Taghi Farvar and John P. Milton, eds., *The Careless Technology*. Garden City, N.Y.: Natural History Press. One of the clearest summaries available.

Alfven, Hannes. 1974. "Fission Energy and Other Sources of Energy," *Science and Public Affairs*, January, pp. 4–8. Superb analysis of the dangers of nuclear energy along with a proposed alternative plan. Highly recommended.

Bryerton, Gene. 1970. *The Nuclear Dilemma*. New York: Ballantine. Superb overview of risks and benefits of nuclear power. Good bibliography.

Cohen, Bernard L. 1974. "Perspectives on the Nuclear Debate," *Bulletin of the Atomic Scientists*, October, pp. 35–39. An outstanding defense of nuclear power. Highly recommended.

Commoner, Barry, Howard Boksenbaum, and Michael Corr, eds. 1974. *Energy and Human Welfare: A Critical Analysis*, 3 vols. New York: Macmillan. Excellent series of articles on the pros and cons of nuclear power.

Cook, Earl. 1972. "Ionizing Radiation," in William W. Murdoch, ed., *Environment: Resources, Pollution and Society*.

Stamford, Conn.: Sinauer. One of the best summaries on effects of radiation and problems of nuclear wastes.

DeNike, L. Douglas. 1974. "Radioactive Malevolence," *Science and Public Affairs,* February, pp. 16–20. Superb and shocking account of the potential for easy highjacking and criminal use of radioactive materials. Try to read this one.

Farney, Dennis. 1974. "Ominous Problem: What to Do with Radioactive Waste," *Smithsonian,* vol. 5, no. 1, 20–26. One of the best nontechnical summaries. Highly recommended.

Gofman, John W., and Arthur A. Tamplin. 1971. *Poisoned Power: The Case against Nuclear Power.* Emmaus, Pa.: Rodale Press. Hard hitting popularized attack on nuclear power plants by two prominent nuclear scientists.

Hammond, Phillip R. 1974. "Nuclear Power Risks," *American Scientist,* vol. 62, 155–160. Excellent presentation of the arguments for nuclear power.

Inglis, David R. 1973. *Nuclear Energy: Its Physics and Social Challenge.* Reading, Mass.: Addison-Wesley. Outstanding presentation by a recognized expert at a slightly higher level. Highly recommended.

Kneese, Allen V. 1973. "The Faustian Bargain," *Resources,* no. 44, September, pp. 1–3. A prominent economist and environmentalist provides a cost–benefit analysis of nuclear power and concludes that we should phase out nuclear fission reactors.

Lovins, Amory B. 1973. "The Case against the Fast Breeder Reactor," *Bulletin of the Atomic Scientists,* March, pp. 29–35. A physicist presents a strong case against the breeder.

Micklin, Philip P. 1974. "Environmental Hazards of Nuclear Wastes," *Science and Public Affairs,* April, pp. 36–42. Superb summary.

Novick, Sheldon. 1973. "Toward a Nuclear Power Precipice," *Environment,* 15:2, 32–40. Fine analysis of the dangers of nuclear power.

Rose, David J. 1974. "Nuclear Electric Power," *Science,* vol. 184, 351–359. An excellent analysis, concluding that the benefits of nuclear power outweigh its risks relative to other energy alternatives but only if we can adequately protect shipments of nuclear materials from accidents and highjacking.

Seaborg, Glenn T., and Justin L. Bloom. 1970. "Fast Breeder Reactors," *Scientific American,* 223:5, 13–21 (November). Excellent introduction.

Seaborg, Glenn T., and William R. Corliss. 1971. *Man and Atom.* New York: Dutton. Vigorous defense of nuclear energy by Nobel Prize winner and former chairman of the Atomic Energy Commission. See pp. 54–85 for a superb summary of the case for nuclear power.

Shapley, Deborah. 1971. "Radioactive Cargoes: Record Good but the Problems Will Multiply," *Science,* vol. 172, 1318–1321. Danger of accidents as nuclear shipments increase.

Speth, J. Gustave, Arthur R. Tamplin, and Thomas B. Cochran. 1974. " Plutonium Cycle: The Fateful Step," *Bulletin of the Atomic Scientists,* November, pp. 15–22. Critical analysis of nuclear fuel cycle by experts.

Starr, Chauncey, and Philip R. Hammond. 1972. "Nuclear Waste Storage," *Science,* vol. 177, 744. Storage of nuclear wastes is not a serious problem.

U.S. Atomic Energy Commission. 1966. *The Genetic Effects of Radiation* (written by Isaac Asimov and Theodosius Dobzhansky). Oak Ridge, Tenn.: USAEC Division of Technical Information Extension. Excellent nontechnical discussion.

U.S. Atomic Energy Commission. 1969. *Atomic Fuel* (by John F. Hogerton). Oak Ridge, Tenn.: USAEC Division of Technical Information Extension. Superb nontechnical discussion of the nuclear fuel cycle.

U.S. Atomic Energy Commission. 1969a. *Radioactive Wastes* (by Charles H. Fox). Oak Ridge, Tenn.: USAEC Division of Technical Information Extension. Excellent nontechnical pamphlet describing methods for dealing with nuclear wastes.

7

Some Energy Alternatives: Fusion, Solar, Geothermal, Wind, and Conservation

Unless the nuclear fission breeder reactor is developed and proves to be safe, we will have to rely after the year 2000 to 2020 on essentially infinite energy sources such as nuclear fusion, solar energy, geothermal energy, and wind power. What chance do we have of developing these sources within the next 30 years? How will their ecological side effects compare with those from fossil fuels and nuclear fission? What sort of research program and how much money will be needed to enhance the probability that they can be developed in time? How can we conserve fossil fuel energy now to buy more time for the development of other energy sources and to decrease our dependence on the breeder reactor?

7-1   Nuclear Fusion

The potential energy locked in the nucleus of an atom can be released by two processes—*nuclear fission* or *nuclear fusion*. In nuclear fission (Chapter 6) a neutron is used to split the nucleus of a heavy atom such as uranium-235 into two lighter fragments with the release of additional neutrons and energy (see 6–3). In nuclear fusion two nuclei of light atoms (such as helium), and energy is released. At present the two most attractive nuclear fusion reactions are (1) the D-D reaction, in which two deuterium or hydrogen-2 nuclei[1] fuse to form a helium-3 nucleus, and (2) nucleus and a tritium (hydrogen-3) nucleus fuse to form helium-4 (Figure 7–1).

Advantages and hazards   A successful fusion reactor has several extremely important advantages over fission reactors.[2]

1. Its fuel sources are essentially limitless and cheap. A few grams (a fraction of an ounce) of deuterium fuel can be

extracted from seawater and used to produce energy equivalent to 300 gallons of gasoline for only a few cents. The deuterium in the ocean could supply all mankind with power at many times present consumption rates for several billion years.

2. It is much less dangerous than nuclear fission. Reactor meltdown with a serious release of radioactive materials, an ever present danger in fission reactors (Chapter 6), could not occur.

3. The amount and hazard of the radioactive materials produced would be much less than with conventional and breeder fission reactors.[3]

4. Massive shipments of radioactive fuels would not be necessary, and far smaller quantities of radioactive wastes would have to be stored (Section 6–4).

5. Thermal pollution of the bodies of water (Section 8–5) used for cooling would be much less than that from fission reactors and about equal to or slightly better than that from fossil fuel plants.

6. The danger of theft of fuel materials, a major problem with conventional fission and breeder reactors (Chapter 6), would be eliminated.

7. Fusion energy could be used for the cheap production of hydrogen gas, which could serve as a much cleaner replacement for natural gas and gasoline (Section 5–2).

8. It could lead to the development of a *fusion torch* (Gough & Eastlund 1971) that would vaporize junk, automobiles, bottles, cars, and other solid wastes and convert them back to their basic elements for recycling (Figures 3–8 and 3–9).

The greatest hazard of a fusion reactor would undoubtedly be the release of radioactive tritium (hydrogen-3) either as a gas or in the water (tritiated water). Tritium has a relatively short half life of 12 years, but it spreads rapidly because it is a light gas and because it can replace normal hydrogen (hydrogen-1) in substances such as water. Tritium is extremely difficult to contain, because at high temperatures and neutron

---

[1] As a crude model, the nucleus of an atom contains *neutrons* (neutrally charged particles) and *protons* (positively charged particles), each with a relative mass of one. The sum of the number of protons plus neutrons in a nucleus is a measure of the atom's mass and is called the *mass number*. Atoms of the same element can have different numbers of neutrons in their nucleus and are called *isotopes*. For example, there are three isotopes of hydrogen and three of uranium.

[2] Unfortunately this statement does not apply to the nuclear fission–fusion hybrid reactor envisioned by some (Leonard 1973), which would have the hazards associated with both nuclear fission and nuclear fusion.

---

[3] For a summary and comparison of the radioactive materials produced in fusion and fission reactors see Steiner 1971.

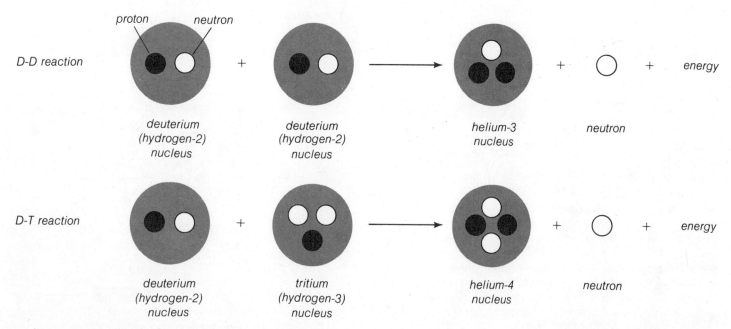

7–1 *Two potentially useful nuclear fusion reactions.*

densities it can diffuse right through metals. It is also produced in fission reactors, and scientists are already testing a number of methods for tritium control.

Problems to overcome Man has mastered *uncontrolled* thermonuclear fusion in the hydrogen bomb, but after 20 years of research by Soviet, American, and other scientists, we have yet to master *controlled* thermonuclear fusion.[4] There are three difficult requirements for achieving a sustained fusion reaction and they must all be attained simultaneously.[5] The basic difficulty is that the positively charged nuclei repel one another, and for fusion to occur they must be pushed and held together with enormous force. This requires: (1) heating the fuel atoms (such as D-D or D-T) to 40 million to several billion °C to convert the atoms into a plasma[6] and to allow ignition of the fusion reaction; (2) holding and pushing the plasma together long enough (1 second) for a sufficient fraction of the fuel atoms to fuse; and (3) recovering enough useful energy to make fusion a profitable source of net energy.

[4] It is impossible for any type of nuclear explosion to occur inside a nuclear fusion reactor.

[5] For summaries of nuclear fusion reactors and their problems see Gough & Eastlund 1971, Lidsky 1972, Rose 1971, Wood & Nuckolls 1972, Hammond et al. 1973, Chapters 13 & 14, Landis 1973, Bova 1971, Alexander 1970, Commoner et al. 1974, vol. 2.

[6] At such high temperatures the nuclei are stripped of their surrounding negatively charged electrons, leaving an intensely hot mixture of positively charged nuclei and negatively charged electrons known collectively as a *plasma.*

Isotope	Mass number: neutrons plus protons in the nucleus	Protons in the nucleus	Neutrons in the nucleus
Hydrogen-1	1	1	0
Hydrogen-2 (deuterium)	2	1	1
Hydrogen-3 (tritium)	3	1	2
Uranium-233	233	92	141
Uranium-235	235	92	143
Uranium-238	238	92	146

Because no known material can contain fuel heated to 40 million degrees or more, research during the past 20 years has concentrated on trying to find a "magic bottle" that could hold and press together (the pinch effect) the hot plasma long enough for self-sustaining fusion to occur. Although there are a number of approaches, the two most promising ones appear to be *magnetic containment* (Metz 1972a, Hammond et al. 1973, Chapter 13, Coppi & Rem 1972) and *laser ignition* (Metz 1972, Hammond et al. 1973, Chapter 14, Lubin & Fraas 1971).

In the magnetic bottle or containment approach an intense magnetic field is used to pinch and hold the plasma of charged nuclei and electrons together. The problem is to find the right shape for the "magnetic bottle" so that the conditions necessary for fusion are obtained. Until recently most of the research has been on the tokamak or toroidal configuration, developed originally by Soviet scientists who lead the world in the amount of money and research on nuclear fusion. The stream of plasma is squeezed by a doughnut shaped

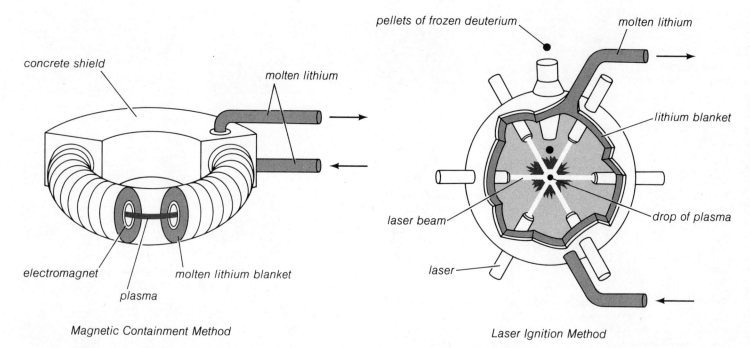

Magnetic Containment Method

Laser Ignition Method

7-2   *Comparison of magnetic containment and laser ignition methods for initiating a nuclear fusion reaction.*

magnetic field (Figure 7-2) into a circle. But in 1974, scientists at Brigham Young University hit upon a new type of doughnut shaped "bottle" that holds the plasma stream in the shape of a fat banana and has much greater promise of keeping the plasma from leaking.[7]

The newer laser ignition approach would use a series of high powered laser beams to bombard and implode a small D-D or D-T fuel pellet from all sides to achieve a temperature high enough to ignite fusion (Figure 7-2). The two major problems are the development of lasers with enough power and the containment and use of the sudden release of energy, which occurs as a shock wave that could damage or destroy the containment vessel.

Building a fusion reactor   Even if the plasma confinement and ignition problems are solved, scientists still face formidable problems in developing a workable nuclear fusion reactor and plant.

One difficult engineering problem is the sharp temperature difference needed over a short distance. At the center of the reactor the plasma may be at 40 million to 100 million °C, but only 2 meters away, where the magnets are located, the temperature must be near absolute zero (−273°C). Another problem is the choice of material for the inner wall of the re-

[7] This new bottle design, known as topolotron, resulted from the application of a field of mathematics known as topology.

actor. It must not react with extremely reactive hot liquid lithium (at 1000°C) and must last at least 10 to 20 years while being bombarded by large numbers of energetic neutrons (which destroy most known materials).

Possible Development of Commercially Feasible Fusion Energy

Step 1: Scientific feasibility—*small scale laboratory experiments showing that the physical process is possible.*
Present program: 1980 to 1985
Crash program: 1980

Step 2: Engineering and ecological feasibility—*successful large scale pilot plant with promise of an economically and ecologically acceptable process.*
Present program: 1990 to 1995
Crash program: 1985 to 1987

Step 3: Ecological, economic, and commercial feasibility—*begin building and operating commercial plants at acceptable costs and environmental side effects.*
Present program: 2000 to 2010
Crash program: 1995 to 1997

Step 4: Process provides significant percentage of needs—*successful large scale building and operation of plants.*
Present program: 2020 to 2030
Crash program: 2010 to 2020

A timetable for fusion power   How soon, *if ever*, might fusion be available? The development of any commercially useful process depends on the successful completion of a number of steps (see insert). Although the technical problems are enormous, many feel one reason we don't have fusion power now or won't have it within a decade or two is our refusal to provide the massive research funding such a potentially useful energy source warrants (Kenward 1972). Most funds are being used to develop the potentially more dangerous conventional fission and breeder reactors. The total funds spent on U.S. controlled fusion research and development since the program began in 1950 are about the same as those spent in one Apollo moon shot. In one year Americans spend more on deodorants than our entire expenditure on fusion from 1950 to 1975.

The $1.45 billion budget proposed (but not authorized) by the AEC (U.S. Atomic Energy Commission 1973c) for the years 1975 to 1979 is not enough to determine whether fusion is a viable alternative to the breeder reactor. With a crash program of several billion dollars between 1975 and 1980, the most promising approaches to fusion could be pursued simultaneously and we would have a much higher probability of demonstrating its feasibility (Feare 1971, Post 1971).

7–2   Solar Energy

Since there is no assurance that nuclear fusion will ever become feasible on the large scale needed, we must develop a parallel crash program for controlled use of another potentially infinite energy source, solar energy.[8]

Some advantages and difficulties   Solar energy has an impressive array of advantages over other energy sources.

1. It is an infinite and readily available energy source. If 30 percent of the solar energy falling on 1 square mile of the earth could be converted to electricity, its output would equal that of the largest nuclear power plant.[9] If only 1 percent of the solar energy falling on the Sahara Desert were converted to electrical power, it would supply all of the world's projected energy needs for electrical power for the year 2000.[10]

2. It is the cleanest and safest of all energy sources (along with wind power, an indirect form of solar energy). It produces no air or water pollution. Large areas of land would be needed for solar collectors, but the amount of land needed and the environmental impact are small compared to coal strip mining and oil refineries and spills. The dangers associated with radioactive materials are not present. Some visual pollution from the array of solar collectors will exist, but this is minor compared to the alternatives.[11] (See Table 4–3).

3. Along with wind power, it provides an escape from entropy or heat trap. Fossil fuel and nuclear energy sources in the long run are limited by the heat or entropy built up in the atmosphere (Sections 2–5 and 8–4), as required by the second energy law. With solar energy the major entropy or heat release occurs in the sun—a gigantic nuclear fusion reactor 93 million miles away.

4. It could be used to produce hydrogen gas as a replacement for oil, natural gas, and gasoline (Section 4–3).

5. No major breakthroughs are needed to make solar energy technologically feasible (Morrow 1973). The major problem at present is its economic feasibility on a large scale. This is in sharp contrast to the fission breeder reactor (Chapter 6) and the nuclear fusion reactor, where both technological and economic feasibility have yet to be demonstrated.

6. Solar energy could be developed into a major energy source within 5 to 10 years as contrasted to the 10 to 30 years needed for nuclear fission and fusion, assuming they work and are safe.

With this array of advantages, why have we not used solar energy to solve our energy problems long ago? There are two major reasons. First, the solar energy reaching the earth's surface is widely dispersed (high entropy) and must be collected over a very large area and concentrated so that it can be used. The second energy law (Sections 2–2 and 2–5) explains why solar energy might not be economically feasible on a large scale, that is, we might have to put more energy (and money) into the system than we get out (Section 4–1).

A second problem with solar energy is that it is not available at night when electrical needs are highest, and its supply varies with cloud cover and the season of the year.[12] Thus, we must also have a method of storing solar energy received in the daytime for use at night or during cloudy spells.

In spite of these difficulties a 1972 National Science Foundation-National Aeronautics and Space Administration panel of distinguished scientists (NSF/NASA Solar Energy Panel 1973) stated that with adequate funding solar energy could supply a sizable portion of future U.S. energy needs. Some of their conclusions are:

---

[8] For more details on solar energy see Tamplin 1973, NSF/NASA Solar Energy Panel 1973, Meinel & Meinel 1971, 1972, Hammond 1973b, Halacy 1973, Glaser 1968, Wolf 1974, Daniels 1964, Morrow 1973, Ford & Kane 1971, Hammond et al. 1973, Chapters 10 & 11, Brinkworth 1974, Commoner et al. 1974, Clark 1974.

[9] David R. Inglis, personal communication.

[10] W. W. Bearinger of the Honeywell Corporation in a speech in February 1972.

[11] If solar energy in houses and buildings become widespread there may be a number of legal suits on sun rights when a neighboring building casts a shadow on someone's solar collector.

---

[12] Air pollution from fossil fuel power plants and smog from automobiles could also reduce the amount of solar energy.

1. Although the cost of useful solar energy is now higher than most conventional sources, the increasing prices of these fuels and new solar technology will make it more competitive in the near future.

2. The cost of solar heating of homes and buildings is already competitive with fossil fuels in some parts of the country and could supply as much as 80 percent of the heat needs in sunny climates.

3. An extensive solar energy research and development program with a budget of $3.5 billion has a good probability of achieving the following goals:

a. Commercially available space heating and cooling of buildings in 5 to 10 years at a research cost of $100 million.

b. Use of solar energy to produce methane and other synthetic fuels from organic materials (bioconversion) such as algae, manure, and urban sewage within 10 years at a cost of $172 million.

c. Large scale solar electric power generation within 10 to 15 years, with $1 billion needed to develop a demonstration plant.

d. By the year 2020 solar energy could potentially provide 35 percent of heating and cooling in buildings, 30 percent of the nation's gaseous fuels, 10 percent of its liquid fuels from bioconversion, and 20 percent of our electrical needs from solar power plants.

Some approaches to harnessing solar energy   Other than photosynthesis in plants, there are two basic approaches for capturing and using solar energy: (1) the absorption and concentration of solar energy as heat, which is either used directly or converted to other forms of energy; and (2) the direct conversion of solar energy into electrical energy using solar or photovoltaic cells. Scientific feasibility for both of these approaches has been demonstrated for decades.

Several million solar water heaters and cookers are in use around the world, especially in Japan, Israel, Australia, Florida, and other areas where electricity or fossil fuel is expensive or in short supply.

Solar energy can be used to heat and cool homes and buildings. Energy collectors coated with a black heat-absorbing substance are mounted on the roof. The top of the collector is covered with glass or plastic to trap heat by use of the greenhouse effect (Section 8–2). Water circulating through the collectors carries the heat into the building's heating system. Heat for use at night and in cloudy weather is stored in water, rocks, or chemical salts maintained in a well-insulated tank. Such systems are used in over 2 dozen homes and small buildings in the United States and the number is increasing rapidly as fuel prices rise. Congress has proposed a solar feasibility experiment that would equip 4,000 homes with solar heating and cooling units between 1975 and 1980 at government expense.

Large solar electrical power plants are a possibility that has not yet been tested. Marjorie and Aden Meinel (1971, 1972), have proposed the building of large desert solar "farms" in Arizona and California to serve as combined solar power and water desalination plants.[13] Pipes coated with plastic films would selectively absorb solar radiation and produce a "super greenhouse effect." Large lenses would concentrate sunlight on hundreds of miles of these pipes laid out like a field in a conventional food growing solar farm. A gas or low boiling liquid (such as sodium) flowing through the pipes would transfer the heat to steam boilers and eventually produce electricity. Excess heat might be stored in chemicals or rock formations which could then be released on cloudy days or used to produce hydrogen gas. By the year 2000, solar farm plants constructed over a 15,000 square mile (39,000 square kilometer) desert area could produce 1 million megawatts of electricity—about half of the projected need for that year. The basic problem is that a solar farm requires a large area of land and might disturb fragile desert ecosystems. However, the farms would require much less land and have much less impact than the strip mining of coal. To minimize the land impact of one gigantic solar farm, a number of smaller solar power farms could be built instead over an eight state area.

Solar power might also be collected by taking advantage of thermal gradients in the sea. Two major problems with land based solar energy power plants are the high cost of collectors and the need to store energy for use at nighttime or on cloudy days. The sea, however, collects and stores solar energy free of charge. The easiest and cheapest method for producing electricity from solar energy might be to use the heat stored in the thermal gradient (temperature difference between the surface and bottom water layers) of the ocean (Tamplin 1973, Metz 1973, Walters 1971, Zener 1973, Othmer & Roels 1973). Large floating platforms in the Gulf Stream or other warm water areas would use warm surface water to vaporize propane or some other liquid at high pressure. The vapor would be used to power a turbine and generate electricity. It could be cooled and circulated for reuse by drawing cold water up from the ocean bottom. The nutrients that were brought up at the same time might make such artificial upwelling areas major fish and shellfish producing areas and aid in providing more protein from the ocean. An ocean gradient plant could also desalinate ocean water to produce fresh water. The technology for such plants is already available, but the economics and a satisfactory method for

---

[13] They estimate that a demonstration plant could be built for a fraction of the cost of a demonstration nuclear breeder plant and that the electricity produced would be competitive in cost with nuclear power.

transmitting the electricity to the land have yet to be worked out. An alternative would be to use the electricity to electrolyze water and produce hydrogen gas, which could be piped or transported in tankers to shore (Tamplin 1973, p. 18). There is also concern over the ecological effects on ocean ecosystems and on climate if a large number of such plants began upsetting normal thermal distributions in the ocean. Because this method is limited to mostly tropical and subtropical areas where sufficient thermal gradients exist, it may become an important source of energy for many developing nations.

Besides absorbing and concentrating heat, the other basic approach for harnessing solar energy is the direct conversion of solar energy into electrical energy through the use of photovoltaic cells like those in space vehicles. Again the technology is available, but the cost is prohibitive and will have to be reduced by a factor of 100 to 300 to be economically feasible (Tamplin 1973, Morrow 1973).

Why we don't have solar energy   Solar energy, like conventional fission, breeder, and nuclear fusion energy will only be developed by a massive government supported research and development program, and only then if the process yields net energy (Section 4–1). Because the fuel for solar energy plants is free, it is not surprising that the oil, coal, natural gas, and uranium companies are not enthusiastic about supporting an approach that would only sell furnaces not fuel. Their political influence, the Atomic Energy Commission's concentration on the breeder reactor, and a lack of awareness among government officials mean that the government appropriated only 2 percent of its energy budget for 1975 for the development of solar energy, compared to 9 percent for fusion and 40 percent for nuclear fission. Nobel Laureate (Chemistry) Sir George Porter put it very well: "I have no doubt we will be successful in harnessing the sun's energy. . . . If sunbeams were weapons of war, we would have had solar energy centuries ago."

7–3   Geothermal and Wind Energy

Wind power   The power of the wind has been tapped for centuries. The windmills of the Netherlands are well known. In the mid-1800s they were widely used in the United States, but with steam engines and electrification they have all but disappeared.

To some (Heronemus 1972, 1972a, Clark 1973, 1974, McCaull 1973) wind is a major untapped source of unlimited, free, and clean energy. A joint National Science Foundation and National Aeronautics and Space Administration Committee suggests that by the year 2000, a major development program in wind power could provide electricity equivalent to the total amount consumed in the United States during 1970

(Clark 1973). Wind power expert Dr. William E. Heronemus (1972) calculates that 957 specially designed wind turbines could supply more than twice the additional electrical power needed by the state of Vermont between 1975 and 1990. He also suggests that a band of about 300,000 giant wind turbines (each about 850 feet high) from Texas to the Dakotas could provide half of the electrical needs in this country. For the heavily populated East Coast wind turbines could be floated on platforms off the Atlantic Coast. In this case the wind energy would probably be used to electrolyze water to produce hydrogen gas, which could be piped or shipped to land as fuel.

Like solar energy this source of power emits no pollution and allows us to escape the heat or entropy trap (Table 4–2). Windmills require even less commitment of land than solar energy. One environmental objection is the visual pollution from large towers dotting the landscape, especially in areas of high prevailing winds where they would be concentrated. Investigations must also be made to determine whether a number of wind turbines in one area could cause changes in the weather or affect migratory bird flight patterns. In addition, far too little information is available on the economic feasibility and net energy yield of these power sources.

One of the windmill's most long standing problems is how to store the energy for use when the wind isn't blowing. Today there are a number of solutions to this problem. For homes and small buildings wind energy can be stored by charging batteries, by producing hydrogen gas to be used as a fuel, or by using a flywheel similar to a spinning top or toy gyroscope. While spinning, the flywheel (a cheaper and more efficient method than battery storage) stores energy, which can be tapped as it "runs down" after the wind stops. A good home flywheel system could provide electrical power for a week of windless days (Clark 1973).

If the electricity were to be fed into the lines of an electric utility, energy from the wind could be stored by using it to pump water into a huge reservoir. The water would be released on windless days to operate an electric generator. Other proposals bypass the need for storage. For example, a series of windmills (probably on top of existing electric transmission towers) could be coupled directly to the regional utility power grid to provide a base of power with no fuel costs. On windless days the system could be augmented by other fuel sources. This approach is technologically and probably economically feasible today and could be developed within a short time.

Although the potential for use of wind power is great in many areas and its technology well-developed, industry and the federal government have shown little interest in developing it. In 1975 the amount requested for wind power research and development in the federal energy budget was only 0.4 percent of the total budget.

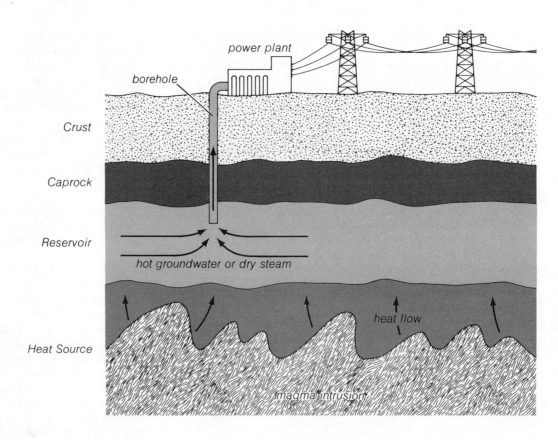

power plant

borehole

Crust

Caprock

**7–3   Schematic view of a
dry (steam) or wet (hot water
or brine plus steam) geothermal
well and power plant.**

Reservoir

hot groundwater or dry steam

heat flow

Heat Source

magma intrusion

Tapping the earth's heat: geothermal energy   Geothermal energy is produced when rocks lying several thousand feet below the earth's surface are heated to high temperatures by energy from the decay of radioactive elements in the earth and by nonradioactive materials such as magma or molten rock. When ground water comes into contact with these hot rock formations it can be heated to high temperatures and in some cases converted to steam. Natural crevices or man-made geothermal wells can then bring this steam or hot water to the surface. At least 80 nations have geological conditions favorable for tapping geothermal energy. Because it is cheap, almost inexhaustible, and relatively clean, it is being developed in some 25 countries including Kenya, Ethiopia, Chile, Turkey, Nicaragua, El Salvador, and Taiwan.[14]

There are three basic types of geothermal wells: (1) natural dry wells that contain superheated dry steam, (2) natural wet wells that contain a mixture of superheated water or brine (mineral laden water) and steam, and (3) man-induced hot rock wells where water is pumped into deliberately fractured layers of deep underground hot rocks, converted to steam,

and then brought to the surface by drilling another well nearby. Only the natural dry well can be easily and economically tapped at present (Figure 7–3).

A large natural dry steam well near Larderello, Italy, has been producing electricity since 1904 and is a major source of power for Italy's electric railroads. Two other major sites producing electricity from dry steam are at Matsukawa, Japan, and at the Geysers steam field located about 90 miles (145 kilometers) north of San Francisco. The Geysers field has been producing electricity since 1960 at costs lower than that for comparable fossil fuel and nuclear plants. Its production is being expanded each year and should be able to supply all of San Francisco's electrical needs by 1977 (Malin 1973). A dry geothermal plant can be put into operation in about three years compared to about 5 for a fossil fuel plant and 8 to 10 years for a nuclear plant.

Although little serious world-wide exploration has been undertaken, it appears that dry steam deposits are relatively rare. Wet (hot water or brine) geothermal fields are much more common. Electrical generating plants based on this type of deposit are found in New Zealand, Mexico, Japan, the Soviet Union, and in Reykjavik, Iceland. In Reykjavik geothermal hot water is pumped directly to hot water faucets and pipes are placed under the sidewalks so that snow melts immediately. Fruits and vegetables are grown in large greenhouses warmed

---

[14] The potential and problems of geothermal energy are discussed in Fenner & Klarman 1971, Malin 1973, Panel on Geothermal Energy Resources 1972, Hickel et al. 1972, Kruger & Otte 1972, Muffler 1973, Rex 1971, Barnea 1972, Robson 1974, Hammond et al. 1973, Chapter 9, Commoner et al. 1974, vol. 2.

by steam, to compensate for Iceland's short growing season. One expert (Rex 1971) estimates that the hot water geothermal resources below Southern California's Imperial Valley could produce enough electrical energy to meet the needs of the entire American Southwest for two or three centuries.

In wet fields, the steam is mixed with hot water or brine, which is laden with dissolved minerals. The steam must be separated from the hot water or a secondary system must be added so that the hot water is converted to steam or is used to vaporize another low boiling liquid that can then be used to drive a turbine. In addition, the mineral laden brine is highly corrosive to metal parts and must be disposed of without polluting nearby water sources—adding to the cost.

Another method now being tested avoids these problems completely. A heat exchanger containing a low boiling liquid (such as isobutane) is immersed in the underground well. The heat from the hot water is used to vaporize the liquid and it is brought to the surface to spin the turbine. Not only does this avoid corrosion and waste water problems, but it leaves the water and steam in the well for continual reheating rather than depleting the resource.

Geothermal wells could be created by drilling into hot rock formations deep below the earth's surface. Artificial cavities could be formed by conventional or nuclear explosives, and water could be circulated from the surface to extract heat from the rock. So far this method has not been developed because of uncertainties about economic feasibility and about the seismic effects of blast waves from the explosions needed to create the cavities.

A more promising version of the hot rock approach is being investigated by the Atomic Energy Commission's Los Alamos Scientific Laboratory in New Mexico (Hammond 1973). A well would be sunk as deep as 20,000 feet (6,600 meters) into underlying hot rock deposits. Cold water would then be fed into the area to crack the rocks and create a network of fissures in which water can circulate and be converted to high pressure steam. A second hole is then drilled and the superheated steam is brought to the surface. In 1974 the ability of cold water to fracture the rock was demonstrated in a test well. If this technique should become economically feasible the potential for the use of geothermal energy throughout the world could be greatly expanded. In the United States potential natural geothermal well sites are mostly confined to the West, but hot-rock formations less than 20,000 feet from the earth's surface probably occur in many regions.

Estimates of the potential for electrical energy from geothermal sources in the United States vary widely from about 0.5 percent to all of our projected electrical energy needs (Theobald et al. 1972, Hickel et al. 1972, Panel on Geothermal Energy Resources 1972, Kruger & Otte 1972, pp. 69–94, Muffler 1973, Robson 1974).

There are some environmental effects from geothermal energy, but most experts consider them to be more readily and cheaply managed than those from fossil fuels and nuclear

power (Table 4–2). Mineral laden water wastes are produced, but they can be reinjected into the deep wells or desalinated to produce water and minerals, which could be sold. The problem of deep well injection needs to be studied, but the injection of brine (as opposed to deadly chemical wastes) may help prevent subsidence (caving in) of fields by replacing some of the water that was removed. Air and odor pollution occurs in most wells from the traces of poisonous hydrogen sulfide (which smells like rotten eggs) and dirt particles that escape in the steam. This could be controlled by emission devices or eliminated by using the underground heat transfer system that avoids bringing the steam or hot water to the surface. Noise pollution also occurs from the ear-splitting hiss of escaping steam, but presumably such wells would not be located near populated areas. As with most energy sources waste heat injected to the atmosphere or bodies of cooling water is a problem (Section 8–5). But it is no greater for geothermal than for fossil fuel and nuclear plants.

Oil and energy companies are interested in developing geothermal sources. Unlike solar and wind energy, which anyone could theoretically tap into, rich geothermal deposits are located in specific underground areas just as fossil fuels are, so the fuel can be sold to customers on a continuing basis. Unlike coal and natural gas, geothermal heat can't be transported and sold in international markets. The potential for geothermal energy remains largely unknown and undeveloped in the United States for two major reasons. First, most rich geothermal deposits are on government owned lands, and until recently the government has been slow in leasing these lands to private companies for exploratory drilling and development. Second, the proposed budget for geothermal energy development for 1975, like that for solar energy, is only 2.5 percent of entire federal energy budget.

7–4 Energy Conservation: Our Most Important and Neglected Option

A tragic and unnecessary waste There are two basic approaches to the present and future energy crises—we can increase the supply or input or we can reduce input by cutting back on per capita energy use and by reducing wasteful uses of energy. It is clear that a massive program for energy conservation should form the basic foundation of any national energy policy.[15] Conservation would save enormous amounts

[15] For summaries of energy conservation see Hammond 1972a, 1974, Hirst 1973a, Hirst & Moyers 1973, Corr & MacLeod 1972, Makhijani & Lichtenberg 1972, Lincoln 1973, Holden 1973, Berg 1973, 1974, 1974a, Hyman 1973, Shell Oil Company 1973a, Office of Emergency Preparedness 1972, Large 1973, Hannon 1974, Rice 1974, Berry & Makino 1974, Novick 1973, Freeman 1971, Committee on Interior and Insular Affairs 1972, Meyer & Todd 1973, Concern, Inc. 1973, Mother Earth News 1974, Commoner et al. 1974, vol. 2.

of energy, reduce international tensions by making us less dependent on foreign imports of fossil fuels, reduce the number of fossil fuel and nuclear power plants we need to build, buy us much needed time to develop and evaluate alternate sources of energy, reduce pollution of our air, water, and land, reduce our balance of payments deficit, and save every individual and business considerable amounts of money.

In spite of much talk about conservation from federal officials and members of Congress, our present national energy policy commits its funding primarily to increasing output rather than conservation (Table 4–2). Over 50 percent of the energy used in this country is wasted (Figure 1–5) — much of it an unavoidable consequence of the second law of thermodynamics (Section 2–2). But with existing knowledge and technology and with little pain to industry or the consumer, at least 25 percent of all the energy used in this country could be conserved. An important but neglected study by the Office of Emergency Preparedness (1972) showed how we could save the equivalent of 7.3 million barrels of oil per day by 1980 — about two-thirds of projected oil imports. Although its recommendations would be the simplest, quickest, and cheapest method for approaching energy independence, very few have been incorporated into national energy policy. Another important study (Makhigani & Lichtenberg 1972) has shown how per capita energy consumption by the year 2000 could be reduced 38 percent below the 1968 level with no significant loss in amenities. These savings can be brought about by a series of changes in our energy use patterns.

Energy savings in transportation   Transportation accounts for about 25 percent of all energy use in the United States. Half of this is used by automobiles which with an overall efficiency of only 10 to 12 percent represent our most wasteful use of energy (Figure 4–3). Ways to reduce transportation energy waste include

1. Reduce the average car weight to 2,500 pounds or less. This would save 2.1 million barrels of oil per day by 1985 and cut our projected balance of payments deficit for 1985 by $2.3 billion (Hyman 1973, p. 7). Cutting the weight of an automobile from 5,000 to 2,500 pounds increases mileage per gallon by 100 percent. (By contrast, emission control devices reduce fuel economy by no more than 10 percent.)

2. Require all cars to get an average of 20 miles per gallon by 1978 and 26 miles per gallon by 1982.[16] Any car not meeting these minimum standards would be heavily taxed.

3. Increase federal funding for the development of new and more efficient engines (Figure 4–3). Provide tax credits for businesses using more efficient engine types, and require

that at least 50 percent of all government purchased cars use more efficient engines.

4. Organize car pools. Offer reduced tolls, free parking, and income tax deductions for those using car pools.

5. Increase the use of bus and rail transit for people and goods within and between cities.

6. Walk and ride bikes. Over 50 percent of all automobile trips in the country are less than 5 miles in length. In time trials comparing bikes and cars for urban trips averaging 5 miles, bicycles won 21 out of 25 races (Hyman 1973, p. 9). Bike paths or reserve lanes on major streets and highways should be required and supported by federal funding from the Highway Trust Fund.[17]

Energy savings in buildings and appliances   Residential and commercial energy consumption accounts for about 35 percent of the annual energy usage in the United States. The biggest energy uses in homes and commercial buildings are space heating (18 percent), water heating (4 percent), air conditioning (2.5 percent), refrigeration (2.2 percent), lighting (1.5 percent), cooking (1.3 percent), and clothes drying (1.1 percent). The Office of Emergency Preparedness (1972) reports that a 14.3 percent reduction in residential and commercial energy consumption could be attained with no inconvenience or hardship in daily life by 1980. This represents a 5.3 percent reduction in total national energy consumption. Over 50 percent of all the electricity used in the United States is used in the construction and operation of residential and commercial buildings. Architect Richard Stein (1972) estimates that at least 25 percent of this energy is wasted.[18] Simple and fairly obvious changes in architectural design, insulation, ventilation, and lighting of buildings could save 11 percent of the forecasted total energy use by 1980 (Office of Emergency Preparedness 1972).
A towering monument to energy waste is the new 110-story World Trade Center in lower Manhattan, which requires as much electricity each year as the entire city of Schenectady, New York, with 100,000 persons. Not a single window in its four towering walls of glass can be opened to take advantage of nature's warming and cooling. Major ways to reduce energy waste in buildings and appliances include:

1. Improve insulation. A minimum of 3.5 inches of wall insulation and 6 inches of ceiling insulation (with 10 inches or more recommended) would cut energy used for heating and

---

[16] Many cars imported into the United States today already meet this requirement.

[17] The extensive use of bicycles in many European cities shows that with careful planning the bicycle can become a significant factor in our urban transportation system.

[18] For more details on energy savings in building design and use see Large 1973, Wells 1973, Hammond 1974, Dubin 1972, Caudill et al. 1974, Rafalik 1974, Berg 1973, Commoner et al. 1974, vol. 3, Abrahamson & Emmings 1973.

cooling by 40 to 50 percent (Berg 1973). The added initial cost would be recouped within 3 years and thereafter savings would be significant. Minimum insulation standards should be required by law on all new constructions, and tax deductions should be allowed for up-grading insulation in existing homes and buildings.

2. Make use of better building design by proper placement with respect to the sun, use of natural ventilation,[19] reduced use of glass, and use of double-pane glass, storm windows, and reflective shades on windows. Year round use of storm windows and doors can save 15 to 20 percent of a house's heating energy and about 8 percent of its cooling energy.

3. Shift from electric heat to gas heat for homes. For space heating natural gas is more than twice as efficient as electricity (Figure 4–3), and a balanced gas-electric house (which uses gas for space heating, water heating, range, and dryer) reduces energy waste and fuel bills by about 40 percent. To make gas available for direct residential space heating it should be prohibited as a fuel to generate electricity in power and industrial plants, where the efficiency is only about one-third of its direct use for heating. Federal laws banning gas pilot lights on gas appliances and elimination of decorative outdoor gas lights would reduce residential use of natural gas by 20 percent and make it available for space heating.

4. Improve the efficiency of hot water heaters and shift to solar hot water heaters. Switching from electrical to gas water heaters (with electrical igniters instead of pilot lights) would increase efficiency. Solar water heaters could replace about half of all conventional water heaters with a saving of 2 percent of total national energy use (Berg 1973).

5. Reduce lighting levels and improve lighting. Recommended lighting levels in buildings have risen 300 percent in the past 15 years with no concrete evidence that such high and energy wasting levels are necessary or desirable. Reducing lighting levels by 50 percent, switching from incandescent to fluorescent lights (which are 4 times as efficient and last 7 to 10 times longer), and making better use of natural daylight could reduce total electricity use by 4 to 5 percent (Stein 1972). Individual light switches for all rooms should be required so that a janitor or late worker doesn't have to light up an entire floor in an office building in order to work.

6. Improve the efficiency of air conditioners, refrigerators, and other appliances. The efficiency of comparable air con-

ditioners vary by a factor of 3.[20] Frost-free refrigerators and side-by-side refrigerator-freezer units require about 50 percent more energy (and money) to operate than standard models. Color TV sets consume twice as much electricity as black and white models, and instant-on TVs and other electrical appliances consume electricity 24 hours a day.[21] Federal laws should require that all appliances meet a minimum energy efficiency requirement and that an energy efficiency rating be clearly displayed on each unit.

Energy savings in industry   Industry consumes more energy than any other sector of the American economy, accounting for 40 to 45 percent of total U.S. energy use. Two industrial uses, direct heating and steam production, account for about 27 percent of national fuel consumption—more than that used by all forms of transportation. The production of primary metals (especially iron, steel, and aluminum), basic chemicals, petroleum refining, textiles, food, paper, glass, and concrete use most of this energy. Berg (1973) estimates that approximately 30 percent of this energy could be saved by applying known conservation techniques to industrial processes.[22] Major ways to reduce energy waste in industry are

1. Convert to more efficient equipment and processes. For example, the aluminum industry, which accounts for 7 percent of all electrical energy use and 4 percent of all industrial energy use, has developed a new process that reduces electrical use by 40 to 70 percent.

2. Initiate crash research programs on improving the energy efficiency of existing processes and developing new, more efficient processes.

3. Extend the useful life of all products by a minimum of a factor of 2, probably by banning harmful or wasteful products and adding a disposal or recovery tax to all products not lasting longer than 10 years.

---

[19] When windows cannot be opened the movement of air must be done by mechanical ventilation systems, which account for 10 percent of the electricity used in high-rise commercial buildings and 5 percent of their total energy consumption.

[20] To determine efficiency, divide the BTU per hour rating (listed on the back of the air conditioner) by the number of watts input. Values will range from 4.7 to 12.2. The higher the number the higher the efficiency. The most efficient units are the larger sizes (more than 10,000 BTU per hour) that use 115 volt (not 220 volt) current. Paying a somewhat higher price for a more efficient unit will save money in a short time by reducing electrical bills and in the process reduce national electrical waste and pollution. This efficiency check can also be used for electric clothes dryers.

[21] If you have any instant-on appliances turn them on and off using the plug or deactivate using the switch frequently found on the back.

[22] Because fuel costs average less than 5 percent of industry's total expenses, rising fuel costs alone may not be enough to trigger replacement or upgrading of energy wasting equipment and processes. However, corporate management can respond to energy conservation measures more rapidly than individual consumers and a federal bureaucracy.

4. Promote extensive recycling. Steel made from scrap in an electric furnace requires only about one-fourth the energy of steel made from virgin ore. Provide economic incentives and favorable transportation rates for secondary (recycled) materials industries and users, require that all materials purchased by government agencies use an average of 50 percent recycled material, and impose a manufacturing tax on all energy intensive products. Virgin materials may have to be taxed to slow down their use and favor recycled materials.

5. Ban advertising by utility and energy companies that promotes the use of electricity or fossil fuels.

6. Reverse the electricity rate structure, which encourages increased and wasteful use of electricity by providing cheaper rates for the largest users. Now, rising fuel costs penalize the poor and the middle class, who should receive the lowest not the highest rates.

7. Increase electrical rates during peak load seasons such as hot summer months and between 4 and 9 P.M. to shift some of the electrical load and to reduce waste. The size and number of electrical power plants is determined by peak loads not by average daily or annual use.

For the individual,[23] for business, and for the nation, conservation is not only a major energy option but is also the quickest and cheapest option available. One of the most important energy issues is why it hasn't become a major part of our national energy policy.

A country that runs on energy cannot afford to waste it.

Bruce Hannon

Discussion Topics

1. Contrast fossil fuel, conventional fission, breeder (Chapter 6), fusion, geothermal, and solar power plants in terms of (a) how they work, (b) their environmental impact, and (c) their technological problems.

---

[23] Individuals who wish to become self-sufficient in energy should consult Hammond 1974, Mother Earth News 1974, and Commoner et al. 1974, vol. 3. Unfortunately, some measure of independence from rising energy costs is feasible primarily for the rich and those living in rural areas. Urban dwellers will find it difficult to get chicken manure to fuel their cars, to install a windmill or solar collector for their apartments or offices, or to start compost heaps and organic gardens on the roofs of their buildings.

2. Criticize the following statements:

a. A nuclear fusion plant can blow up like a hydrogen bomb.

b. Nuclear fusion plants could release large amounts of radioactive materials.

c. Solar power plants shouldn't be developed because they will take up 10 percent of the desert area in the United States.

d. Development of solar and wind energy should be left up to private enterprise rather than the federal government.

e. Windpower is not feasible at present.

f. Natural dry geothermal fields offer a clean and abundant source of energy.

g. Electric toothbrushes and carving knives waste large amounts of energy and should be abolished.

h. Emission controls on cars are the major culprit in reduced gas mileage and should not be required on new cars.

i. A requirement of 26 miles per gallon for all cars is unreasonable and should not be required by law.

3. Fusion, solar, geothermal, wind energy, and conservation are all proposed as significant and less harmful energy sources than fossil fuel and nuclear fission energy. Assuming this is valid, explain in each case why they haven't been developed. Outline a plan for their development.

4. Outline the major advantages and disadvantages of nuclear fusion, solar energy, wind power, and geothermal energy. In each case explain how they are limited by the first and second laws of thermodynamics. How do these limitations compare with those on fossil fuel and nuclear fission energy?

5. Distinguish between direct use of solar energy as heat, its conversion into electricity, and solar power from ocean thermal gradients. Which is the most promising and has the least environmental impact?

6. Distinguish between the three types of geothermal energy wells in terms of their operation, potential availability, and environmental impact.

7. Explain why energy conservation should form the basis of any individual, corporate, or national energy plan. Does it form a significant portion of your personal energy plan or lifestyle? Why or why not? Is it a significant factor in our national energy policy? Why?

8. Outline major ways to conserve energy in transportation, in appliances, and in the construction and use of homes and buildings.

9. Draw up a personal energy conservation plan. Outline a plan for your own personal energy self-sufficiency by 1985 (see Hammond 1974 and Mother Earth News 1974).

10. Make an energy use study of your campus or school, and use the findings to develop an energy conservation program.

Further Reading

Clark, Wilson. 1974. *Energy for Survival: The Alternative to Extinction.* New York: Doubleday Anchor. Superb discussion of alternative.

Clark, Wilson. 1973. "Interest in Wind is Picking Up as Fuels Dwindle," *Smithsonian,* 4:8, 70–78, November. Outstanding nontechnical summary of wind power potential.

Gough, William C., and Bernard J. Eastlund. 1971. "The Prospects of Fusion Power," *Scientific American,* February, pp. 56–64. Superb overview.

Halacy, D. S., Jr. 1973. *The Coming Age of Solar Energy.* 2nd Ed. New York: Harper & Row. One of the best summaries.

Hammond, Allen L. 1974. "Individual Self-Sufficiency in Energy," *Science,* vol. 184, 278–282. Excellent overview of how one can become independent from the utility and oil companies.

Hammond, Allen L., William D. Metz, and Thomas H. Maugh, II. 1973. *Energy and the Future.* Washington, D.C.: American Association for the Advancement of Science. Outstanding description and evaluation of all major energy options at a slightly higher technical level. Highly recommended.

Hannon, Bruce. 1974. "Options for Energy Conservation," *Technology Review,* February, pp. 24–31. Superb overview.

Heronemus, W. E. 1972. "The United Energy Crisis: Some Proposed Gentle Solutions," paper presented at the joint meeting of the American Society of Mechanical Engineers and the Institute of Electrical and Electronics Engineers, West Springfield, Mass., Jan. 12. Available from the author. University of Massachusetts, Amherst, Mass. 01002.

Hirst, Eric, and John C. Moyers. 1973. "Efficiency of Energy Use in the United States," *Science,* vol. 179, 1299–1304. Results of Oak Ridge study showing how we can greatly reduce our waste of energy.

Holden, Constance. 1973. "Energy: Shortages Loom, but Conservation Lags," *Science,* vol. 180, 1155–1158. Superb overview of methods for energy conservation.

Hyman, Barry I. 1973. *Initiatives in Energy Conservation.* Staff Report prepared for the Committee on Commerce, United States Senate. Washington, D.C.: Government Printing Office. Stock No. 5270–01960. One of the best summaries available. Highly recommended.

Large, David B. 1973. *Hidden Waste: Potentials for Energy Conservation.* Washington, D.C.: The Conservation Foundation. Excellent summary.

Lidsky, Lawrence M. 1972. "The Quest for Fusion Power," *Technology Review,* January, pp. 10–21. Outstanding summary of nuclear fusion energy.

McCaull, Julian. 1973. "Windmills," *Environment,* January–February, 6–17. (Jan./Feb.) Excellent overview of potential of wind power.

Makhigani, A. B., and A. J. Lichtenberg. 1972. "Energy and Well-Being," *Environment,* June, pp. 11–18. How we can reduce our per capita energy use by almost 40 percent by the year 2000.

Malin, H. M. 1973. "Geothermal Heats Up," *Environmental Science and Technology,* 7:8, 680–681, August. Superb summary.

Meinel, Aden B., and Marjorie P. Meinel. 1971. "Is It Time for a New Look at Solar Energy?" *Bulletin of the Atomic Scientists,* October, pp. 32–37. How we can build large scale solar energy power plants in the desert now.

Office of Emergency Preparedness. 1972. *The Potential for Energy Conservation.* Washington, D.C.: Government Printing Office. Stock No. 4102–00009. One of the most important and neglected government documents published in the last decade. Extensive bibliography.

Robson, Geoffrey R. 1974. "Geothermal Electricity Production," *Science,* vol. 184, 371–375. Excellent overview of potential.

Stein, Richard G. 1972. "A Matter of Design," *Environment,* October, pp. 17–29. How better building design could reduce our use of electricity by at least 25 percent.

Tamplin, Arthur R. 1973. "Solar Energy," *Environment,* June, 16–34. Probably the single best summary of the potential and methods for utilizing solar energy. Good bibliography.

Wells, Malcolm B. 1973. "Confessions of a Gentle Architect," *Environmental Quality,* July, pp. 51–57. A magnificent article showing how an architect or home builder can work with nature.

Our knowledge about global climate can be summed up in one word—ignorance.

Anonymous

8

Energy Use, Heat, and Climate: The Ultimate Problem

8-1   Climate and Human Activities

Potential impact   Until recently it was assumed that human impact on global and regional climatic patterns was negligible compared to changes from natural phenomena such as volcanic eruptions and forest fires. Despite our general lack of accurate knowledge about global climate there is some tentative evidence that human activities are already affecting local climates and may affect regional and even global climatic patterns in the future. There are several ways in which these activities could alter regional and global climate (MacDonald 1969, 1971, Bryson 1968, 1974, Hobbs et al. 1974, Fleagle 1969, Fletcher 1969, Kellogg & Robinson 1971, Landsberg 1970a, SCEP 1970, SMIC 1971, Singer 1970):

1. Increasing the carbon dioxide content of the atmosphere by burning fossil fuels (Brown 1971, Manabe 1971, Peterson 1969, Plass 1959).
2. Decreasing atmospheric transparency by injecting particulate matter (dust, sulfates, liquid droplets) into the atmosphere from industry, automobiles, space heating, agriculture, and land clearing activities (Bryson & Petersen 1968, Rasool & Schneider 1971, Watt 1972).
3. Changing the *albedo* (the percentage of incoming solar radiation that is directly reflected outward) of the earth's surface through irrigation, urbanization, deforestation, and agriculture.
4. Direct heating of the atmosphere by burning fossil and nuclear fuels (Budyko 1970, 1972, Petersen 1973, Harte & Socolow 1971, Holdren 1971, MacDonald 1972, Washington 1972, Sellers 1970, Weinberg & Hammond 1972).
5. Altering the rate of thermal energy transfer between the oceans and the atmosphere by oil films from spills and blowouts (Section 5-3).

8-2   Carbon Dioxide and the Greenhouse Effect: Is the Atmosphere Warming?

Carbon dioxide levels are increasing   Carbon dioxide (CO_2) is a normal component of the atmosphere, and until recently has not been considered an air pollutant.

Average global CO_2 concentrations have been increasing since 1860, with a sharp increase since 1940 and an even sharper increase since 1958. During the past 100 years the CO_2 content of the atmosphere has risen almost 10 percent, from around 290 parts per million by volume (ppm) to its present value of about 323 ppm (Callendar 1958, Bolin & Bischoff 1971). Calculations based on a crude model of the atmosphere (Machta 1971) indicate that the CO_2 level could rise to around 375 to 384 ppm by the year 2000—a 20 percent increase over 1958 levels.

The oceans, as part of the carbon cycle, dissolve about one-third to one-half of any carbon dioxide within 2 to 5 years after it is injected into the atmosphere (Manabe & Bryan 1969, Berger & Libby 1969). Without this major sink, the global values would have increased up to twice as much. Excess CO_2 could also be removed to a lesser extent over relatively short periods by increasing the amount of trees and green plants on earth, but of course man is doing the opposite by clearing more and more land for agriculture, housing, and industrialization. Even if this were not the case we would need to add almost 3 billion acres of new forest (greater than the area of the United States) each year to absorb the man-made additions of CO_2. It is highly improbable that we can devise a method for removing CO_2 from the atmosphere, and CO_2 levels will continue to rise as more and more fossil fuels are burned.

The greenhouse effect   Although the carbon dioxide content of the atmosphere is only about 0.032 percent, it is a major factor in determining average global temperature, in what is known as the *greenhouse effect*. Incoming sunlight consists of many wavelengths including ultraviolet, visible, and near infrared radiation (Figure 3-1). But ozone in the upper atmosphere filters out most of the shorter wavelength ultraviolet light, and water vapor and CO_2 in the atmosphere absorb much of the incoming infrared radiation. So mostly visible light reaches the earth. It is absorbed by land, sea, and cloud portions of the earth's surface and is reradiated into the atmosphere as longer wavelength infrared (IR) radiation, or heat, as the earth cools (Figure 3-1).

At this point we encounter the greenhouse effect. Much of this IR radiation is absorbed by carbon dioxide.[1] The

---

[1] Water vapor and ozone also absorb IR radiation, but since their concentrations are not being altered appreciably by man they do not enter into this discussion.

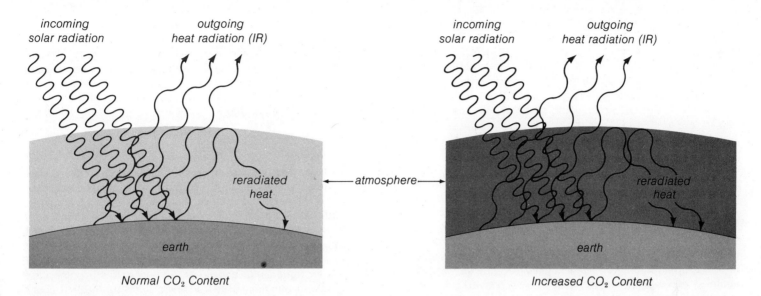

8–1   *The greenhouse effect. Short wavelength solar radiation strikes the earth and is transformed into longer wavelength heat radiation, some of which is absorbed and reradiated back to the earth by the CO_2 in the atmosphere. As CO_2 content increases more heat is retained and the atmosphere becomes warmer.*

carbon dioxide then radiates a portion of absorbed heat energy back to the earth so that some of the heat that would normally be lost fairly rapidly to space is reradiated to warm the atmosphere (Figure 8–1).

Somewhat like the glass in a greenhouse or a car window[2] on a sunny day the CO_2 (along with water vapor and several other substances) acts as a one-way filter that allows visible light to enter but prevents longer wavelength heat radiation from leaving. Assuming that energy is arriving at a constant rate from the sun and that the earth's albedo (reflectivity) is constant, then as the level of CO_2 increases the average global surface temperature should rise. In accordance with the first law of thermodynamics (Section 2–1) energy input equals output over time, but the wavelengths of input and output differ as solar energy is degraded to heat in accordance with the second law (Section 2–2 and Figure 3–3).

Possible effects on climate   This possible effect of CO_2 on the earth's climate was first suggested in 1863 by J. Tyndall, but the question was ignored until 1956 with the work of G. N. Plass. Probably the best mathematical model for projecting future changes in CO_2 content is that of S.

Manabe and R. T. Wetherald (1967, Manabe 1971). They found that the projected increase in CO_2 concentration from 320 to 375 ppm between 1967 and 2000 could cause the average air temperature near the earth to increase about 0.5°C, (0.9°F),[3] assuming that relative humidity and other factors remain constant. A doubling of CO_2 levels, which with increasing fossil fuel consumption might occur by 2050, could raise the average temperature by about 2°C (3.6°F).

A 1° to 2°C change would significantly modify global climate. It could trigger the relatively rapid melting of the floating Arctic ice pack, which by decreasing the albedo could cause further warming (SMIC 1971, pp. 125–129, 159–161). Eventually glaciers and even Antarctic ice might slowly melt,[4] further decreasing the earth's albedo since ice has a higher reflectivity than land. Another self-amplifying or runaway effect could occur because the solubility of carbon dioxide in the ocean decreases with increasing temperature, thus releasing even more CO_2, which would raise temperatures further. Once set in motion these self-amplifying changes would be irreversible and probably would last for millions of years.

---

[3] 1°C = 1.8°F.
[4] Some scientists, however, suggest that melting the Arctic ice pack could have the reverse effect, triggering a new ice age instead of massive melting and flooding. In other words, we know relatively little about this complex matter, and climate change predictions are subject to considerable disagreement.

---

[2] Strictly speaking the term *greenhouse effect* is misleading. A greenhouse, or a closed car on a sunny day, not only traps heat energy but also reduces heat exchange with the wind.

Gradual melting of the land-based Antarctic ice could eventually raise world sea levels 200 to 300 feet. This would flood about 20 percent of the planet's present land area including most of the world's major population centers and the flood plains that produce most of our food. Despite stories in the popular press predicting imminent global flooding, this process, if it occurred, would probably take place very slowly over at least 1,000 years.

Melting of the Arctic ice cap and the glaciers, however, could be much more rapid. Since the Arctic ice pack is afloat, its melting would *not* raise the water level in the oceans. But the absence of polar ice would change ocean currents and undoubtedly would trigger major unpredictable changes in climate. Subpolar regions would probably become warmer, and weather in many other parts of the world (including the United States) would become much drier (Fletcher 1969), thus affecting water supplies and food growing capacity.

According to this "greenhouse model," the earth's average temperature should have increased by about 0.2°C because of the increase in CO_2 between 1860 and the present. But facts run counter to these predictions. Between 1880 and 1940 the average global temperature rose about 0.6°C, but it has fallen about 0.3°C since 1945 (SMIC 1971, p. 42)—the period of greatest expansion in the burning of fossil fuels.

8–3   Particles in the Atmosphere: Is the Atmosphere Cooling?

Other possible climatic factors   Obviously there must be additional man-made or natural factors affecting global climate patterns. For example, the concentration of water vapor, ozone, and the average degree of cloud cover also have major effects on the global heat balance. Since water vapor content and cloud cover vary considerably with location and time, we have no reliable measurements indicating whether they have decreased or increased on the average. Möller (1963) estimates that a 10 percent increase in CO_2 could be counterbalanced by a 3 percent increase in water vapor content or a 1 percent increase in average cloudiness.

Other scientists (SMIC, 1971, pp. 114–122), however, indicate that increasing water vapor content would enhance the greenhouse effect because water is also an infrared absorber like CO_2. They also point out that changes in the amount of cloud cover or cloud height could either decrease or increase mean temperatures. Increased low-level cloudiness tends to increase albedo and thus cool the atmosphere by decreasing the amount of solar radiation reaching the earth's surface (Bryson 1968). On the other hand, increased high-level cloudiness reduces radiative heat loss to space and tends to warm the earth. The balance between the two opposing tendencies depends on the type and height of the

clouds, and it is not presently possible to determine which tendency predominates.

It has also been assumed that the intensity of solar radiation reaching the earth's surface has remained constant since 1860. This may not be the case. No one really knows if any of these factors have affected the changes in global temperature since 1860.

Particle pollution—a new ice age?   Some scientists feel that a new ice age rather than a flood is more likely. They suggest that the atmosphere may be cooling rather than heating because of increased amounts of dust, soot, and other solid and liquid particles being injected into the atmosphere by natural causes such as salt sea spray, volcanoes, forest fires, and dust storms and by man-made sources such as smokestacks, automobiles, and the burning and clearing of land for agricultural and urban purposes. It is hypothesized that about one-third of the warming trend up to 1940 could be the result of the greenhouse effect, while the drop in temperature since 1940 could result from decreased atmospheric transparency as increased particulate levels more than compensate for the increase in CO_2 concentration. If mean global temperature were to drop only 2° to 3.5°C and be maintained for several years, a new ice age could be triggered (SCEP 1970, pp. 10, 220, Rasool & Schneider 1971). Again a runaway process could occur because as the ice caps enlarged they would increase the earth's reflectivity, lowering temperatures even more.

How reasonable is this hypothesis? In general, atmospheric transparency increased between 1886 and 1940 and has decreased since that time (Budyko 1970). As you might imagine accurate determination of average global transparency is exceedingly difficult even with modern methods. Furthermore, atmospheric transparency is not solely a function of particulate levels. It is also affected by the percentage of cloud cover, water vapor concentration, and other poorly understood factors.

Furthermore, the idea that particulates serve only to decrease atmospheric temperature is not necessarily valid. They can raise or lower the temperature depending on their size, reflective properties, and height in the atmosphere. If the dust is "whiter" than the normal atmospheric cover, it will reflect more incoming solar radiation and cause a drop in average temperature. If the dust is "blacker," it absorbs heat energy and radiates it back toward the earth, thus raising the temperature (Landsberg 1970a). In reality both processes are occurring, and the net effect depends on the balance between the two opposing tendencies and the height of the dust layer. If the layer is high enough, then the cooling process probably dominates and average temperatures near the earth's surface drop (SMIC 1971, p. 220).

There are also disagreements over whether man is the major source of atmospheric particulates. Present estimates indicate that between 5 and 45 percent of all atmospheric particulate matter is produced by man (SMIC 1971, p. 187). Natural injection totals 773 million to 2.2 billion metric tons per year, while man-made emissions total 185 to 415 million metric tons per year. Approximately 50 to 70 percent of the man-made emissions are sulfate particles from fossil fuel power plants. This massive injection almost equals sulfate emissions from natural sources and represents a major intrusion into the sulfur cycle.

Most particulate emissions near the earth's surface have a residence time of days to a few weeks before they fall out or are washed out by rain. Although they can have significant effect on local weather patterns they are not a major factor in global climate. On the other hand, very small particles that rise or are injected into the stratosphere have a residence time of 1 to 5 years and can affect global climate. It is argued that since most man-made particulates are injected into the lower atmosphere, their climatic effects are primarily local rather than global.

SSTs and the environment—glimmerings of ecological sanity   Recently there has been concern that man might increase the particulate, water vapor, and especially nitrogen oxide inputs into the stratosphere by the development of a world-wide fleet of supersonic transport planes (SSTs). Although we do not know enough to predict the effects of these emissions into the stratosphere, they could not only affect global climate but also partially deplete the ozone that protects us from harmful and eventually lethal wavelengths of ultraviolet radiation.[5] Harold Johnston (1972), a leading authority in atmospheric chemistry, has projected that 500 SSTs could halve the amount of ozone in the atmosphere within a time as short as 1 year. One possible effect could be an increase in skin cancer from the higher levels of harmful ultraviolet radiation.

An international team of atmospheric scientists (SMIC 1971, pp. 262–275) recommended that no large scale operation of SSTs in the stratosphere be allowed until further research determines their effects. A study panel of the National Academy of Sciences (1972a) found that these predictions could be off by a factor of 10 *either way*. Nevertheless, they found Johnston's arguments credible and expressed "general agreement" that nitrogen oxides from SSTs "can have important effects on the ozone concentration." They also pointed out that a 5 percent decline in ozone would produce at least 8,000 additional cases of skin cancer per year among the U.S. white population.

The SST program is a prime example of "frontier" as opposed to "earthmanship" thinking—doing something merely because it is technologically feasible. It is a very expensive program that will benefit only the affluent few while millions suffer from inadequate food, housing, and health care. Fortunately, the U.S. Congress abolished the taxpayers' support of this program in spite of intense presidential and industrial pressure. This defeat may be one of the most significant and hopeful political and ecological events of the twentieth century. It marked the first time that an industrialized society refused to develop a technology just because it could be done. Even if further research shows the risk for climate change and ozone depletion[6] to be negligible, this program should have a very low global, national, and human priority.

8–4   Heat: The Ultimate Pollutant

To exist is to heat the atmosphere   Take a breath, raise your arm, turn on a light, drive a car, air condition your house or car, and you add heat to the environment. To exist is to produce waste heat and to exist in an industrial society is to inject enormous amounts of heat into the environment.[7] No technological or scientific breakthrough can be expected to repeal the laws of thermodynamics (Section 2–2).

The man-induced thermal load on the environment depends on three factors—the number of energy users, their per capita energy use, and the thermodynamic efficiency of the energy conversion processes. The second law limits our ability to increase thermodynamic efficiency. Thus, as long as population and per capita energy consumption increase, heat is the ultimate pollutant for any closed system.

Such thermal pollution of the atmosphere is already altering the weather of urban regions (Lowry 1967, Petersen 1969) and could alter regional and world-wide climate patterns directly from the heat producing activities of man or from the combined effects of heat and increasing CO_2 content. What is the heat limit of the earth's atmosphere? How long might it take for man to reach this limit? Again we have no precise answers to these complex and important questions, but we can make some crude estimates.

---

[5] One primary earthmanship rule is that we should never do anything that could potentially upset the life saving ozone layer. In 1974 researchers (Cicerone et al. 1974) warned that the gradual atmospheric buildup of freon from aerosol spray cans and leaking refrigerants from air conditioners could reduce the ozone layer by 10% within 50 years.

[6] Noise pollution and damage from excess takeoff noise and sonic booms are also problems, but they are less serious than potential global climate changes. Noise levels could probably be reduced with increased costs and improved technology.

[7] For example, one human being at rest emits about 113,000 calories of heat energy per hour. A 4,000 pound automobile traveling at 70 miles per hour emits about 188,000 calories per hour. Refining 1 barrel of crude oil emits about 38,000,000 calories.

Table 8–1   Increase in man's energy consumption and environmental heat load

Cultural stage of man	Per capita energy use (kcal per day)	Per capita continuous heat load (watts)
Early hunter–gatherer	2,000	100
Advanced hunter–gatherer	4,000	200
Primitive agricultural	12,000	600
Advanced agricultural	25,000	1,250
Early industrial	70,000	3,500
World average in 1972*	40,000	2,000
World average in 2000	100,000?	5,000?
Modern industrial:		
U.S. citizen in 1972	250,000	12,500
U.S. citizen in 2000	1,250,000?	62,500?

Source: Cook 1971, MacDonald 1972.

* The figure is lower because most of the world still exists at an intermediate agricultural level, with about 30 percent at the modern industrial level.

Global heat limit   An adult living on a diet of about 2,000 kilocalories per day radiates heat continuously at about the same rate as a hundred-watt light bulb.[8] As shown in Table 8–1 the heat load from early man as a hunter–gatherer to advanced industrial man in the United States in 1972 increased over 100-fold, and this level could increase by a factor of 5 or more before the year 2000. When we consider all direct and indirect energy uses, each American is now injecting a heat load into the environment equivalent to 125 hundred-watt light bulbs burning continuously. And energy use in the United States is rising rapidly (Figure 1–3).

How does this man-induced heat input compare with the portion of incoming solar energy that affects the heat balance of the earth? Although man's input seems large it represents only about 0.005 to 0.01 percent of the net solar input,[9] so that at present the sun's contribution to our heat load is 10,000 to 20,000 times that of man (Holdren 1971, Weinberg & Hammond 1972, Brown 1971).

Many meteorologists (Budyko 1970, 1972, Sellers 1970, 1973, Ferguson 1968) feel that global climate could be

seriously affected if man's input ever reaches 0.5 to 1 percent of the solar contribution. World-wide energy consumption is presently increasing at about 5 to 6 percent per year, corresponding to a doubling time of 12 to 14 years. At a 6 percent rate, we would reach the 0.5 percent limit in about 80 years and the 1 percent limit in 92 years (Holdren 1971, Weinberg & Hammond 1972). If we consider the radiation balance only over land areas rather than the entire earth's surface climate could be affected within 60 years. If energy use grows at about 5 percent per year then a noticeable global climatic warming would probably occur within 100 to 125 years (Petersen 1973, Budyko 1972).

Let's look at these projections in a different way. Suppose we have a world population of 7 billion and we somehow bring the average energy use for the entire world up to the present U.S. rate of about 12,500 watts per person. This would still represent only about 0.08 percent of the solar input. A population of 15 billion living at a per capita energy consumption of 25,000 watts, twice the present U.S. rate, would yield about 0.35 percent of the solar input. Using only land masses of the earth's surface, however, this population of four times our present one would probably reach the limit for climate effects.

Thus, we can see that changes in the global climate solely from man's heat producing activities are not an immediate environmental problem. They could become a problem, however, in 60 to 200 years (perhaps somewhat sooner if the heat and carbon dioxide effects interact to raise the average global temperature).

8–5   Thermal Water Pollution

A growing problem   Thermal water pollution[10] occurs when water needed for cooling industrial plants, especially fossil fuel and nuclear power plants, is withdrawn from a lake, river, or other body of water and returned to that body at such a high temperature that undesirable ecological changes occur in the aquatic system (the second law again). Again judgments of what constitutes undesirable ecological change differ. Environmentalists tend to speak of adding heat to bodies of water as *thermal pollution,* while some industrialists and others see some potential benefits and speak of it as *thermal enrichment.*[11]

By 1990 power plants will require an estimated 470 billion gallons of water per day for cooling. A single 1,000 megawatt plant requires about 500,000 gallons of cooling water per minute—equivalent to the gross water usage of the city of

[8] A kilocalorie (abbreviated kcal) equals 1,000 calories. Thus, a daily energy diet of 2,000 kcal equals 2,000,000 calories. Power is the rate of energy use, or the work done per unit of time. An energy input of about 2,000 kcal per day represents a heat output of about 25 calories per second, or 100 watts.

[9] The large variation in these estimates results from our lack of knowledge and from the use of different definitions of net solar input. For calculations in this section the lower value of 0.005 percent is assumed.

[10] Good summaries of thermal pollution are found in Schurr 1971, Cairns 1971, 1972, Clark 1969, Brown 1971, Mihursky 1967, Staff report 1970a, 1973a, U.S. Department of Interior 1968a, Brook & Baker 1972.

[11] "Heat Pollution or Enrichment?" *Industrial Research,* July 1968, p. 51.

Chicago. Since average stream flow in the United States is about 1,200 billion gallons per day, we can see why many are concerned about thermal pollution. Although some cooling will be done with lake water instead of stream water, at least 25 percent of all freshwater flow in the country will be used to cool power plants by the year 2000. This percentage could double during the summer or whenever stream flow is greatly reduced. These averages, however, mask the fact that some streams because of their location will be intensely heated while other isolated ones may receive little heating. And although the average temperature increase of a body may not be too high, most of the hot water will be discharged near the shoreline. In a lake the shoreline zone is where fish spawn and young fish spend their first few weeks. Both spawning ability and young fish are especially susceptible to temperature increases.

We also have the problem of the threshold effect. One or several power plants may use a given body of water without serious damage—thus giving the misleading impression that others can be built. Eventually the operation of one additional plant can completely disrupt the system as its threshold level is exceeded.

Undesirable effects   Excess heat in an aquatic ecosystem can produce many harmful effects. The most dangerous threat is degradation of the ecosystem, which may occur so slowly that the effects will not be apparent for a number of years. Other detrimental effects are:

1. Thermal shock—the sudden death of aquatic life from sharply increased or decreased temperature. Thermal tolerance varies widely not only with different species but also by the stage of life. Heat shock can occur for existing species when the plant opens but new heat resistant species that take their place could be completely disrupted when a nuclear plant periodically shuts down for fuel replacement or repair and the temperature suddenly drops.

2. Increased susceptibility of aquatic organisms to parasites, disease, and chemical toxins.

3. Disruption of migration patterns.

4. Decreased oxygen concentrations at a time when increased temperature raises the organisms' need for oxygen.

5. Enhanced eutrophication rate from increased temperature and decreased oxygen content, which encourages growth of undesirable blue-green algae.

6. Decreased spawning success and survival of young fish with less temperature tolerance.

7. Disruption of food chain by loss of one or several key species, especially plankton, at lower levels of the food chain.

8. Shift of species composition toward less desirable species. Fishing may increase near power plants, but usually only less desirable fish can survive in the heated water. Two of the most heat tolerant organisms are blue-green algae and stinging nettles.

Other problems are indirectly related to the use of cooling water, but not caused by heat. For instance, some fish kills and other effects may be caused by the chlorine or copper sulfate used as a biocide in the nuclear plant cooling system to avoid fouling of pipes by bacteria and other growths.

Beneficial effects   Not all effects of thermal addition are bad. Warmer water can lengthen commercial fishing seasons and increase catches by attracting warm water species (frequently less desirable species) to heated areas, reduce winter ice cover, and increase the recreational use of very cold water bodies. In some locations the hot water could be used to cultivate catfish, shrimp, carp, and other desirable food species and perhaps to irrigate croplands (Carter 1969a). Although aquaculture won't be viable for some plants because of climate, chemical content of the water, or other conditions, it could be used in numerous areas if it proves to be economically feasible (Lee 1972). This potential use of heated water should be considered in the siting of all future nuclear power plants.

Although it is difficult, heated water from a power plant could also be used to heat buildings and domestic water supplies, to remove snow, to desalt ocean and brackish water, and to provide heat for some chemical and industrial processes. To be used for these purposes, however, nuclear plants would have to be located near urban centers, which would increase the danger to humans if a nuclear accident ever occurred.

Some possible solutions   The sites of most existing and future power plants, however, make them unsuitable for making use of their enormous outputs of hot water. This leaves us with several alternatives.

Input Approaches

1. Decrease our wasteful and growing use of energy (Chapter 7).

2. Strictly limit the number of power and industrial plants (if any) allowed to use a given body of water.

Table 8–2   *Man and energy flow in the ecosphere*

Man's activities	Probable effects	Present area of impact	Years before global impact	Potential for controlling
Burning of fossil fuels	Warming due to greenhouse effect	Local and regional	100–200	Poor
Release of particulate matter	Cooling	Local and regional	100–200	Fair to poor
Stratospheric injections from jet aircraft, especially SSTs	Cooling, partial destruction of ozone layer	Negligible	30–100	Good
Freon from aerosol sprays and refrigeration units	Partial destruction of ozone layer	Negligible	20–30	Good to fair
Clearing land, diverting waters, building dams	Variable	Local and regional	100–200	Fair to poor
Building cities	Heating	Local and regional	100–200	Fair to poor
Man-generated heat	Heating	Local and regional	100–200	Poor

Output Approaches

1. Return heated water in a way that minimizes damage (for instance, away from the fragile shore zone).

2. Dissipate some of the heat in man-made cooling ponds or canals (applicable only where ample land is available at a reasonable cost).

3. Transfer heat to the air either by evaporation (wet cooling towers) or by conduction and convection (dry cooling towers). A typical cooling tower may rise as high as a thirty-story building and measure more than a block in diameter at its base.

Perhaps the real question we should ask ourselves is whether we really need all of this electricity.

8–6   Needed: A Global Plan

Even the scanty evidence we have shows that man is already drastically affecting energy flow and climate in urban areas and that more serious regional effects may occur in the near future. Man also has the potential to alter global climate within perhaps 20 to 200 years. Steps for prevention must begin now because such changes, if initiated, would be essentially irreversible for thousands of years. A summary of man's effects on energy flow in the ecosphere is given in Table 8–2.

As a top priority we need to develop a global plan of research and sophisticated computer simulation of climatic effects. This should be coupled with a world-wide atmospheric monitoring system, using satellite reconnaissance and rapid analysis of the vast amounts of data this program will generate.

If this research indicates that man is modifying global climate, then we may have to consider reducing the burning of fossil fuels, limiting the use of automobiles with internal combustion engines, not building SSTs, reducing energy use, and preventing the formation of megalopolises. In effect we would have to institute "entropy rationing" that would limit man's heat and pollution producing activities.

When you understand all about the sun and all about the atmosphere and all about the rotation of the earth, you may still miss the radiance of the sunset.

Alfred North Whitehead

Discussion Topics

1. *Trace all of the direct and indirect effects you had today on local and global climate. Classify these activities as essential, desirable, or frivolous.*

2. *Criticize the following statements:*

a. *A new ice age could spread across the United States by the year 2050.*

b. *Massive global flooding would occur if we melted the floating Arctic ice pack.*

c. *Massive global flooding near seacoasts could occur by the year 2050.*

3. *Debate the pros and cons of the SST program. If the government revises plans for this program, would you support such efforts? Explain. SSTs are still being built by other nations. What should be our attitude and actions? Consider carefully the economic, political, and human pros and cons of such actions.*

4. *What effect on the climate might each of the following have: (a) oil spills, (b) increased land under cultivation, (c) driving an air-conditioned automobile, (d) switching on a light, (e) air-conditioning your home or place of work, (f) strip mining, (g) using an electric dryer to dry hair or clothing, (h) switching from oil and coal power plants to nuclear power plants, (i) switching from fossil fuel and nuclear power plants to solar energy power plants?*

5. *Criticize the statement that "man's actions will not affect global climate for 20 to 200 years, so we need not be concerned with the problem now."*

6. *Criticize the following statements:*

a. *Power company executive: This talk about thermal pollution is just a scare tactic by environmentalists. Near the hot water output at both of our plants on Lake Lovely the fishing has never been better.*

b. *Environmentalist: No more power plants should be built on Lake Lovely because they can upset the ecological balance of the lake.*

Would you allow a third plant to be built? What evidence would you require before approval or what alternatives would you suggest, assuming there is a definite need for more power in the area?

Further Reading

Brown, T. L. 1971. *Energy and the Environment.* Columbus, Ohio: Charles E. Merrill. One of the best presentations at a level slightly above that in this chapter.

Bryson, R. A. 1968. "All Other Factors Being Constant—A Reconciliation of Several Theories of Climatic Change," *Weatherwise,* April, p. 68. Useful discussion of the many complex theories of climate change.

Cairns, John, Jr. 1971. "Thermal Pollution—A Cause for Concern," *Journal of the Water Pollution Control Federation,* 43:1, 55–66. Outstanding summary of problems and solutions.

Fletcher, J. O. 1969. "Controlling the Planet's Climate," *Impact of Science on Society,* 19:2. Excellent summary of man's potential impact on global climate along with a summary of major schemes proposed to deliberately tamper with climate.

Holdren, J. P. 1971. "Global Thermal Pollution," in J. P. Holdren and P. R. Ehrlich, eds., *Global Ecology.* New York: Harcourt Brace Jovanovich. Pp. 85–88. Remarkably clear summary of the calculations and principles involved in predicting the heat limits of our atmosphere.

Johnston, Harold. 1972. "The Effect of Supersonic Transport Planes on the Stratospheric Ozone Shield," *Environmental Affairs,* 1:4, March, pp. 735–781. Summary of Johnston's important work on potential effects of SSTs.

Landsberg, Helmut E. 1970. "Man-Made Climatic Changes," *Science,* vol. 170, 1265–1274. Outstanding balanced summary. Highly recommended. Good bibliography.

MacDonald, G. J. F. 1971. "Pollution, Weather and Climate," in W. W. Murdoch, ed., *Environment: Resources, Pollution and Society.* Stamford, Conn.: Sinauer. Pp. 326–335. Excellent summary of man's potential effects on climate by a recognized expert.

Petersen, James T. 1973. "Energy and the Weather," *Environment,* 15:8, 4–9. Excellent summary of potential effects of heat on climate and weather.

Peterson, Eugene K. 1969. "Carbon Dioxide Affects Global Ecology," *Environmental Science and Technology,* vol. 3, 1162–1169. Good nontechnical summary of CO_2 problem.

SCEP (Study of Critical Environmental Problems). 1970. *Man's Impact on the Global Environment.* Cambridge, Mass.: M.I.T. Press. Summary and recommendations by a panel of leading scientists in preparation for the 1972 United Nations Conference on the Human Environment. Probably the most useful and authoritative source available along with the SMIC report listed below.

SMIC (Study of Man's Impact on Climate). 1971. *Inadvertent Climate Modification.* Cambridge, Mass.: M.I.T. Press. Authoritative summary by a panel of prominent scientists. This and the SCEP study are the best sources for up-to-date information.

Weinberg, A. M., and R. P. Hammond. 1972. "Global Effects of Increased Use of Energy," *Science and Public Affairs,* March, pp. 5–8, 43–44. Optimistic view of man's effect on climate by two distinguished scientists.

*One cannot build life from refrigerators,
politics, credit statements, and crossword
puzzles. That is impossible. Nor can one
exist for any length of time without poetry,
without color, without love.*

Antoine de Saint-Exupéry

9

What We Must Do!

9-1   Hope: The People Are Stirring

My purpose has not been to show you what the future will necessarily be, but to show you where we appear to be heading if present trends continue. But as Rene Dubos reminds us, "trend is not destiny." We can say no!

Biological evolution takes millions of years, but cultural change can occur rapidly, even more rapidly today because of the speed and potential power of mass communication (Livingston 1973). Possible futures based on extrapolation of present trends will probably occur only if we give up in despair and assume they are inevitable.

We are sufficiently self-aware and equipped to avoid or alter catastrophic trends, if we choose to accept the sacrifices and joy that all important transitions produce. Glenn T. Seaborg (1970) urges us to look at the present and future with new eyes:

What we are seeing today in all our social upheavals, in all our alarm and anguish over an environmental feedback and, in general, the apparent piling of crisis upon crisis to an almost intolerable degree, is not a forecast of doom. It is the birthpangs of a new world. It is a period of struggle in which we are making the physical transition from men to mankind.

Or as Samuel Beckett put it, "We are between a death and a difficult birth."

If the change that occurs in man's behavior and institutions in the next 30 to 50 years is half as significant as those that have occurred during the past 30 to 50 years, we can make the transition to an earthmanship society.

Adopting an earthmanship consciousness means that we can no longer expect clean air and still drive large cars with internal combustion engines instead of developing efficient mass transportation. We can no longer justify our monstrous use and waste of the world's mineral and energy resources that literally means misery and death for other human beings. We cannot continue to make self-righteous pronouncements about peace, honor, brotherhood, justice, freedom, and elimination of poverty, while wasting enormous amounts of money and finite resources on armaments.

Achieving this dream means we must make choices: we can have more of this only if there is less of something else. We can increase the quality of life only by limiting the number of passengers and their energy-consuming and entropy-producing activities. Industrialist Irwin Miller (1971, p. 36) has expressed the reality that we as Americans must face.

The real price of the future is our willingness to grow up and become an adult people—to make choices rather than to avoid them. . . . We never thought Americans would have to choose. For the first time we are beginning to realize that we can't have everything. The price of the future, then, will be found in the things we give up *in order to gain the things that are compatible with the limitations of living on a spaceship"* (italics mine).

J. M. Stycos has observed that major social changes go through four stages:

Phase 1:   No talk, no do
Phase 2:   Talk, no do
Phase 3:   Talk, do
Phase 4:   No talk, do

During the short period between 1965 and the present most U.S. citizens have become aware of and concerned about our environment. Now, for pollution, we have already moved into phase 3 with real progress being made on several environmental problems and more progress expected during the next decade. Since 1968 air pollution has been declining in 82 metropolitan areas. In water pollution we are only holding our own, but by 1980 it is expected that this problem will also have begun to decline.

With regard to population the United States has made some hopeful movements into phase 3. Zero population growth is probably at least 50 years away because of the momentum from our youthful age structure, but the birth rate and total fertility rate have fallen dramatically since 1968 and in 1972 fell below the replacement level. If this level can be held, especially through 1987, the United States could have a stable population by 2020 and perhaps as early as 2010.

Of course many far more difficult problems remain, such as the energy crises, depletion of nonrenewable resources, agricultural pollution, recycling of our wasted solids, long term handling and storage of radioactive materials, land use, the automobile, and possible long term effects on global climate. Awareness, research, and some action are occurring on all of these fronts, but solving or at least controlling most of these problems will require that we change to an earthmanship society within the next 30 to 50 years.

I am not suggesting that everything is going well. We have only begun to recognize our predicament, much less decide on courses of action. Some cynics say that ecology is a fad. If it is, it will be the last fad. There will be much confusion and disagreement and many early converts will drop out or oppose the environmental movement once they realize the really fundamental economic, political, social and ethical changes it requires. But awareness is growing that no individual, country, or ecosystem is an island. The secret is to begin now, where you are, as you are.

Three human attitudes can kill us: (1) *the blind technological optimism* of those who believe that some scientific innovation or unknown factor will always save us; (2) *the gloom-and-doom pessimism* of those who have given up hope; and (3) *the greed, apathy, and refusal to face reality* of those who have given up concern and involvement through easy fatalism or a naive view of reality.

9-2 *The Four Levels of Environmental Awareness and Action*

The first level—pollution There are four levels of awareness of our ecological crisis. The first level is that of discovering the symptom, *pollution*. In only a few years' time pollution has become one of the major issues for most citizens. Although this is most encouraging it is also dangerous. As soon as we discover a problem, we want to fix blame and find a quick solution. We are now engaged in an unhealthy and counterproductive phase of the environmental crisis—a "pollution witch hunt." We blame industry, government, technology, doctors and health officials, the poor, Christianity —anyone, of course, but ourselves. We have not accepted the fact that we are the enemy. We must rigorously point out and curtail irresponsible acts of pollution by large or small organizations and resist being duped by eco-pornography. But we must at the same time change our own lifestyles. We have all been drilling holes in a leaky boat. Arguing over who is drilling the biggest hole only diverts us from working together to keep the boat from sinking.

Another danger in remaining at the pollution awareness level is that it leads people to view the crisis simplistically as a problem comparable to a "moon shot." Spend $30 billion and go to the moon; spend $300 billion (the bill is much higher) and clean up the environment. Have technology fix us up, send me the bill at the end of the month, but don't ask me to change my way of living. Using technology and spend-

ing enormous amounts of money will be absolutely necessary, but this alone will not solve the problem. By dealing with the symptoms we may buy enough time to deal with the diseases of overpopulation, overconsumption, and the misuse of technology.

The problem at the pollution level is that each individual and industry perceives their impact as negligible. This tragedy of the commons (Hardin 1968a) is that each person sees himself or herself as insulated from others and from the environment. Eventually we must realize that we are all part of the ecosphere and that preserving it must be our ultimate loyalty for ourselves as well as for others.

The second level—overpopullution Many have already moved to the second level of awareness, *the overpopullution level*. The cause of pollution is not just people but their level of consumption and the environmental impact of various types of production. At the overpopullution level the answers seem obvious. We must simultaneously reduce the number of passengers and their levels and wasteful patterns of consumption.

The third level—spaceship earth But these actions will not even begin to happen unless a reasonable number of our leaders and citizens move to a third plateau of awareness, *the spaceship earth level*. At this point we recognize the finiteness of the earth and the potential vulnerability of our life-support system. We are forced to recognize that all human beings are mutually dependent and that we must not impair, destroy, or waste the resources that sustain us.

The danger of the spaceship earth level, as perceived by many, is that we use the astronauts as the model for solving our problems. To protect them and their life-support system, every natural function must be subject to deliberate and rigid control in a programmed existence. Instead of novelty, spontaneity, joy, freedom, and those things that make life meaningful, the spaceship model is based on cultural homogenization, social regimentation, artificiality, monotony, sameness, and gadgetry. We must control and manage parts of the ecosphere, but using a spaceship crew as the ultimate model for solving our problems poses a dire threat not only to individual freedom but also to ecosphere stability through the creation of a highly vulnerable human monoculture.

The fourth level—earthmanship Recognizing our finiteness and interdependence and moving from a frontier world view to a spaceship world view is an important step. But it is not enough. Somehow we must move to the *earthmanship* level. It perceives that the solution to our problems lies in harmonious collaboration with nature, in selective control

Table 9-1   The stages of cultural and ecological evolution

Characteristic	Primitive	Frontier or industrial	Spaceship	Earthmanship
Relationship to nature	Man in nature but controlled by nature	Man vs. nature: increased control	Man vs. nature: attempt at complete control	Man and nature: selective control
Goals	Survival	Survival, high standard of living	Survival, high standard of living	Survival, high quality of life
Method	Try to secure enough food, clothes, and shelter to stay alive	Produce, use, acquire as much as possible in one's lifetime	Complete technological and social control of nature and man to avoid exceeding the limits of the earth	Selective control based on ecological understanding, diversity, harmonious collaboration, and caring to avoid exceeding the limits of the earth
Social units	Individual, tribe	Family, community, corporation, nation	Family, community, earth	Family, community, earth
Reward	Staying alive	Profit, efficiency, power	Survival, comfort, power	Survival, joy, a purpose to life
Population	Reproduction to survive	Reproduction determined by economic and social factors	Reproduction controlled by the state	Reproduction controlled by a balance of voluntary action and mutual coercion through laws
Environmental quality	Not always a meaningful idea	A free good to be used and abused at will	A basic concept of critical value	A basic concept of critical value

based on ecological understanding and an ethic of creative earth stewardship. The important differences between the spaceship and earthmanship views (Figures 3–9 and 3–10, and Table 9–1) are the recognition of *freedom* (versus control), *humility* (versus the assumption of total knowledge and control), and deliberate preservation of *diversity* (versus man-made over-simplification).

Some see earthmanship as "going back to nature." But this approach is based on an idealized and romanticized view that nature's ways are somehow always kind, beautiful, and gentle. Those who romanticize about nature do not know its frequently harsh realities. They confuse a desire to feel close to nature with living close to nature. A mass return to natural living would also mean death for billions of human beings. Long ago we exceeded the population carrying capacity for a world living at such a low technological level. This option is available to only a few in an overcrowded world that has lost its technological and social virginity.

But this does not mean we can't convert our lifestyles to ones more harmonious with natural cycles and our mind

rhythms to a philosophy of enoughness. Important examples of low consumption, high quality, and ecologically sane alternatives to "growthmania" can be seen in the myriad of fragile but crucial experiments now being carried out in America and Western Europe. Out of these rural and urban communes, extended families, organic farming, free schools and clinics, neighborhood rap centers, and numerous other attempts to break out of the conventional urban–industrial trap will come a diverse range of meaningful alternatives. As in any transition period, many and perhaps most of these experiments will fail. But by commitment to a search for new meaning instead of apathy and despair, a few will survive to show others the way (Roszak 1972, p. 394).

9-3   What We Must Do: An Integrated Energy Plan for the United States

Major elements of a national energy plan   So far the consumer's and the federal government's response to the

The Four Levels of Environmental Awareness

First level: **Pollution** — *Discovering the symptoms.*

Second level: **Overpopullution** — *Population × per capita consumption × environmental impact = ecosystem disruption and pollution.*

Third level: **Spaceship earth** — *Seeing the problem as a complex mix of physical, social, political, and economic factors. Everything is connected to everything and our job is to run and preserve the ship by controlling everything in a pseudo-holistic world view.*

Fourth level: **Earthmanship** — *Seeing the problem as a complex mix of physical, social, political, economic, and ethical factors. Everything is connected to everything and our job is to preserve stability, ambiguity, diversity, and human dignity and freedom by harmonious cooperation with nature. Because we can never know how everything or even most things are interconnected, true holism involves restraint and humility.*

1973–74 energy policy crisis have been to view it only as a short term "situation" that will not interfere with wasteful energy lifestyles and ever increasing total and per capita energy demands. The 1975 plan for achieving energy self-sufficiency by 1980 projects a thirteen-fold increase in nuclear energy, expansion of the coal industry by over 50 percent, a 30 percent rise in domestic oil production, a voluntary energy conservation program rather than laws that would be strongly opposed by automobile and oil companies, and little funding for solar, wind, and other alternate energy sources. The cost of this program is estimated at a staggering $750 billion.

This short-sighted policy could produce a temporary and highly misleading energy glut. But based on the thermodynamic, ecological, and cybernetic principles presented in this book, it could in the long run lead to a series of national and global energy, environmental, and human catastrophes. Using up the world's high quality natural gas and oil supplies over the next few decades would leave us no high net energy resources to phase in other energy options should they become feasible and will decrease our ability to produce food for a rapidly growing world population. Finally, the laws of thermodynamics will determine the energy realities on this planet, not political or industrial pronouncements about self-sufficiency and estimates of energy resources based on total rather than net energy yield.

With our background of energy principles and evaluation of the various energy options, it should be possible to develop the elements of an alternate energy plan.   (See pp. 239–240.) Our present energy policy, however, fails to incorporate most of these principles. Even though energy is the lifeblood of our society, the total 1975 government budget is no more than we spend on one nuclear powered aircraft carrier or

Table 9–2   *Proposed government energy research and development expenditures for 1975*

Program	Proposed expenditures* (millions of dollars)	Percentage of total energy budget	Approximate expenditure equivalents
Nuclear fission ($473.4 or 26% for the liquid metal fast breeder)	$724.7	40.0	One conventional aircraft carrier
Coal	415.5	23.0	Two nuclear powered submarines
Pollution control	178.5	9.8	One destroyer
Nuclear fusion	168.6	9.3	One nuclear powered submarine
Conservation	128.6	7.1	One destroyer escort
Miscellaneous	52.8	2.9	One C-5A transport plane
Solar	50.0	2.7	One conventional submarine
Geothermal	44.7	2.5	One B-1 bomber
Oil, gas, and oil shale	41.8	2.3	One B-1 bomber
Wind	7.0	0.4	One fighter plane
Total	$1815.5	100.0	One nuclear powered aircraft carrier

* Proposed expenditures do not represent increases or decreases in budget by Congress or any refusal of the administration to spend allocated funds. For a more detailed summary, see *Science,* vol. 183, 15 Feb. 1974, p. 637.

submarine with missiles (Table 9–2). And this budget is a "crash program" response to the energy crisis, representing a three-fold increase over the 1973 budget.

---

[1] For other (and sometimes conflicting) energy plans see Anthrop 1974, Rose 1974, David 1973, Auer 1974, Sporn 1974, Hammond 1973a, 1974c, U.S. Atomic Energy Commission 1973a, Office of Emergency Preparedness 1972, Lovins 1974, Udall 1973, Wilson 1972, Policy Study Group 1974, Clark 1974.

Major Elements of a National Energy Plan

1. Establish a Cabinet-level National Energy Agency *to plan, implement, and regulate national energy policy and research and development. (This agency should include all of the 61 fragmented government agencies that now contribute to and confuse the nation's energy decisions.)*

2. *As one of the National Energy Agency's first tasks,* establish a national energy policy based on evaluation of short term (present to 1985), intermediate term (1985 to 2000), and long term (2000 to 2020) energy options and strategies. *Also establish a national energy data bank on all energy resources and uses in the country.*

3. Institute thermodynamic bookkeeping for all energy resources and options. *Fund a crash research program to evaluate and report all energy resources in terms of estimated net energy yield instead of total energy reserves.*

4. Break up the horizontal and vertical monopolistic practices or potential of individual energy companies and of groups of companies acting directly or indirectly as energy cartels. *There are four ultimate monopolies—control of air, water, food, and energy. Regardless of whether one believes that energy companies have conspired directly or indirectly to control energy supplies and prices, it is clear that the potential is there and that this potential will increase in the future. Vertical integration of many oil companies, control of every step of oil production from exploration, refining, and distribution to sale of products, already exists (Peach 1973, Netscheat 1971, Sherill 1972). But the real danger in the long run is horizontal integration of many big oil companies. A U.S. Senate investigation in 1973 revealed that the large oil companies now control not only the oil and oil shale deposits but more than 70 percent of the U.S. natural gas supply, between 30 and 60 percent of the nation's coal, more than 50 percent of the uranium supply, and are rapidly moving to take over U.S. geothermal reserves and the new coal gasification industry (Lovins 1974).[2] Such power to control energy prices and policy regardless of what energy options we select cannot be tolerated in a free society that runs on energy. Breaking up this potential monopoly over the next 10 years will require intensive political efforts by citizens. It will cause some decrease in the efficiency of national energy production but the dangers of an energy monopoly are too great to ignore.*

5. Slow down the expansion of nuclear fission power until its net energy yield can be evaluated, its risks decreased, and other safer and perhaps more net energy yielding alternatives can be evaluated. *Nuclear power plants would not be allowed to produce more than 10 percent of our total electricity and 2 percent of our total energy per year by 1985,* at which time this policy would be reevaluated. No commercial breeders would be put into operation until at least 1995. All nuclear plants would be built underground at acceptable geological sites away from urban centers (Lovins 1974).[3] Greatly increase research on net energy evaluation, nuclear safety, protection of shipments of nuclear materials, thermal water pollution, and long term storage of radioactive wastes. Decrease funding for the breeder reactor.

6. Reduce the average per capita rate of energy growth. *Cut the present average of 1.4 percent per year to 1 percent by 1985. This could be accomplished with no serious impact by reducing the growth of per capita energy consumption to 0.3 percent per year and making up the difference by savings of 0.7 percent per year through energy conservation.*[4]

7. *Institute a massive energy conservation program (Section 7–4). Improve the efficiency of energy conversion systems; adopt extensive recycling and eliminate throw-away containers; shift to smaller cars and more efficient and less polluting engines; establish mandatory gas mileage minimums on all cars and tax autos not meeting these standards; develop para and mass transit; require minimum thermal insulation for all buildings; use solar energy for hot water heating and space heating and cooling; substitute natural gas for electrical heating in homes and buildings; ban the use of natural gas for electrical power generation; improve the efficiency of air conditioners, freezers, refrigerators, and electric hot water heaters and require that they all meet minimum efficiency standards; require energy efficiency labels on all products; use wasted heat from power plants for agriculture, aquaculture, and space heating; rely more on trains and less on trucks for freight; reduce lighting levels in buildings and switch from incandescent to fluorescent lights; reduce nighttime building lighting and advertising displays; design buildings with windows that open and shutters that reflect the sun in warm weather so that air conditioning will not be necessary in many areas; offer tax breaks to individuals and corporations that install energy saving equipment and improvements and that use recycled materials; reverse the present rate structures so that large electrical users are charged the highest rates with even higher rates at peak load hours and seasons; ban promotion of increased energy use by utilities and energy companies; tax all electricity use by the kilowatt-hour with funds used for research and development of new energy sources, mass transportation, and pollution control (similar to the Highway Trust Fund).*

---

[2] The investigation revealed that at least nine of the 20 companies had fuel interests in all five fuel categories: oil, gas, coal, uranium, and oil shale.

[3] This recommendation was made in 1962 by the AEC and in 1965 by Edward Teller, but it was rejected, presumably because awkward questions might be raised about reactors already built on the surface. The cost is about the same as that for above ground plants.

[4] The Council on Environmental Quality has proposed a similar but less stringent plan that would allow annual growth to continue at 1.4 percent per year by reducing consumption to 0.7 percent per year and saving 0.7 percent per year through conservation.

8. Stimulate exploration and development of domestic supplies of oil, natural gas, coal, oil shale, and coal gasification, but only in conjunction with increased environmental controls and the mandatory energy conservation program described above. *This plan, combined with a strong conservation program, appears to be the only alternative for the short term (present to 1985 and perhaps to 1990) that will allow nuclear slowdown and provide the time needed for evaluation and development of other intermediate and long range energy options.*

9. Locate and develop, but set aside, a two-year supply of oil and natural gas by 1980 and no later than 1985 (Odum 1973). *This will prevent energy price blackmail by other countries and reduce chances of international conflict over fossil fuel resources. Perhaps a National Energy Company should be established with this goal (not to compete with commercial energy companies but to be part of our national security). This company would also have the goal of evaluating and developing alternate "free fuel" energy sources, such as solar and wind power.*

10. Institute a crash research program for the evaluation and development of energy options and of pollution control *with emphasis on solar, nuclear fusion, wind, geothermal, coal gasification, MHD conversion to improve efficiency of fossil fuel power plants, improved pollution control for particulates and sulfur oxides, and alternatives to the internal combustion engine.*

11. Shift economic incentives from primary mineral resources industries to recycling (secondary materials) industries to reduce consumption of nonenergy resources and to save energy. *Remove or sharply decrease depletion allowance and tax writeoffs for virgin materials and shift them to recycled materials. Remove transportation rates that now make it more expensive to ship many recycled materials than virgin materials. National, local, and state governments should require a certain percentage of recycled materials in all products they purchase and industries and businesses instituting such specifications would be given tax breaks.*

12. Stabilize U.S. population by 2010. *Integrate energy plans with the U.S. and world population plans.*

13. Carefully integrate energy plans with plans for food, water use and pollution, air pollution, solid wastes, and land use. *For example, major deposits of oil shale, geothermal energy, and coal, the proposed site for a national solar energy farm, the largest fossil fuel plant complex in the country (the Four Corners plant), and a possible site for permanent storage of radioactive wastes are all located in the five-state area of Utah, Colorado, Arizona, Nevada, and New Mexico. Clearly some of these energy options cancel others out, and care must be taken to determine which energy options are allowed and in what order so that long term land and water resources in this arid region are also preserved. To date these multiple pressures and possibilities have not been evaluated in any systematic way because the various responsibilities are divided among a number of different agencies.*

A more detailed energy plan   A more detailed version of the energy plan delineates specific suggestions on a short term (present to 1985), intermediate term (1985 to 2000), and long term (2000 to 2020) basis.

Integrated Energy Plan for the United States

Phase 1: Short Term (Present to 1985)

1. *By 1976 establish a National Energy Agency at the cabinet level. By 1978 this agency is to develop a national policy for the next 40 to 50 years, with a preliminary report due by 1977.*

2. *By 1977 establish a national data bank on all energy resources and use patterns.*

3. *By 1977 institute thermodynamic bookkeeping for all energy resources and options, based on estimated net energy yields and reserves rather than our present total energy reserves.*

4. *Declare 1978 as energy education year to inform the American public of the true nature of the four energy crises and to outline what we must do over the short, intermediate, and long term.*

5. *Reduce growth rate of energy consumption to 1.2 percent per year by 1980 and to 1 percent by 1985 with a 0.7 percent per year reduction to occur through energy conservation.*

6. *Begin breaking up the vertical and horizontal monopolistic structure of energy companies by 1977 and complete it by 1984.*

7. *Slow down the licensing and building of conventional nuclear power plants. They are not to produce more than 7 percent of our electricity by 1980 or more than 10 percent by 1985. Preference to be given to plants not located near urban centers. All new plants to be constructed 500 feet underground in geologically safe areas.*

8. Decrease funding for building breeder reactors and move the completion date for a single demonstration plant to 1990. No commercial breeders allowed before at least 1995.

9. By 1977 enact stricter regulations on the licensing and operation of nuclear fuel reprocessing plants and on transportation of nuclear fuel and wastes.

10. By 1976 greatly increase research funding for nuclear safety, transportation, and long-term storage of radioactive materials and for thermal water pollution.

11. By 1976 implement a crash research program at $5 billion to $6 billion per year to evaluate and develop alternate energy options with emphasis on solar energy, geothermal energy, nuclear fusion, wind power, coal gasification, improved pollution control for sulfur oxides and particulates, MHD energy conversion, alternatives to the internal combustion engine, and mass transit.

12. By 1976 begin to implement a mandatory energy conservation program (see item 7 in list of major elements and Section 7–4). The goal is to reduce energy waste by 10 percent of 1973 levels by 1982 and 15 percent by 1985.

13. Institute taxes by 1977 on sulfur oxides, heat, and particulate emissions from power and industrial plants and on horsepower and weight of all automobiles. Proceeds to go to a national pollution control and resource development fund to support the research programs mentioned above.

14. Stimulate exploration and development of domestic supplies of oil, natural gas, coal, oil shale, and coal gasification, but only in conjunction with stringent environmental regulations and a mandatory energy conservation program.

15. Beginning in 1977, build 3 to 5 oil refineries per year until 1985, all with strict environmental controls. These should be built on inland rather than coastal areas.

16. Develop and set aside a two-year supply of oil and natural gas by 1980 and no later than 1985 to be used only if foreign supplies become unavailable or too expensive or to relieve or prevent international tensions based on competition for imports.

17. By 1977 establish a National Energy Company with two goals: locating and developing the two-year reserve supply of oil and natural gas, and developing and evaluating wind, solar, and geothermal energy sources.

18. By 1978 require all new cars to achieve an average 20 miles per gallon or be taxed proportionately. Mileage requirement to be raised to 22 miles per gallon by 1980 and to 26 miles per gallon by 1982.

19. Beginning in 1977 charge large electricity and natural gas users the highest rates, institute higher peak load rates during the summer and during peak hour periods, and ban all advertising promoting the use of energy.

20. To help fund energy research and the National Energy Company, institute a kilowatt hour or energy BTU tax on all electricity use and a tax on all new cars failing to meet minimum gas mileage standards. Funds to go into an Energy Resource, Pollution Control, and Mass Transportation Trust Fund.

21. By 1977 ban new construction of all-electric homes and buildings and ban the use of natural gas by electrical power plants.

22. By 1977 greatly increase funding for para and mass transit with at least half of the funds in the Highway Trust Fund diverted from highways to mass transit. Provide incentives and, if necessary, legislation to discourage use of cars in cities.

23. By 1978 increase air pollution control standards on power plants, other stationary sources, and automobiles. Present air pollution standards and goals are not to be relaxed.

24. By 1976 pass laws banning contour strip mining in fragile areas and requiring extensive land reclamation (probably at an average cost of $2,000 per acre) in all other areas.

25. By 1977 establish minimum insulation requirements and reduce lighting levels in all new buildings. By 1985 all older structures to meet new insulation standards with tax breaks allowed for owners who comply before that time.

26. By 1977 enact "truth in energy" legislation requiring all new appliances to meet efficiency levels corresponding to the highest available in products during 1975. Each appliance to carry an energy efficiency label.

27. By 1976 eliminate discriminatory transportation rates for recycled materials, and by 1977 provide economic incentives for secondary materials (recycling) industries. Require all government purchases to specify a certain fraction of recycled material (where possible).

28. Between 1976 and 1985 gradually remove economic incentives (depletion allowances and tax writeoffs) from primary or virgin materials industries.

29. Greatly increase recycling of paper, aluminum, and steel with a goal of 50 percent by 1980 and 60 percent by 1985.

30. Greatly increase solar space heating and cooling and hot water heating in buildings and homes by 1980.

31. Greatly increase the use of wind turbines to supplement the electrical power grid and for individual homes and small buildings by 1980.

32. Coordinate this plan with a population stabilization program.

33. Integrate energy plans with those for land use, food, water use, water pollution, air pollution, and solid wastes.

Phase 2: Intermediate Term (1985 to 2000)

1. *Continue earlier programs as needed.*

2. *Have pilot demonstration power plants for solar energy and nuclear fusion ready hopefully by 1990 and for a breeder reactor by 1990.*

3. *Make a full scale evaluation of nuclear energy in 1985 to determine whether the risks warrant increase in nuclear power plants compared with other energy options.*

4. *Phase in coal gasification, wind power, solar heating in homes and buildings, geothermal energy plants, and electrical power plants with increased efficiency (perhaps by MHD).*

5. *Increase recycling of paper, aluminum, and steel with a goal of 50 percent by 1990 and of 70 percent by 2000.*

6. *Greatly strengthen pollution controls.*

7. *Initiate a major building program for urban mass and para transit systems.*

8. *Greatly increase recycling of all critical materials.*

9. *Phase out the internal combustion engine completely, with none to be built after 1985 and all old cars replaced by 1995.*

10. *Complete the phasing in of an energy conservation program with a goal of reducing energy waste by 20 percent of 1973 levels by 1990, 25 percent by 1995, and 30 percent by 2000. Evaluate energy conservation progress and add new controls and taxes to reduce use, if needed.*

11. *Population stabilization goals almost completed.*

12. *Coordinate this plan with other integrated plans.*

Phase 3: Long Term (2000 to 2020)

1. *Continue earlier policies as needed.*

2. *Begin the major shift of energy to solar, geothermal, and/or fusion energy depending on technological, ecological, economic, and thermodynamic feasibility.*

3. *Recycle all critical minerals.*

4. *Refine mass and para transit systems.*

5. *Achieve highly sophisticated pollution control in all segments of society.*

6. *Redistribute population to relieve localized energy problems and urban heat islands.*

7. *Achieve a steady state economic system.*

8. *Achieve U.S. population stabilization.*

9–4　What Can You and I Do?

Finally, it all comes down to what you and I are willing to do as individuals and in groups. We must bring about a caring explosion coupled with the creative use of politics to make the transition to an earthmanship society. To begin:

1. *You can sensitize yourself to your environment.* Stand up, look around, compare what is with what could and should be. Look around your room and your home, your school, your place of work, your street, your city, state, nation, and world. What things around you really improve the quality of your life? What are your own environmental bad habits?

2. *You can become ecologically informed.* Give up your "frontier," or linear, thinking and immerse yourself in earthmanship thinking. Specialize in one particular area of the ecological crisis and pool your specialized knowledge with others. Everyone doesn't need to be an ecologist but you do need to ecologize your particular profession or job.

3. *You can choose a simpler lifestyle, reducing your energy and matter consumption and entropy production.* Go on an energy and entropy diet. For every high energy or entropy thing you do (having a child, buying a car, living or working in an air-conditioned building) give up a number of other things. Such a lifestyle will be cheaper and it may add more joy as we learn how to break through the plastic, technological membrane that separates us from nature and from one another.

4. *You can remember that environment begins at home.* Before you start converting others begin by changing your own living patterns. Be prepared for the fact that if you become an ecological activist everyone will be looking for and pointing out your own ecological sins.

5. *You can avoid the extrapolation to infinity syndrome as an excuse for not doing anything,* the idea that if we can't change the entire world quickly then we won't change any of it. While most people are talking about the difficulties of changing the system, others (such as Ralph Nader) go ahead and by doing their homework and using political action change the system.

6. *Above all, you can become politically involved on a local and national level.* Start or join a local environmental group and also join national organizations. Become the ecosphere citizen of your block or school. Use positive

synergy to amplify your results. We would see major improvements in the environment if each of us donated $5 apiece to six politically active environmental organizations. Hire professional lobbyists and lawyers to work for you.

7. *You can do the little things.*[5] Individual acts of consumption, litter, and so on, have contributed to the mess. When you are tempted to say this little bit won't hurt, multiply it by 214,000,000 Americans saying the same thing. Picking up a single beer can, not turning on a light, using a car pool, writing on both sides of a piece of paper, not buying a grocery product with packages inside of packages are all very significant acts. Each small act reminds us of ecological thinking and leads to other ecologically sound practices. Start now, where you are, with a small concrete personal act, and expand into ever-widening circles. Little acts can be used to expand our awareness of the need for fundamental changes in our entire political, economic, and social system over the next few decades. These specific acts also help us avoid psychic numbness when we realize the magnitude of the job to be done.

8. *You can work on the big polluters and big problems,* primarily through political action. Individual actions help reduce pollution, give us a sense of involvement, and help us develop a badly needed ecological consciousness. Our awareness must then expand to recognize that large scale pollution and environmental disruption are caused by some industries, municipalities, and big agriculture. Picking up a beer can is significant but not if it means we allow uncontrolled strip mining in Montana.

9. *You can start a counter J curve of awareness and action.* The world is changed by changing the two people next to you. For everything, big or little, that you decide to do, make it your primary goal to convince two others to do the same thing and convince them in turn to convince two others. Carrying out this doubling process only 28 times would convince everyone in the United States; you need only persuade about 5 to 10 percent for action. After 32 doublings everyone in the world would be convinced.

10. *Don't make people feel guilty.* If a couple has a number of children or someone is overconsuming don't make them feel bad. Instead, find the things that each individual is willing to do to help our environment. There is plenty to do and no one can do everything. Use positive rather than negative reinforcement. We need to nurture, reassure, and understand rather than threaten one another.

The secret of sustained action is to think and work on two levels simultaneously. We must continually whittle away at making major changes in our political and economic systems and our world view. At the same time we must do a number of little daily things to give us the time needed for the major changeover to an exciting, dynamic steady-state world. Daily

accomplishments also give us the psychic energy to keep working on long range changes, where progress will be slow.

Begin at the individual level and work outward in ever-widening circles. Join with others and amplify your actions. This is the way the world is changed. Envision the world as made up of all kinds of circles in an incredibly beautiful and diverse web of interrelationships and an ever-changing kaleidoscope of patterns and rhythms whose very complexity and multitude of potentials remind us that cooperation, honesty, humility, and love must be the model for our behavior toward one another and the earth.

Indifference is the essence of inhumanity.

George Bernard Shaw

---

[5] There are a number of action guides. Among the best are Cailiet et al. 1971, Sickle 1971, Saltonstall 1971, Koestner et al. 1971.

Discussion Topics

1. Do you agree with Pogo's oft-quoted statement that "we have met the enemy and he is us"? Why or why not? Criticize this statement from the viewpoint of the poor; from the viewpoint that large corporations and government are the really big polluters.

2. Distinguish carefully between the "spaceship earth" and "earthmanship" world views.

3. Do you agree with the characteristics of the human cultural and ecological stages summarized in Table 9–1? Can you add other characteristics?

4. Do you agree or disagree with the following propositions? Defend your choice.

a. To conserve finite and dwindling supplies of oil and natural gas we should shift back to coal and ease air pollution and strip mining regulations to make this possible.

b. The energy crisis of the early 1970s was staged by the major oil companies to drive prices up, increase profits, and eliminate competition from independent gas stations.

c. To conserve finite and dwindling supplies of oil and natural gas and to decrease our reliance on other countries for supplies, we should shift to nuclear power, especially the breeder reactor, as soon as possible.

d. The price of electricity and fossil fuels in the United States should be doubled or increased significantly in order to decrease environmental impact and demand for our rapidly dwindling fossil fuels.

e. We should not be overly concerned about foreign oil imports because it is a way to improve international ties and relationships and it prevents us from depleting our own remaining oil and natural gas supplies.

f. The United States uses far too much energy relative to our needs, and we should institute a program designed to cut our energy use by at least 35 percent.

g. We should greatly slow down or declare a moratorium on the building and licensing of all nuclear power plants until we can be more assured of their safety and of the feasibility of safe transportation and long term storage of nuclear wastes.

h. A massive energy conservation program should form the basis of our energy policy; the program must be mandatory to be effective.

i. The vertical and horizontal structure of the major oil or energy companies must be broken up within the next 10 years.

j. A National Energy Company, supported by taxes, should be established to develop and control about one-fourth to one-third of our energy resources in competition with major energy companies in order to protect the consumer from rising prices.

k. A National Energy Company should be created but, instead of competing directly with private energy companies, its mission should be to develop a two-year reserve supply of oil and gas and to test the feasibility of solar, wind, and other energy sources not dependent on conventional fuel supplies.

l. A requirement of 26 miles per gallon for all cars should be mandatory by 1982, if not sooner.

5. Why is it so important to do the little things? Discuss this in terms of thermodynamics and cybernetics. Why are these actions not enough? As a class make a list of all the little things you can do.

Further Reading

See also references for Chapter 4.

Callahan, Daniel. 1973. *The Tyranny of Survival.* New York: Macmillan. Magnificent analysis of what I mean by earthmanship ethics that lie between the tyranny of survival, or spaceship, ethics and the tyranny of superindividualism. Try to read this book.

Esfandiary, F. M. 1970. *Optimism One: The Emerging Radicalism.* New York: W. W. Norton. Superb antidote to pessimism, although he gets carried away at the end.

Elder, Frederick. 1970. *Crisis in Eden: A Religious Study of Man and Environment.* Nashville: Abingdon Press. Reply to Lynn White's charge that Christianity is the culprit. Calls for a theology of nature based on reverence for all life.

Fackré, Gabriel. 1971. "Ecology and Theology," *Religion in Life*, vol. 40, 210–224. Superb overview.

Fromm, Eric. 1968. *The Revolution of Hope: Toward a Humanized Technology.* New York: Harper & Row. Superb analysis of hope that takes us beyond the typical superficial approach. Effective antidote to despair.

Gardner, John W. 1970. *The Recovery of Confidence.* New York: W. W. Norton. Hope is the driving force of human action. Highly recommended.

Hardin, Garrett. 1974. "Living on a Lifeboat," *Bioscience*, 24:10, 561–568. Superb analysis of ecological ethics by one of our best thinkers.

Livingston, John A. 1973. *One Cosmic Instant.* Boston: Houghton Mifflin. Superb and readable summary of man's cultural evolution and his relationship to nature.

Platt, John R. 1966. *The Step to Man.* New York: Wiley. One of the most important and insightful books I have ever read by one of the most brilliant ecosphere thinkers on this planet. Don't fail to read this important collection of essays.

Sickle, D. V. 1971. *The Ecological Citizen.* New York: Harper & Row. Excellent handbook of what you can do.

Watt, Kenneth E. F. 1974. *The Titanic Effect: Planning for the Unthinkable.* Stamford, Conn.: Sinauer. Superb overview of our problems and possible solutions. Highly recommended.

When there is no dream, the people perish.

Proverbs 29:18

Epilogue

This book is based on nine deceptively simple theses:

1. The ecological crisis is not only more complex than we think but more complex than we can ever think.
2. In Garrett Hardin's terms, the basic principle of ecology is "that everything and everyone are all interconnected." Truly accepting this and trying to learn how things are interconnected will require a fundamental change in our patterns of living. But because we can never completely know how everything is connected we must function in the ecosphere with a sense of humility and creative cooperation rather than blind domination.
3. On a closed spaceship there are no consumers, only users of materials. We can never really throw anything away. This is a threat in a linear or frontier society but an opportunity in an earthmanship society.
4. Because of the first law of thermodynamics we cannot get something for nothing, and because of the second law of thermodynamics almost every action of man has some undesirable impact on our environment, or life-support system. As a result, there can be no completely technological solution to pollution on a spaceship, although technology can help. A continued increase in the number of passengers and their wasteful uses of energy and materials must insure a continuing decline in the quality of life and threaten survival for a large number of passengers.
5. Because we have rounded the bend on a J or exponential curve of increasing population, use of resources and energy, and pollution, we now have the potential to seriously disrupt our life-support system.
6. The implication of these ideas is that each of us, and particularly those in the affluent middle and upper classes, must now give up certain things and patterns in our lives to prevent a continuing decrease in freedom and in the quality of life for all. We may live to experience the future we deserve.
7. Our primary task must be to transform from simplistic, linear thinking to cyclic thinking harmonious with the ecological cycles that sustain us—forming a dynamic, diverse, adaptable, steady state that is in keeping with the fundamental biorhythms of life.
8. Informed action based on hope rather than pessimism, blind technological optimism, or apathy offers mankind its greatest opportunity to come closer to that elusive dream of peace, freedom, brotherhood, and justice for all.
9. It is not too late, if. . . . There is time—30 to 50 years—to deal with these complex problems if enough of us really care. It's not up to "them," but it is up to "us." Don't wait.

References

* = Recommended for basic environmental library.

*Abrahamson, Dean E. 1970. *Environmental Cost of Electrical Power*. New York: Scientists Institute for Public Information.

*Abrahamson, Dean E. 1972. "Ecological Hazards from Nuclear Power Plants," in M. T. Farvar and J. P. Milton, eds., *The Careless Technology: Ecology and International Development*. Garden City, N.Y.: Natural History Press.

Abrahamson, Dean E., and Steven Emmings, eds. 1973. *Energy Conservation*. Minneapolis: School of Public Affairs, University of Minnesota.

Ackerman, Adolph J. 1972. "Atomic Power: Fallacies and Facts," *IEEE Transactions on Aerospace and Electronic Systems*, vol. AES-8, no. 5, 576–582.

Alexander, Tom. 1970. "The Hot New Promise of Fusion Power," *Fortune*, vol. 81, no. 6, 94.

*Alfven, Hannes. 1974. "Fission Energy and Other Sources of Energy, *Bulletin of the Atomic Scientists*, January, pp. 4–8.

*Alfvén, Hannes, and Kerstin Alfvén. 1972. *Living on the Third Planet*. San Francisco: Freeman.

Allaby, Michael. 1972. *The World Food Problem: Can We Solve It?* London: Tom Stacy, Ltd.

*American Chemical Society. 1969. *Cleaning Our Environment: The Chemical Basis for Action*. Washington, D.C.: American Chemical Society.

*Anthrop, Donald F. 1974. "The Need for a Long-Term Policy," *Bulletin of the Atomic Scientists*, May, 33–37.

Averitt, Paul. 1969. *Coal Resources of the United States*. U.S. Geological Survey Bulletin 1275. Washington, D.C.: Government Printing Office.

Babcock, Lyndon R., Jr. 1970. "A Combined Pollution Index for Measurement of Total Air Pollution," *Journal of Air Pollution Control Association*, vol. 20, 653–659.

Bair, W. J., and R. C. Thompson. 1974. "Plutonium: Biomedical Research," *Science*, vol. 183, 715–721.

*Barnea, J. 1972. "Geothermal Power," *Scientific American*, vol. 226, no. 1, 70.

*Barnett, Harold J. 1967. "The Myth of Our Vanishing Resources," *Transactions—Social Sciences & Modern Society*, June, pp. 7–10.

Battelle Memorial Institute. 1967. *Oil Spillage Study: Literature Search and Critical Evaluation for Selection of Promising Techniques to Control and Prevent Damage*. Richland, Wash.: Battelle.

*Bengelsdorf, Irving. 1971. "Are We Running Out of Fuel?" *National Wildlife Magazine*, February/March.

*Berg, Charles A. 1973. "Energy Conservation through Effective Utilization," *Science*, vol. 181, 128–138.

*Berg, George G. 1973a. "Hot Wastes from Nuclear Power," *Environment*, vol. 15, no. 4, 36–44.

Berg, Charles A. 1974. "Conservation in Industry," *Science*, vol. 184, 264–270.

*Berg, Charles A. 1974a. "A Technical Basis for Energy Conservation," *Technology Review*, February, pp. 15–23.

Berger, R., and W. F. Libby. 1969. "Equilibration of Carbon Dioxide with Sea Water," *Science*, vol. 164, 1395.

*Berkowitz, David A., and Arthur M. Squires, eds. 1971. *Power Generation and Environmental Change*. Cambridge, Mass.: MIT Press.

*Berry, Stephen R. 1970. "Perspectives on Polluted Air—1970," *Bulletin of the Atomic Scientists*, April, pp. 33–42.

*Berry, Stephen R., and Hiro Makino. 1974. "Energy Thrift in Packaging and Marketing,"*Technology Review*, February, pp. 33–43.

*Billings, W. D. 1970. *Plants, Man, and the Ecosystem*, 2nd ed. Belmont, Calif.: Wadsworth. 708–712.

*Blaustein, Elliott H. 1972. *Anti-Pollution Lab*. New York: Sentinel Books.

*Blumer, Max. 1971. "Scientific Aspects of the Oil Spill Problems," *Environmental Affairs*, vol. 1, 54–73.

*Bockris, J. O'M. 1972. "A Hydrogen Economy," *Science*, vol. 176, 1323.

Bolin, B., and W. Bischoff. 1971. *Tellus*, vol. 22, 431.

*Borgstrom, Georg. 1973. *Focal Points*, New York: Macmillan.

*Borgstrom, Georg. 1973a. *The Food and People Dilemma*. North Scituate, Mass.: Duxbury.

Borgstrom, Georg. 1973b. *World Food Resources*. New York: Intext.

*Boulding, Kenneth E. 1964. *The Meaning of the Twentieth Century*. New York: Harper & Row.

Bova, Ben. 1971. *The Fourth State of Matter: Plasma Dynamics and Tomorrow's Technology*. New York: St. Martin's.

Brinkworth, B. J. 1974. *Solar Energy for Man*. New York: Halsted Press.

*Brodine, Virginia. 1972a. "Running in Place," *Environment*, vol. 14, no. 1, 2–11, 52.

*Brodine, Virginia. 1973. *Air Pollution*. New York: Harcourt, Brace, Jovanovich.

Brook, Alan J., and Alan L. Baker. 1972. "Chlorination at Power Plants: Impact on Phytoplankton Productivity," *Science*, vol. 176, 1414–1415.

Brookhaven National Laboratory. 1957. *Theoretical Possibilities and Consequences of Major Accidents in Large Nuclear Power Plants*, WASH-740: Atomic Energy Commission, March.

*Brown, Lester R. 1970. "Human Food Production as a Process in the Biosphere," *Scientific American*, vol. 223, no. 3, 166–170.

*Brown, Harrison. 1970a. "Human Materials Production as a Process in the Biosphere," *Scientific American*, September.

*Brown, Theodore L. 1971. *Energy and Environment*. Columbus, Ohio: Charles E. Merrill.

*Brown, Lester R., and Gail W. Finsterbusch, 1972. *Man and His Environment: Food*. New York: Harper & Row.

Brown, Harrison, et al. 1957. *The Next Hundred Years*. New York: Viking Press.

*Brubaker, Sterling. 1972. *To Live on Earth*. Baltimore: Johns Hopkins Press for Resources for the Future. (Also available in paperback from New American Library.)

*Bryerton, Gene. 1970. *The Nuclear Dilemma*. New York: Ballantine.

*Bryson, R. A. 1968. "All Other Factors Being Constant—A Reconciliation of Several Theories of Climatic Change," *Weatherwise*, April, p. 68.

*Bryson, R. A. 1974. "A Perspective on Climatic Change," *Science*, vol. 184, 753–759.

Bryson, R. A., and J. T. Petersen. 1968. "Atmospheric Aerosols: Increased Concentration during the Last Decade," *Science*, vol. 162, October 4.

Budyko, M. J. 1970. "Comments," *Journal of Applied Meterology*, vol. 9, 310.

Budyko, M. J. 1972. "The Future Climate," *EOS, Transactions of the American Geophysical Union*, vol. 153, no. 11, 868–874.

*Cailiet, G., et al. 1971. *Everyman's Guide to Ecological Living*. New York: Macmillan.

*Cairns, John, Jr. 1971. "Thermal Pollution—A Cause for Concern," *Journal of the Water Pollution Control Federation*, vol. 43, no. 1, 55–66.

*Cairns, John, Jr. 1972. "Coping with Heated Waste Water Discharges from Steam-heated Electric Power Plants," *Bioscience*, vol. 22, no. 7, 411–419.

*Callahan, Daniel. 1973. *The Tyranny of Survival*. New York: Macmillan.

Callendar, G. S. 1958. "On the Amount of Carbon Dioxide in the Atmosphere," *Tellus*, vol. 10, 243–248.

*Cambel, Ali B. 1970. "Impact of Energy Demands," *Physics Today*, December, pp. 38–45.

*Cameron, Eugene N., ed. 1973. *The Mineral Position of the United States, 1975–2000*. Madison: University of Wisconsin Press.

Carnow, Bertram W. 1970. "Population Invites Disease," *Saturday Review*, July 4.

Carruthers, W., et al. 1967. "1.2-Benzanthracene Derivatives in Kuwait Mineral Oil," *Nature*, vol. 213, 691–692.

Carter, Luther J. 1969a. "Warm-water Irrigation: An Answer to Thermal Pollution," *Science*, vol. 165, 478–480.

*Caudill, William W., et al. 1974. *A Bucket of Oil: The Humanistic Approach to Building Design for Energy Conservation*. New York: Cahners Books.

Chemical and Engineering News. 1966. "Chemistry and the Atmosphere." March 28, pp. 1A–54A.

*Cheney, Eric S. 1974. "U.S. Energy Resources: Limits and Future Outlook," *American Scientist*, vol. 62, January/February, pp. 14–22.

*Chourci, Nazli. 1972. "Population, Resources and Technology: Political Implications of the Environmental Crisis" in D. Kay and E. B. Skolnikoff, eds., *World Eco-Crisis.* Madison: University of Wisconsin Press. Pp. 9–47.

*Clapham, W. B., Jr. 1973. *Natural Ecosystems.* New York: Macmillan.

*Clark, John R. 1969. "Thermal Pollution and Aquatic Life," *Scientific American,* March.

*Clark, Wilson. 1973. "Interest in Wind is Picking Up as Fuels Dwindle," *Smithsonian,* vol. 4, no. 8, 70–78.

*Clark, Wilson. 1974. *Energy for Survival: The Alternative to Extinction.* New York: Anchor/Doubleday.

*Clark, Wilson, et al. 1974. *The Case for a Nuclear Moratorium.* Washington, D.C.: Environment Action Foundation.

*Cloud, Preston E., Jr. 1968. "Realities of Mineral Distribution," *Texas Quarterly,* vol. 11, 103–126.

*Cloud, Preston E., Jr. 1969. "Mineral Resources from the Sea" in National Academy of Sciences, *Resources and Man.* San Francisco: Freeman. Pp. 135–156.

Coan, Eugene. 1970. "Oil Pollution," *Sierra Club Bulletin.*

*Cochran, Thomas B. 1974. *The Liquid Metal Fast Breeder Reactor: An Economic and Environmental Critique.* Baltimore: Johns Hopkins Press for Resources for the Future.

Cohen, Bernard L. 1967a. *The Heart of the Atom.* Garden City, N.Y.: Doubleday-Anchor Books. P. 83.

*Cohen, Bernard L. 1974. "Perspectives on the Nuclear Debate," *Bulletin of the Atomic Scientists,* October, pp. 35–39.

*Cole, Lamont C. 1958. "The Ecosphere," *Scientific American,* April, pp. 11–16.

*Cole, Lamont C. 1968. "Man and the Air," *Population Bulletin,* vol. 24, 103–113.

Committee on Interior and Insular Affairs, U.S. Senate. 1971. *A Bibliography of Congressional Publications on Energy from the 89th Congress to July 1, 1971.* Washington, D.C.: Government Printing Office.

Committee on Interior and Insular Affairs, U.S. Senate. 1971a. *A Bibliography of Nontechnical Literature on Energy.* Washington, D.C.: Government Printing Office.

*Committee on Interior and Insular Affairs, U.S. Senate. 1972. "Conservation of Energy," Serial No. 92–18. Washington, D.C.: Government Printing Office.

Committee on Interior and Insular Affairs, U.S. Senate. 1972a. *A Supplemental Bibliography of Publications on Energy.* Washington, D.C.: Government Printing Office.

*Committee on Interior and Insular Affairs, U.S. Senate. 1973. "Report of the Cornell Workshop on Energy and the Environment." Washington, D.C.: Government Printing Office.

*Commoner, Barry. 1970. "The Ecological Facts of Life" in H. D. Johnson, ed., *No Deposit-No Return.* Reading, Mass.: Addison-Wesley. Pp. 18–35.

*Commoner, Barry. 1970b. "Nuclear Power: Benefits and Risks" in Harvey Foreman, ed., *Nuclear Power and the Public.* Minneapolis: University of Minnesota Press. Pp. 224–239.

*Commoner, Barry, et al. 1974. *Energy and Human Welfare: A Critical Analysis.* 3 vols. New York: Macmillan.

*Concern, Inc. 1973. *Eco-Tips #5—Energy Conservation.* 2233 Wisconsin Ave., N.W., Washington, D.C.: Concern, Inc.

Conservation Foundation. 1972a. *CF Letter,* June.

*Cook, Earl. 1971. "The Flow of Energy in an Industrial Society," *Scientific American,* September, pp. 83–91.

*Cook, Earl. 1971a. "Ionizing Radiation," in William W. Murdoch, ed., *Environment: Resources, Pollution and Society.* Stamford, Conn.: Sinauer.

*Cook, Earl. 1972. "Energy for Millenium Three," *Technology Review,* December, pp. 16–23.

Coppi, Bruno, and Jan Rem. 1972. "The Tokamak Approach in Fusion Research," *Scientific American,* vol. 227, no. 1, 65.

*Corr, Michael, and Don MacLeod. 1972. "Getting It Together," *Environment,* vol. 14, no. 9, 2–45.

*Cottrell, Fred. 1955. *Energy and Society.* New York: McGraw-Hill.

*Council on Environmental Quality. 1970–1973 (annual). *Environmental Quality.* Washington, D.C.: Government Printing Office.

*Council on Environmental Quality. 1973a. *Energy and the Environment.* Washington, D.C.: Government Printing Office.

*Curtis, Richard, and Elizabeth Hogan. 1970. *Perils of the Peaceful Atom.* New York: Doubleday and Ballantine.

*Daniels, Farrington. 1964. *Direct Use of the Sun's Energy.* New Haven: Yale University Press.

*Darling, Frank F., and Raymond F. Dasmann. 1969. "The Ecosystem View of Human Society," *Impact of Science on Society,* vol. 19, 109–121.

*Darmstadter, Joel. 1971. *Energy in the World Economy.* Baltimore: Johns Hopkins Press for Resources for the Future.

Darmstadter, Joel. 1972. "Energy Consumption Trends and Patterns," in Sam H. Schurr, ed., *Energy, Economic Growth and Environment.* Baltimore: Johns Hopkins Press for Resources for the Future.

*Darnell, Rezneat M. 1973. *Ecology and Man.* Dubuque, Iowa: Wm. C. Brown.

*Dasmann, Raymond F. 1972. *Environmental Conservation,* 3rd ed. New York: Wiley.

Deevey, Edward S., Jr. 1951. "Life in the Depths of a Pond," *Scientific American,* vol. 185, 68–72.

*DeNike, L. Douglas. 1974. "Radioactive Malevolence," *Bulletin of the Atomic Scientists,* February, pp. 16–20.

Devanney, John W., III. 1974. "Key Issues in Offshore Oil," *Technology Review,* January, pp. 21–25.

Dreschhoff, Gisela, et al. 1974. "International High Level Nuclear Waste Management," January, pp. 28–33.

Dubin, F. S. 1972. "Energy Conservation Needs New Architecture and Engineering," *Public Power,* March–April.

*Ehrlich, Paul R., and Anne H. Ehrlich. 1972. *Population, Resources, and Environment: Issues in Human Ecology.* 2nd ed. San Francisco: Freeman.

*Energy Policy Project. 1974. *Exploring Energy Choices—A Preliminary Report.* Washington, D.C.: Ford Foundation Energy Policy Project.

*Environment Information Center. 1973. *The Energy Index.* Environment Information Center, Inc., 124 East 39th St., New York, N.Y. 10016.

Environmental Protection Agency. 1971c. *Estimates of Ionizing Radiation Doses in the United States, 1969–2000.* Washington, D.C.: U.S. Government Printing Office.

*Esfandiary, F. M. 1970. *Optimism One: The Emerging Radicalism.* New York: W. W. Norton.

*Ewell, Raymond. 1970. "U.S. Will Lag U.S.S.R. in Raw Materials," *Chemical and Engineering News,* vol. 48, 42–46.

*Faltermayer, Edmund. 1972. "The Energy 'Joyride' is Over," *Fortune,* September, pp. 99–101, 178, 191.

*Farney, Dennis. 1974. "Ominous Problem: What to Do with Radioactive Waste," *Smithsonian,* vol. 5, no. 1, 20–26.

*Fay, James A. 1970. "Oil Spills: The Need for Law and Science," *Technology Review,* January.

*Feare, Thomas E. 1971. "Fusion Scientists Optimistic over Progress," *Chemical and Engineering News,* December 20, pp. 33–37.

Fenner, David and Joseph Klarman. 1971. "Power from the Earth," *Environment,* vol. 13, no. 10, 19–34.

Ferguson, H. L. 1968. *Atmosphere,* vol. 6, 133.

Fisher, John C. 1974. *Energy Crises in Perspective.* New York: Wiley.

Fisher, Joseph L., and Neal Potter. 1971. "The Effects of Population Growth on Resource Adequacy and Quality" in National Academy of Sciences, *Rapid Population Growth: Consequences and Policy Implications.* Baltimore: Johns Hopkins Press. Pp. 222–244.

Fleagle, R. G., ed. 1969. *Weather Modification: Science and Public Policy.* Seattle: University of Washington Press.

*Fletcher, J. O. 1969. "Controlling the Planet's Climate," *Impact of Science on Society,* vol. 19(2).

*Forbes, J. A., et al. 1972. "Cooling Water," *Environment,* vol. 14, no. 1, 41.

Ford, Norman C., and Joseph W. Kane. 1971. "Solar Power," *Bulletin of the Atomic Scientists,* vol. 27, no. 8, 27.

*Ford, D. F., and H. W. Kendall. 1972. "Nuclear Safety," *Environment,* vol. 14, no. 7.

*Foreman, Harvey, ed. 1971. *Nuclear Power and the Public.* Minneapolis: University of Minnesota Press.

*Freeman, S. David. 1971. "Toward a Policy of Energy Conservation," *Bulletin of the Atomic Scientists,* October.

Freeman, A. Myrick, III, et al. 1973. *The Economics of Environmental Policy.* New York: Wiley.

*Frischman, Leonard L., and Hans H. Landsberg. 1972. "Adequacy of Nonfuel Minerals and Forest Resources" in Ronald G. Ridker, ed., *Population, Resources and Environment, The Commission on Population Growth and the American Future Research Reports.* Vol. III. Washington, D.C.: Government Printing Office. Pp. 77–100.

*Fromm, Eric. 1968. *The Revolution of Hope: Toward a Humanized Technology.* New York: Harper & Row.

*Gardner, John W. 1970. *The Recovery of Confidence.* New York: W. W. Norton.

*Garvey, Gerald. 1972. *Energy, Ecology, Economy.* New York: Norton.

*Gates, David M. 1971. "The Flow of Energy in the Biosphere," *Scientific American,* September.

*Geesaman, Donald P., and Dean E. Abrahamson. 1974. "The Dilemma of Fission Power," *Bulletin of the Atomic Scientists,* November, pp. 37–42.

General Accounting Office. 1971. "Progress and Problems in Programs for Managing High-Level Radioactive Wastes," B164052, *Report to Joint Committee on Atomic Energy.* January 29. Washington, D.C.: GAO.

*Gillette, Robert. 1973. "Nuclear Safeguards: Holes in the Fence," *Science,* vol. 182, 1112–1114.

*Gillette, Robert. 1973a. "Radiation Spill at Hanford: The Anatomy of an Accident," *Science,* vol. 181, 728–730.

Gillinsky, Victor. 1971. "The Military Potential of Civil Nuclear Power" in Willrich, Mason, ed. *Civil Nuclear Power and International Security.* New York: Praeger.

*Glaser, Peter E. 1968. "Power from the Sun: Its Future," *Science,* vol. 162, 857–861.

*Gofman, John W., and Arthur R. Tamplin. 1970. "Low Dose Radiation and Cancer," *IEEE Transactions on Nuclear Science,* vol. N5–17, no. 1, 1–9.

*Gofman, John W., and Arthur R. Tamplin. 1970a. "Radiation: The Invisible Casualties," *Environment*, April, p. 12.

*Gofman, John W., and Arthur R. Tamplin. 1971. *Poisoned Power: The Case against Nuclear Power.* Emmaus, Pa.: Rodale Press.

Goldsmith, J. R., and S. A. Landaw. 1968. "Carbon Monoxide and Human Health," *Science*, vol. 162, 1352–1359.

*Gough, William C., and Bernard J. Eastlund. 1971. "The Prospects of Fusion Power," *Scientific American*, February, pp. 56–64.

Graef, W., and C. Winter. 1968. "3,4-Benzopyrene in Frodel," *Archives of Hygiene*, vol. 152, no. 4, 289–293.

*Greenburg, William. 1973. "Chewing It Up at 200 Tons a Bite: Strip Mining," *Technology Review*, February, pp. 46–55.

*Gregory, Derek P. 1973. "The Hydrogen Economy," *Scientific American*, vol. 228, no. 1, 13–21.

Griggin, W. C., Jr. 1965. "America's Airborne Garbage," *Saturday Review*, May 22, pp. 32–34, 95–96.

*Halacy, D. S., Jr. 1973. *The Coming Age of Solar Energy.* 2nd ed. New York: Harper & Row.

*Hambleton, William W. 1972. "The Unsolved Problem of Nuclear Wastes," *Technology Review*, March/April, pp. 15–19.

*Hammond, A. L. 1972a. "Conservation of Energy: The Potential for More Efficient Use," *Science*, vol. 178, 1079–1081.

*Hammond, A. L. 1973a. "Energy and the Future: Research Priorities and National Policy," *Science*, vol. 179, 164–166.

*Hammond, A. L. 1973b. "Solar Energy: Proposal for a Major Research Program," *Science*, vol. 179, 1116. See also "Solar Energy: The Largest Resource," *Science*, vol. 177, 1088–1090 (1972).

*Hammond, A. L. 1974. "Individual Self-Sufficiency in Energy," *Science*, vol. 184, 278–282.

*Hammond, R. Phillip, 1974b. "Nuclear Power Risks," *American Scientist*, vol. 62, 155–160.

*Hammond, A. L. 1974c. "A Timetable for Expanded Energy Availability," *Science*, vol. 184, 367–369.

*Hammond, A. L., et al. 1973. *Energy and the Future.* Washington, D.C.: American Association for the Advancement of Science.

*Hannon, Bruce M. 1974. "Options for Energy Conservation," *Technology Review*, February, pp. 24–31.

*Hardin, Garrett. 1968a. "The Tragedy of the Commons," *Science*, vol. 162, 1243–1248.

Harte, J., and R. H. Socolow. 1971. "Energy" in J. Harte and R. H. Socolow, eds., *Patient Earth.* New York: Holt, Rinehart and Winston. Pp. 276–294.

*Healy, Timothy J. 1974. *Energy, Electric Power and Man.* San Francisco: Boyd and Fraser.

Hendricks, T. A. 1965. *Resources of Oil, Gas and Natural Gas Liquids in the United States and the World.* U.S. Geological Survey Circular 522. Washington, D.C.: Government Printing Office.

*Heronemus, W. E. 1971. "Extraction of Pollution Free Energy from the Winds," reprinted in *Congressional Record*, 92nd Congress, vol. 117, no. 190, pp. S. 20776–80, December 7.

Heronemus, W. E. 1972. "Power from Offshore Winds," Proceedings of the 8th Annual Marine Technology Society Conference, Washington, D.C.

*Heronemus, W. E. 1972a. "The United Energy Crisis: Some Proposed Gentle Solutions," presented at the joint meeting of the American Society of Mechanical Engineers and the Institute of Electrical and Electronics Engineers, West Spring-field, Mass., January 12. Available from the author, University of Massachusetts, Amherst, Mass. 01002.

*Hickel, Walter S., et al. 1972. *Geothermal Energy.* Fairbanks, Alaska: University of Alaska.

*Hinch, Nylds. 1969. "Air Pollution," *Journal of Chemical Education*, vol. 46, 93–95.

*Hirst, Eric. 1973. "The Energy Cost of Pollution Control," *Environment*, vol. 15, no. 8, 37–45.

*Hirst, Eric. 1973a. "Transportation Energy Use and Conservation Potential," *Bulletin of the Atomic Scientists*, Nov., pp. 31–42.

*Hirst, Eric. 1974. "Food-Related Energy Requirements," *Science*, vol. 184, 134–138.

*Hirst, Eric, and John C. Moyers. 1973. "Efficiency of Energy Use in the United States," *Science*, vol. 179, 1299–1304.

Hobbs, P. V., et al. 1974. "Atmospheric Effects of Pollutants," *Science*, vol. 183, 909–914.

*Hodges, Laurent. 1973. *Environmental Pollution.* New York: Holt, Rinehart and Winston.

Holcomb, R. W. 1969. "Oil in the Ecosystem," *Science*, vol. 166, 204–206.

*Holcomb, R. W. 1970a. "Radiation Risk: A Scientific Problem?" *Science*, vol. 167, 853–855.

*Holden, Constance. 1973. "Energy: Shortages Loom, but Conservation Lags," *Science*, vol. 180, 1155–1158.

*Holdren, John P. 1971. "Global Thermal Pollution" in J. P. Holdren and P. R. Ehrlich, eds., *Global Ecology.* New York: Harcourt Brace Jovanovich. Pp. 85–88.

*Holdren, John P. 1974. "Hazards of the Nuclear Fuel Cycle," *Bulletin of the Atomic Scientists*, October, pp. 14–23.

*Holdren, John P., and Philip Herrera. 1971. *Energy.* San Francisco: The Sierra Club.

*Hottel, H. C., and J. B. Howard, 1972. *New Energy Technology: Some Facts and Assessments.* Cambridge, Mass.: MIT Press.

*Hubbert, M. King. 1962. *Energy Resources: A Report to the Committee on Natural Resources.* Washington, D.C.: National Academy of Sciences. Publication 1000-D.

*Hubbert, M. King. 1969. "Energy Resources," in National Academy of Sciences, *Resources and Man.* San Francisco: Freeman. Pp. 157–247.

*Hubbert, M. King. 1971. "The Energy Resources of the Earth," *Scientific American*, September. Briefer summary of 1969 work.

*Hull, Andrew P. 1971. "Radiation in Perspective: Some Comparisons of the Risks from Nuclear and Fossil Fueled Power Plants," *Nuclear Safety*, vol. 12, no. 3, May.

*Hutchinson, G. Evelyn. 1970. "The Biosphere," *Scientific American*, September. Reprinted in Scientific American Editors, *The Biosphere*, San Francisco: Freeman. Pp. 1–11.

*Hyman, Barry I. 1973. *Initiatives in Energy Conservation.* Staff Report prepared for the Committee on Commerce, U.S. Senate. Washington, D.C.: Government Printing Office. Stock No. 5270–01960.

*Inglis, David R. 1973. *Nuclear Energy: Its Physics and Social Challenge.* Reading, Mass.: Addison-Wesley.

*Institute of Ecology. 1971. *Man in the Living Environment.* Madison: University of Wisconsin Press.

Jaffe, L. S. 1968. "Photochemical Air Pollutants and Their Effects on Man and Animals: Adverse Effects," *Archives of Environmental Health*, vol. 16, no. 2, 241–255.

*Jensen, William A., and Frank B. Salisbury, 1972. *Botany: An Ecological Approach.* Belmont, Calif.: Wadsworth.

*Johnston, Harold. 1972. "The Effect of Supersonic Transport Planes on the Stratospheric Ozone Shield," *Environmental Affairs*, vol. 1, no. 4, 735–781.

*Joint Committee on Atomic Energy. 1973. *Understanding the National Energy Dilemma.* Washington, D.C.: Government Printing Office.

Karsch, Robert F. 1970. "The Social Costs of Surface Mined Coal" in Alfred J. Van Tassel, ed., *Environmental Side Effects of Rising Industrial Output.* Lexington, Mass.: Heath.

*Kasper, William C. 1974. "Power from Trash," *Environment*, vol. 16, no. 2, 34–39.

Kellogg, W. W., and G. D. Robinson, eds. 1971. *Man's Impact on Climate.* Cambridge, Mass.: MIT Press.

Kenward, M. 1972. "Fusion Power Politics in the U.S.," *New Scientist*, May 18, pp. 380–382.

*Kneese, Allen V. 1973. "The Faustian Bargain," *Resources*, no. 44, September, pp. 1–3.

*Koestner, E. J., et al. 1971. *The Do-It-Yourself Environmental Handbook.* Boston: Little, Brown.

*Kormondy, Edward J. 1969. *Concepts of Ecology.* Englewood Cliffs, N.J.: Prentice-Hall.

Kruger, P., and C. Otte, eds. 1972. *Geothermal Energy.* Stanford, Calif.: Stanford University Press.

*Krutch, Joseph W. 1960. *The Desert Year.* New York: Viking Press.

*Kubo, Arthur S., and David J. Rose. 1973. "Disposal of Nuclear Wastes," *Science*, vol. 182, 1205–1211.

Lambert, P. M., and D. D. Reid. 1970. "Smoking, Air Pollution, and Health," *The Lancet*, April 25..

Landis, John W. 1973. "Fusion Power," *Journal of Chemical Education*, vol. 50, no. 10, 658–662.

Landsberg, Hans H. 1964. *Natural Resources for U.S. Growth: A Look Ahead to the Year 2000.* Baltimore: Johns Hopkins Press for Resources for the Future.

*Landsberg, H. E. 1970a. "Man-Made Climatic Changes," *Science*, vol. 170, 1265–1274.

*Landsberg, Hans H. 1974. "Low-Cost, Abundant Energy: Paradise Lost?" *Science*, vol. 184, 247–253.

*Lapp, Ralph E. 1971. "The Nuclear Plant Controversy—Safety," *New Republic*, January 23, p. 18.

*Lapp, Ralph E. 1973. *The Logarithmic Century.* Englewood Cliffs, N.J.: Prentice-Hall.

*Lapp, Ralph E. 1973a. "The Ultimate Blackmail," *New York Times Magazine*, February 4.

*Large, David B. 1973. *Hidden Waste: Potentials for Energy Conservation.* Washington, D.C.: The Conservation Foundation.

*Lave, Lester B., and Eugene B. Seskin. 1970. "Air Pollution and Human Health," *Science*, vol. 169, 723–732.

*Leachman, Robert B., and Phillip Althoff, eds. 1971. *Preventing Nuclear Theft: Guidelines for Industry and Government.* New York: Praeger.

*League of Women Voters. 1970. *A Congregation of Vapors.* Washington, D.C.: League of Women Voters.

*Lee, William C. 1972. "Thermal Aquaculture: Engineering and Economics," *Environmental Science and Technology*, vol. 6, no. 3, 232–237.

*Lehr, William E. 1973. "Marine Oil Pollution Control," *Technology Review*, February, pp. 13–22.

Leonard, R. R., Jr. 1973. "A Review of Fusion-fission (hybrid) Concepts," *Nuclear Technology*, vol. 10, 161–178.

*Lewis, Richard S. 1972. *The Nuclear Power Rebellion: Citizen vs. Atomic Industrial Establishment.* New York: Viking Press.

*Lieberman, E. James. 1970. "A Case for the Small Family," *Population Reference Bureau Selection No. 32.* Population Reference Bureau, April.

*Lincoln, G. A. 1973. "Energy Conservation," *Science,* vol. 180, 155–162.

Lindop, Patricia, and J. Rotblat. 1971. "Radiation Pollution of the Environment," *Bulletin of the Atomic Scientists,* September, pp. 17–24.

*Linton, Ron M. 1970. *Terracide: America's Destruction of Her Living Environment.* Boston: Little, Brown.

*Livingston, John A. 1973. *One Cosmic Instant.* Boston: Houghton Mifflin.

Lovering, T. S. 1968. "Non-Fuel Mineral Resources in the Next Century," *Texas Quarterly,* Summer, pp. 127–147.

*Lovins, Amory B. 1973. "The Case against the Fast Breeder Reactor," *Bulletin of the Atomic Scientists,* March 1973, pp. 29–35.

*Lovins, Amory B. 1974. "World Energy Strategies, Parts 1 and 2," *Bulletin of the Atomic Scientists,* May and June, pp. 14–32.

*Lowry, W. P. 1967. "The Climate of Cities," *Scientific American,* August.

Lubin, Moshe J., and Arthur P. Fraas. 1971. "Fusion by Lasers," *Scientific American,* vol. 224, no. 6, 21.

*Luten, Daniel B. 1971. "The Economic Geography of Energy," *Scientific American,* September.

McCaull, Julian. 1969. "The Black Tide," *Environment,* vol. 11, no. 9, 2–16.

*McCaull, Julian. 1973. "Windmills," *Environment,* vol. 15, no. 1, 6–17 (January/February).

MacDonald, Gordon J. 1969. "Human Modification of the Planet," *Technology Review,* vol. 72, no. 1.

*MacDonald, Gordon J. 1971. "Pollution, Weather and Climate" in W. W. Murdoch, ed., *Environment: Resources, Pollution and Society.* Stamford, Conn.: Sinauer. Pp. 326–335.

MacDonald, Gordon J. 1972. "Energy in the Environment" in Sam H. Schurr, ed., *Energy, Economic Growth and Environment.* Baltimore: Johns Hopkins Press for Resources for the Future. Pp. 103–104.

*McHale, John. 1970. *The Ecological Context.* New York: Braziller.

Machta, L. 1971. "The Role of the Oceans and the Biosphere in the Carbon Dioxide Cycle," *Nobel Symposium,* vol. 20, August (Gothenburg, Sweden.).

*McKelvey, Vincent E. 1972. "Mineral Resource Estimates and Public Policy," *American Scientist,* vol. 60, 32–40.

*McKelvey, Vincent E. 1974. "Approaches to the Minimal Supply Problem," *Technology Review,* March/April, pp. 13–23.

*McLean, J. G. 1972. *The United States Energy Outlook and Its Implications for National Policy.* Stamford, Conn.: Continental Oil Co.

McPhee, John. 1974. *The Curve of Binding Energy.* New York: Farrar, Straus, and Giroux.

Macrae, Norman. 1974. "The Coming Energy Glut," *Saturday Review/World,* April 20, pp. 6, 10–11.

*Makhigani, A. B., and A. J. Lichtenberg. 1972. "Energy and Well-Being," *Environment,* June, pp. 11–18.

*Malin, H. M. 1973. "Geothermal Heats Up," *Environmental Science and Technology,* vol. 7, no. 8, 680–681.

Manabe, S. 1971. "Estimate of Future Change of Climate Due to the Increase of Carbon Dioxide Concentration in the Air" in W. H. Matthews,

et al. eds., *Man's Impact on Climate.* Cambridge, Mass.: MIT Press. Pp. 249–264.

Manabe, S., and R. T. Wetherald. 1967. "Thermal Equilibrium of the Atmosphere with a Given Distribution of Relative Humidity," *Journal of Atmospheric Sciences,* vol. 24, 241–259.

Manabe, S., and K. Bryan. 1969. "Climate Calculations with a Combined Ocean Atmosphere Model," *Journal of Atmospheric Sciences,* vol. 26, 786.

*Marcus, Henry S. 1973. "The U.S. Superport Controversy," *Technology Review,* March/April, pp. 49–57.

Marion, Jerry B. 1974. *Energy in Perspective.* New York: Academic Press.

*Marquis, Stewart. 1968. "Ecosystems, Societies, and Cities," *The American Behavioral Scientist,* July/August, pp. 11–15.

Marshall, J. 1968. *The Air We Live In.* New York: Coward-McCann, Inc.

Maugh, Thomas H., II. 1972a. "Fuel Cells: Dispersed Generation of Electricity," *Science,* vol. 178, 1273–1274.

*Maugh, Thomas H., II. 1972b. "Fuel from Wastes: A Minor Energy Source," *Science,* vol. 178, 599–602.

*Maugh, Thomas H., II. 1972c. "Gasification: A Rediscovered Source of Clean Fuel," *Science,* vol. 178, 44–45.

*Maugh, Thomas H., II. 1972d. "Hydrogen: Synthetic Fuel of the Future," *Science,* vol. 178, 849–852.

Mayo, Anna. 1974. "Critical Mass on Capitol Hill," *Bulletin of the Atomic Scientists,* April, pp. 8–9.

*Meadows, Dennis L., and Donella H. Meadows. 1973. *Toward Global Equilibrium: Collected Papers.* Cambridge, Mass.: Wright-Allen Press.

*Meinel, Aden B., and Marjorie P. Meinel. 1971. "Is It Time for a New Look at Solar Energy?" *Bulletin of the Atomic Scientists,* October, pp. 32–37.

*Meinel, Aden B., and Marjorie P. Meinel. 1972. "Physics Looks at Solar Energy," *Physics Today,* vol. 25, no. 2, 44.

Menck, H. R., et al. 1974. "Industrial Air Pollution: Possible Effect on Lung Cancer," *Science,* vol. 183, 210–211.

*Metillo, Jerry M. 1972. *Ecology Primer.* West Haven, Conn.: Pendulum Press.

*Metz, William A. 1972. "Laser Fusion: A New Approach to Thermonuclear Power," *Science,* vol. 177, 1180–1182.

*Metz, William A. 1972a. "Magnetic Containment Fusion: What Are the Prospects?" *Science,* vol. 178, 291–293.

*Metz, William A. 1973. "Ocean Temperature Gradients: Solar Power from the Sea," *Science,* vol. 180, 1266–1267.

Metzger, H. Peter. 1972. *The Atomic Establishment.* New York: Simon & Schuster.

Meyer, Charles F., and David V. Todd. 1973. "Conserving Energy with Heat Storage Wells," *Environmental Science and Technology,* vol. 7, no. 6, 512–516.

*Micklin, Philip P. 1974. "Environmental Hazards of Nuclear Wastes," *Bulletin of the Atomic Scientists,* April, pp. 36–42.

Mihursky, J. A. 1967. "On Possible Constructive Uses of Thermal Additions to Estuaries," *Bioscience,* vol. 17, no. 10, 698–702.

Miller, Albert. 1966. *Meteorology.* Columbus, Ohio: Charles E. Merrill.

*Miller, G. Tyler, Jr. 1972. *Replenish the Earth: A Primer in Human Ecology.* Belmont, California: Wadsworth.

*Miller, G. Tyler, Jr. 1975. *Living in the Environment: Concepts, Problems, and Alternatives.* Belmont, California: Wadsworth.

*Miller, J. Irwin. 1971. "Changing Priorities: Hard Choices: New Price Tags," *Saturday Review,* January 23.

Mills, G. Alex. 1971. "Gas from Coal: Fuel of the Future," *Environmental Science and Technology,* vol. 5, no. 12, 1178–1182.

*Mills, G. Alex, et al. 1971. "Fuels Management in an Environmental Age," *Environmental Science and Technology,* vol. 5, no. 1, 30–38.

*Mines, Samuel. 1971. *The Last Days of Mankind.* New York: Simon and Schuster.

Möller, F. 1963. "On the Influence of Changes in CO_2 Concentration in Air on the Radiation Balance of the Earth's Surface and on the Climate," *Journal of Geophysical Research,* vol. 68, 3877–3886.

Morgan, Karl Z. 1971. "Never Do Harm," *Environment,* vol. 13, no. 1, 28–38.

Morrow, Walter E., Jr. 1973. "Solar Energy: Its Time is Near," *Technology Review,* December, pp. 31–40.

*Morse, R. S. 1967. *The Automobile and Air Pollution.* Washington, D.C.: U.S. Department of Commerce.

*Mother Earth News. 1974. *The Mother Earth News Handbook of Homemade Power.* New York: Bantam.

Muffler, L. J. P. 1973. *U.S. Geological Survey Professional Paper No. 820.* Washington, D.C.: Government Printing Office.

*Murphy, P. M. 1972. "Future Possibilities in Nuclear Fuel Processing" in Proceedings of Connecticut Clean Power Symposium, St. Joseph College, West Hartford, Conn., May 13.

*National Academy of Sciences. 1969b. *Resources and Man.* San Francisco: Freeman.

National Academy of Sciences. 1972a. *Biological Impacts of Increased Intensities of Solar Ultraviolet Radiation.* Washington, D.C.: National Academy of Sciences.

National Academy of Sciences. 1973. *Man, Materials and Environment.* Cambridge, Mass.: MIT Press.

National Coal Association. 1968. *Bituminous Coal Facts.* Washington, D.C.: National Coal Association.

*National Petroleum Council. 1971. *U.S. Energy Outlook.* Vol. 1, July.

National Research Council. 1972. News release on study of relationship between urban air pollution and lung cancer, September 6. See summary in *Chemistry and Engineering News,* September 18, 1972, p. 17.

*National Tuberculosis and Respiratory Disease Association. 1969. *Air Pollution Primer.* New York: National Tuberculosis and Respiratory Disease Association.

Nephew, E. A. 1973. "The Challenge and Promise of Coal," *Technology Review* December, 21–29.

*Netscheat, Bruce C. 1971. "The Energy Company: A Monopoly Trend in Energy Markets," *Bulletin of the Atomic Scientists,* October, pp. 13–19.

Newell, R. E. 1971. "The Global Circulation of Atmospheric Pollutants," *Scientific American,* vol. 224, 32.

*Novick, Sheldon. 1969. *The Careless Atom.* Boston: Houghton Mifflin.

*Novick, Sheldon. 1969a. "A Mile from Times Square," *Environment,* vol. 14, no. 1.

*Novick, Sheldon. 1973. "Looking Forward," *Environment,* vol. 15, no. 4, 4–15.

*Novick, Sheldon. 1973a. "Toward a Nuclear Power Precipice, *Environment,* vol. 15, no. 2, 32–41.

*NSF/NASA Solar Energy Panel. 1973. *Solar Energy as a National Resource.* College Park, Md.: Department of Mechanical Engineering, University of Maryland.

Oakley, Donald T. 1972. *Natural Radiation Exposure in the United States*. Washington, D.C.: Environmental Protection Agency. For a summary of this report see *Environment*, vol. 15, no. 10, 31–35 (December 1973).

Odum, Eugene P. 1962. "Relationships between Structure and Function in an Ecosystem," *Japanese Journal of Ecology*, vol. 12, 108–118.

*Odum, Howard T. 1971. *Environment, Power and Society*. New York: Wiley-Interscience.

*Odum, Eugene P. 1971a. *Fundamentals of Ecology*. 3rd ed. Philadelphia: W. B. Saunders.

*Odum, Eugene P. 1972. "Ecosystem Theory in Relation to Man" in John A. Wiens, ed., *Ecosystem Structure and Function*. Corvallis: Oregon State University Press. Pp. 11–24.

*Odum, Howard T. 1973. "Energy, Ecology and Economics," paper invited by Royal Swedish Academy of Science. Available from author, Dept. of Environmental Engineering Sciences, University of Florida, Gainesville, Fla. 32611.

*Office of Emergency Preparedness. 1972. *The Potential for Energy Conservation*. Washington, D.C.: Government Printing Office. Stock No. 4102-00009.

Office of Scientific Technology. 1972. *Patterns of Energy Use in the United States*. Washington, D.C.: Government Printing Office.

Olson, T. A., and F. J. Burgess, eds. 1967. *Pollution and Marine Ecology*. New York: Interscience.

*Oort, Abraham H. 1970. "The Energy Cycle of the Earth," *Scientific American*, September. Reprinted in Scientific American Editors, *The Biosphere*. San Francisco: Freeman, 1970. Pp. 13–23.

*Osborn, Elburt F. 1974. "Coal and the Present Energy Situation," *Science*, vol. 183, 477–481.

Othmer, Donald F., and Oswald A. Roels. 1973. "Power, Fresh Water, and Food from Cold, Deep Sea Water," *Science*, vol. 182, 121–125.

*Panel on Geothermal Energy Resources. 1972. *Assessment of Geothermal Energy Resources*. Washington, D.C.: Government Printing Office.

*Park, Charles F., Jr. 1968. *Affluence in Jeopardy*. San Francisco: Freeman.

*Pauling, Linus. 1970. "Genetic and Somatic Effects of High Energy Radiation," *Bulletin of the Atomic Scientists*, September, pp. 3–7.

*Peach, W. N. 1973. *The Energy Outlook for the 1980's*. Washington, D.C.: Government Printing Office. Stock No. 5270–02113.

*Perry, Harry. 1974. "The Gasification of Coal," *Scientific American*, vol. 230, no. 3, 19–25.

*Perry, Harry and Harold. Berkson. 1971. "Must Fossil Fuels Pollute?" *Technology Review*, December, pp. 34–43.

Petersen, Peter G. 1971. *The United States in the Changing World Economy*. Vol. II. Washington, D.C.: Government Printing Office.

*Petersen, J. T. 1973. "Energy and the Weather," *Environment*, vol. 15, no. 8, 4–9.

Peterson, J. T. 1969. "The Climate of Cities: A Survey of Recent Literature," Pub. AP-59, National Air Pollution Control Administration, Raleigh, N.C.

Peterson, Eugene K. 1969. "Carbon Dioxide Affects Global Ecology," *Environmental Science and Technology*, vol. 3, 1162–1169.

*Peterson, Bruce. 1970. *ZPG Reporter*, October.

*Pfeiffer, J. E. 1972. *The Emergence of Man*. Rev. ed. New York: Harper & Row.

*Phillipson, John. 1966. *Ecological Energetics*. New York: St. Martin's Press.

*Pimentel, D., et al. 1973. "Food Production and the Energy Crisis," *Science*, vol. 182, 443–449.

Plass, G. 1956. "The Carbon Dioxide Theory of Climate Change," *Tellus*, vol. 8, 140–156.

Plass, G. 1959. "Carbon Dioxide and Climate," *Scientific American*, vol. 201, 41.

*Platt, John R. 1966. *The Step to Man*. New York: Wiley.

*Population Reference Bureau. 1970. "Population and Resources: The Coming Collision." *Population Bulletin*, vol. 26, no. 2.

Post, R. E. 1971. "Fusion Power: The Uncertainty Certainty," *Bulletin of the Atomic Scientists*, October, pp. 42–48.

Potter, Jeffrey. 1973. *Disaster by Oil*. New York: Macmillan.

*Pryde, Lucy T. 1973. *Environmental Chemistry: An Introduction*. Menlo Park, Calif.: Cummings.

*Rabinowitch, Eugene. 1973. "Challenges of the Scientific Age," *Bulletin of the Atomic Scientists*. September, pp. 4–8.

Radcliffe, Donna, and Thomas A. Murphy. 1969. *Biological Effects of Oil Pollution—Bibliography*. Department of Interior, Federal Water Pollution Control Administration.

Rafalik, Dianne. 1974. "Architecture's Towering Energy Costs," *Environmental Action*, April 13, pp. 11–14.

*Ramey, James T. 1970. "Nuclear Power: Benefits and Risks," in Harvey Foreman, ed., *Nuclear Power and the Public*. Minneapolis: University of Minnesota Press. Pp. 210–223.

Rasool, S. I., and S. H. Schneider. 1971. "Atmospheric Carbon Dioxide and Aerosols: Effects of Large Increases on Global Climate," *Science*, vol. 173, 138–141.

*Reid, Keith. 1970. *Nature's Network*. Garden City, N.Y.: Natural History Press.

Resources for the Future. 1974. "Air Pollution and Human Health," *Annual Report, 1973*, pp. 15–20. Washington, D.C.: Resources for the Future.

Rex, R. W. 1971. "Geothermal Energy: The Neglected Energy Option," *Bulletin of the Atomic Scientists*, vol. 27, no. 8, 52.

*Rice, Richard A. 1974. "Toward More Transportation with Less Energy," *Technology Review*, February, pp. 45–53.

Robinson, Elmer, and Robert C. Robbins. 1970. "Gaseous Atmospheric Pollutants from Urban and Natural Sources" in S. Fred Singer, ed., *Global Effects of Environmental Pollution*. New York: Springer-Verlag. Pp. 50–64.

*Robson, Geoffrey R. 1974. "Geothermal Electricity Production," *Science*, vol. 184, 371–375.

*Rocks, Lawrence, and Richard P. Runyon. 1972. *The Energy Crisis*. New York: Crown.

Rose, David J. 1971. "Controlled Nuclear Fusion: Status and Outlook," *Science*, vol. 172, 797–808.

*Rose, David J. 1974. "Energy Policy in the U.S.," *Scientific American*, vol. 230, no. 1, 20–29.

*Rose, David J. 1974a. "Nuclear Electric Power," *Science*, vol. 184, 351–359.

*Roszak, Theodore. 1972. *Where the Wasteland Ends*. New York: Doubleday.

Sagan, L. A. 1972. "Human Costs of Nuclear Power," *Science*, vol. 177, 487–493.

*Sagan, L. A., and Rolf Eliassen. 1974. *Human and Ecologic Effects of Nuclear Power Plants*. Springfield, Illinois: Charles C Thomas.

Saltonstall, Richard. 1971. *Your Environment and What You Can Do about It*. New York: Walker.

*Saltonstall, Richard, Jr., and James K. Page, Jr. 1972. *Brownout and Slowdown*. New York: Walker.

SCEP (Study of Critical Environmental Problems). 1970. *Man's Impact on the Global Environment*. Cambridge, Mass.: MIT Press.

*Schurr, Sam H. 1971. *Energy Research Needs*. Washington, D.C.: Government Printing Office.

*Schurr, Sam H., ed. 1972. *Energy, Economic Growth, and Environment*. Baltimore: Johns Hopkins Press for Resources for the Future.

*Scientific American Editors. 1970. *The Biosphere*. San Francisco: Freeman.

*Scientific American Editors. 1971. *Energy and Power*.

*Seaborg, Glenn T. 1972. "The Erehwon Machine: Possibilities for Reconciling Goals by Way of a New Technology in Sam H. Schurr, ed., *Energy, Economic Growth and Environment*. Baltimore: Johns Hopkins Press for Resources for the Future. Pp. 125–138.

*Seaborg, Glenn T., and Justin L. Bloom. 1970. "Fast Breeder Reactors," *Scientific American*, vol. 223, no. 5, 13–21.

*Seaborg, Glenn T., and William R. Corliss. 1971. *Man and Atom*. New York: Dutton.

*Seager, Spencer L., et al. 1975. *Energy: From Source to Use*. Glenview, Illinois: Scott Foresman.

Sellers, William D. 1970. "A Global Climatic Model Based on the Energy Balance of the Earth-Atmosphere System," *Journal of Applied Meteorology*, vol. 8, 392–400.

Sellers, William D. 1973. "A New Global Climate Model," *Journal of Applied Meteorology*, vol. 12, no. 2, 241–54.

*Shell Oil Company. 1973. "The National Energy Outlook." Available free from Shell Oil Company, Public Affairs, P.O. Box 2467, Houston, Texas, 77001.

*Shell Oil Company. 1973a. "The National Energy Problem: Potential Energy Savings. Houston, Texas: Shell Oil Co.

*Sherrill, Robert 1972. "The Industry's Fright Campaign," *The Nation*, June 26, pp. 816–820.

*Shy, Carl M., and John F. Finklea. 1973. "Air Pollution Affects Community Health," *Environmental Science and Technology*, vol. 7, no. 3, 204–208.

*Sickle, D. V. 1971. *The Ecological Citizen*. New York: Harper & Row.

Singer, S. Fred., ed. 1970. *Global Effects of Environmental Pollution*. New York: Springer-Verlag.

*Skinner, Brian J. 1969. *Earth Resources*. Englewood Cliffs, N.J.: Prentice-Hall.

SMIC (Study of Man's Impact on Climate). 1971. *Inadvertent Climate Modification*. Cambridge, Mass.: MIT Press.

*Smith, J. E., ed. 1968. *Pollution and Marine Life*. Cambridge, England: Cambridge University Press.

*Smith, Robert L. 1974. *Ecology and Field Biology*, 2nd ed. New York: Harper & Row.

*Southwick, C. H. 1972. *Ecology and the Quality of the Environment*. New York: Van Nostrand-Reinhold.

*Speth, J. Gustave, et al. 1974. "Plutonium Recycle: The Fateful Step," *Bulletin of the Atomic Scientists*, November, pp. 15–22.

*Sporn, Philip. 1974. "Multiple Failures of Public and Private Institutions," *Science*, vol. 184, 284–286.

Staff report, 1970a. "Canals Offer Vast Cooling Potential," *Environmental Science and Technology*, April, p. 287.

*Staff report. 1970c. "Sulfur Oxide Control: A Grim Future," *Science News*, vol. 98, 187.

Staff report. 1973a. "Canals Cool Hot Water for Reuse," *Environmental Science and Technology*, vol. 7, no. 1, 29–31.

*Starr, Chauncey. 1971. "Energy and Power," *Scientific American*, September, pp. 3–15.

*Starr, Chauncey. 1973. "Realities of the Energy Crisis," *Bulletin of the Atomic Scientists*, September, pp. 15–20.

*Starr, Chauncey, and R. Philip Hammond. 1972. "Nuclear Waste Storage," *Science*, vol. 177, 744.

*Stein, Richard G. 1972. "A Matter of Design," *Environment*, October, pp. 17–29.

*Steiner, Don. 1971. "The Radiological Impact of Fusion," *New Scientist*, December 16.

*Steinhart, Carol E., and John S. Steinhart. 1972. *Blowout: A Case Study of the Santa Barbara Oil Spill*. North Scituate, Mass.: Duxbury.

*Steinhart, Carol E., and John S. Steinhart. 1974. *Energy: Sources, Use, and Role in Human Affairs*. North Scituate, Mass.: Duxbury.

*Steinhart, John S., and Carol E. Steinhart. 1974a. "Energy Use in the U.S. Food System," *Science*, Vol. 184, 307–315.

Stern, A. C., ed. 1968. *Air Pollution*. 2nd ed. New York: Academic Press.

*Stoker, H. S., and Spencer L. Seager. 1972. *Environmental Chemistry: Air and Water Pollution*. Glenview, Ill.: Scott, Foresman.

*Stokinger, H. E. 1969. "The Spectre of Today's Environmental Pollution—U.S.A. Brand," *American Industrial Hygiene*, vol. 30, 195–217.

*Strange, James O. 1969. "The Urbanite's Interest in Rural Land Use Planning," *Journal of Soil and Water Conservation*, vol. 24, no. 5.

*Surface Mining Research Library. 1972. *Energy and the Environment: What's the Strip Mining Controversy All About?* Charleston, W. Va.: Surface Mining Research Library, 1218 Quarrier St. Charleston, W. Va. 25301.

*Surrey, A. J., and A. J. Bromley. 1973. "Energy Resources" in H.S.O. Cole, et al., *Models of Doom: A Critique of Limits to Growth*. New York: Universe Books.

*Tamplin, Arthur R. 1973. "Solar Energy," *Environment*, vol. 15, no. 5, 16–34.

*Tamplin, Arthur R., and John W. Gofman. 1970. *Biological Effects of Radiation—Population Control Through Nuclear Pollution*. Chicago: Nelson-Hall.

Tamplin, Arthur R., and T. B. Cochran. 1974. *Radiation Standards for Hot Particles*. Washington, D.C.: Natural Resources Defense Council.

*Tansley, A. G. 1935. "The Use and Abuse of Vegetational Concepts and Terms," *Ecology*, vol. 16, 284–307.

*Technology Review. 1972. *Energy Technology in the Year 2000*. Cambridge, Mass.: Technology Review.

*Theobald, P. K., et al. 1972. *Energy Resources of the United States*. U.S. Geological Survey Circular 650: Washington, D.C.: Government Printing Office.

*Train, Russell E. 1973. "Energy Problems and Environmental Concern," *Bulletin of the Atomic Scientists*, November pp. 43–47.

Trice, H. M., and P. M. Roman. 1970. "Delabeling, Relabeling, and Alcoholics Anonymous," *Social Problems*, vol. 17, 538–540.

Treshow, Michael. 1971. *Whatever Happened to Fresh Air?* Salt Lake City: University of Utah Press.

Turk, Amos, et al. 1972. *Ecology, Pollution, and Environment*. Philadelphia: Saunders.

*Udall, Stewart L. 1973. "The Energy Crisis: A Radical Solution," *World*, May 8, pp. 34–36.

U.S. Atomic Energy Commission. 1966. *The Genetic Effects of Radiation* (written by Isaac Asimov and Theodosius Dobzhansky). Oak Ridge, Tenn.: USAEC Division of Technical Information Extension.

U.S. Atomic Energy Commission. 1967. *Licensing of Power Reactors*. Washington, D.C.: Government Printing Office.

*U.S. Atomic Energy Commission. 1967a. *Nuclear Reactors* (by John F. Hogerton). Oak Ridge, Tenn.: USAEC Division of Technical Information Extension.

*U.S. Atomic Energy Commission. 1969. *Atomic Fuel* (by John F. Hogerton). Oak Ridge, Tenn.: USAEC Division of Technical Information Extension.

U.S. Atomic Energy Commission. 1969a. *Radioactive Wastes* (by Charles H. Fox). Oak Ridge, Tenn.: USAEC Division of Technical Information Extension.

U.S. Atomic Energy Commission. 1973. *AEC Task Force Report: Study of Reactor Licensing Process*. Washington, D.C.: Atomic Energy Commission.

*U.S. Atomic Energy Commission. 1973a. *The Nation's Energy Future*. Washington, D.C.: Government Printing Office.

U.S. Atomic Energy Commission. 1973b. "Nuclear Fuel Supply," USAEC Report *WASH 1242* and *WASH 1243*. Washington, D.C.: Atomic Energy Commission.

U.S. Atomic Energy Commission. 1973c. "Report on Investigation of 106T Tank Leak at Hanford Reservation, Richland, Wash." Washington, D.C.: AEC (July).

*U.S. Bureau of Mines. Annual. *Minerals Yearbook*. Washington, D.C.: Government Printing Office.

*U.S. Bureau of Mines. 1970. *Mineral Facts and Problems*. Washington, D.C.: Government Printing Office. Issued every 5 years.

U.S. Department of Health, Education, and Welfare. 1970d. *Nationwide Inventory of Air Pollution Emissions—1968*. Pub. AP-73. Washington, D.C.: Government Printing Office.

*U.S. Department of the Interior. 1967. *Surface Mining and Our Environment*. Washington, D.C.: Government Printing Office.

U.S. Department of the Interior. 1968a. *Industrial Waste Guide on Thermal Pollution*. Corvallis, Oregon: Pacific Northwest Water Laboratory.

*U.S. Geological Survey. 1973. *United States Mineral Resources*. Washington, D.C.: Government Printing Office.

*Vitti, Joseph A., and William P. Staker. 1972. "The Breeder's Role in the Future Power Generation" in Proceedings of Connecticut Clean Power Symposium, St. Joseph College, West Hartford, Conn., May 13.

*Wade, Nicholas. 1973. "World Food Situation: Pessimism Comes Back into Vogue," *Science*, vol. 181, 634–638.

*Wade, Nicholas. 1974. "Raw Materials: U.S. Grows More Vulnerable to Third World Cartels," *Science*, vol. 183, 185–186.

*Waldbott, George L. 1973. *Health Effects of Environmental Pollutants*. St. Louis: C. V. Mosby.

Walters, S. 1971. "Power in the Year 2001, Part 2—Thermal Sea Power," *Mechanical Engineering*, October, pp. 21–25.

Washington, W. 1972. "Numerical Climatic Change Experiments: The Effect of Man's Production of Thermal Energy," *Journal of Applied Meteorology*, vol. 11, no. 5, 768–772.

Watt, Kenneth E. F. 1966. *Systems Analysis in Ecology*. New York: Academic Press.

Watt, Kenneth E. F. 1968. *Ecology and Resource Management*. New York: McGraw-Hill.

*Watt, Kenneth E. F. 1972. "Tambora and Krakatau: Volcanoes and the Cooling of the World," *Saturday Review*, December 23, pp. 43–44.

*Watt, Kenneth E. F. 1973. *Principles of Environmental Science*. New York: McGraw-Hill.

*Watt, Kenneth E. F. 1974. *The Titanic Effect: Planning for the Unthinkable*. Stamford, Conn.: Sinauer.

*Weaver, Kenneth F. 1972. "The Search for Tomorrow's Power," *National Geographic*. November, pp. 649–681.

*Weinberg, A. M. 1972. "Social Institutions · and Nuclear Energy," *Science*, Vol. 177, 27–34.

*Weinberg, A. M. 1973. "Technology and Ecology—Is There a Need for Confrontation?" *Bioscience*, Vol. 23, No. 1, 43 (January).

*Weinberg, A. M., and Philip R. Hammond. 1972. "Global Effects of Increased Energy Use," *Bulletin of the Atomic Scientists*, March, pp. 7–13.

*Weinberg, A. M., and R. P. Hammond. 1972. "Global Effects of the Increased Use of Energy," *Bulletin of the Atomic Scientists*, March, pp. 5–8, 43–44.

Weisz, John A. 1970. "The Environmental Effects of Surface Mining and Mineral Waste Generation" in Alfred J. Van Tassel, ed., *Environmental Side Effects of Industrial Output*. Lexington, Mass.: Heath.

*Wells, Malcolm B. 1973. "Confessions of a Gentle Architect," *Environmental Quality*, July, pp. 51–57.

White, David C. 1973. "The Energy-Environment-Economic Triangle," *Technology Review*, December, pp. 11–19.

*Whittaker, Robert H. 1970. *Communities and Ecosystems*. New York: Macmillan.

*Whittemore, F. Case. 1973. "How Much in Reserve?" *Environment*, vol. 15, no. 7, 16–37.

Williams, Robert H. 1972. "When the Well Runs Dry, *Environment*, June, pp. 19–31.

*Williamson, Samuel J. 1973. *Fundamentals of Air Pollution*. Reading, Mass.: Addison-Wesley.

*Willrich, Mason, and Theodore B. Taylor. 1974a. *Nuclear Thefts: Risks and Safeguards*. Cambridge, Mass.: Ballinger.

*Wilson, Richard. 1972. "Power Policy—Plan or Panic," *Bulletin of Atomic Scientists*, May, pp. 29–30.

*Wilson, Thomas W., Jr. 1972a. *World Energy, The Environment and Political Action*. New York: International Institute for Environmental Affairs.

*Wilson, W., and R. Jones. 1974. *Energy, Ecology and the Environment*. New York: Academic Press.

Wilson, R. D., et al. 1974. "Natural Marine Oil Seepage," *Science*, vol. 184, 858–865.

*Winsche, W. E., et al. 1973. "Hydrogen: Its Future Role in the Nation's Energy Economy," *Science*, vol. 180, 1321–1332.

*Wolf, Martin. 1974. "Solar Energy Utilization by Physical Methods," *Science*, vol. 184, 382–386.

*Wolman, Abel. 1965. "The Metabolism of Cities," *Scientific American*, March, pp. 179–190.

Wood, Lowell, and John Nuckolls. 1972. "Fusion Power," *Environment*, vol. 14, no. 4, pp. 29–33.

*Woodwell, G. M. 1970a. "The Energy Cycle of the Biosphere," *Scientific American*, September. Reprinted in Scientific American Editors. *The Biosphere*. San Francisco: Freeman. Pp. 25–36.

*World Environment Newsletter. 1974. "Alternate Energy Sources," *Saturday Review/World*. February 23, 29–32.

*World Environment Newsletter. 1974a. "New Energy Sources," *Saturday Review/World*, February 9, 47–50.

*Woodwell, G. M. 1974. "Success, Succession and Adam Smith," *Bioscience*, vol. 24, no. 2, 81–87.

Zener, Clarence. 1973. "Solar Sea Power," *Physics Today*, vol. 26, no. 1, 48.

Index

Figure = (f), Footnote = (n), Table = (t)